For B, as always

DAVID BEATY

The Complete Skytraveller

A Methuen Paperback

First published in Great Britain in 1979
This fully revised and updated edition first published in 1986
by Methuen London Ltd
11 New Fetter Lane, London EC4P 4EE
Copyright © 1978 and 1986 by David Beaty

Made and printed in Great Britain
by Richard Clay Ltd, Bungay, Suffolk

British Library Cataloguing in Publication Data

Beaty, David
  The complete skytraveller.—2nd ed.
  1. Air travel—Handbooks, manuals, etc.
  I. Title
  387.7'42   HE9768

  ISBN 0 413 56220 4

Contents

Foreword

I have already acknowledged the help kindly given me by many people in the first edition of this book. I would now like to repeat my gratitude to them in this new edition. Once again, David Hurst and Ray Berry of the British Airports Authority have given unstinted help, and I am particularly grateful to BAA for allowing me to use the information they sent me. Similarly, the Civil Aviation Authority have been generous and their Public Relations Officers most helpful. So have the Public Relations Officers of Manchester, Birmingham, Luton, Bristol and Cardiff Airports.

British Caledonian Airways and their staff have been most helpful. Ken Brealey who heads Gatwick Air Traffic Contol has kindly given me useful information. *Flight International*, as always, has been invaluable, together with numerous newspapers or magazines too many to mention. I would also like to thank my editors, Ann Mansbridge and Anne Askwith, for their invaluable help.

The first big problem in a book like this is what to leave out – there is so much. The second big problem is that flying changes so fast. I have done my best to make sure the information is accurate as the book goes to press. Telephone numbers may, of course change. But time doesn't stand still, and inevitably things in aviation change quickly.

The views and opinions in the book are of course my own, and do not reflect those of people kind enough to help me.

The author and publisher are grateful to David and Charles Ltd and Mel Equipment Company Ltd for the illustration on page 215. The diagrams and maps were drawn by John Booth.

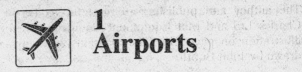

1
Airports

My first flight to a civil airport was on 17 December 1945 from RAF Oakington to Paris, Orly. Liberator J-Jig was a clapped-out, draughty, anti-U-boat veteran, Leigh searchlight removed from her starboard wing and bomb-bay stripped, who shook in every plate at engine run-up and whose battle-scars were plastered with dope and fabric. The object of the exercise was to transport an equipment officer to negotiate for (which in 1945 Britain meant beg, borrow or steal) strips of artificial runway with which to lengthen our own.

At 07.00 hours on a cool, misty Fen morning, I awaited my passenger by the aircraft.

She turned out to be, not the Squadron Leader I was expecting, but a young WAAF Section Officer, clutching a large paper bag. She sat in the jump-seat between myself and my second pilot, with the bag on her knee, as J-Jig rattled and roared down the runway and then climbed steadily up through the overcast sky into the dazzling clear of sunrise.

Orly in contrast was overcast with intermittent rain. There was only one runway in use and that with a bumpy surface. Facilities were a mixture of civilian and military. The WAAF Section Officer seemed to find her way unerringly to where the action was. In a remarkably short time, an American officer had appeared to inspect our hold capacity. Truck loads of artificial runway (punctured metal strips like wide girders) were coming, the Section Officer told me, and while it was being loaded, could she have permission to pop into Paris?

She'd never seen it. There was a truck going in. She could get a lift. She'd be back before our scheduled take-off at 15.00 hours.

I had the odd qualm. The girl was young. Paris at the end of the war was notorious for thieves and black marketeers. But I had other things on my mind. At that time I had been gazetted to a permanent commission, and I was hovering between the RAF and going into civil aviation with BOAC. There was also an oil leak in number four engine, and it didn't look as though any fitter was going to get around to fixing it.

Fifteen hundred hours came and went, and there was no sign of the Section Officer. We were full to the gills with artificial runway, and while J-Jig stood waiting on the tarmac, a couple of American GIs asked if they could thumb a lift back to the UK. I paced up and down cursing the WAAF. I told them they could scramble aboard.

She arrived, in a battered French Citroën, minus her paper bag, in a cloud of expensive perfume. She had other bottles bulging in her uniform pockets. She was saddened but unrepentant by my lecture.

It appeared that she had had as successful an afternoon as morning. Her paper bag had contained cigarettes from the Mess. She had simply sailed into the most exclusive-looking perfumery in the Champs-Elysées and bartered them for scent. I felt it was all wrong and said so. The Section Officer began an argument unbecoming to a very junior officer on why money should be more moral than cigarettes. After take-off there was an icy silence on the flight deck. I was almost glad when rain rattled on the windscreen and dribbled down our necks from the leaky roof.

But the weather worsened. The sky ahead was one black anvil-head, every few seconds lit up by lightning. The aircraft bucked and rattled as if she was going to fall apart. The WAAF Section Officer nursed her bottles on her knee, at one stage removing her cap to act as padding.

12

I could hardly see the runway lights at Oakington through the vast curtain of rain.

My landing was less than perfect. As this was a commercial flight, a makeshift customs had been set up in the aircrew canteen. I looked round for my two GI passengers to acquaint them of this fact, but they had disappeared into the darkness. I never heard of them again. I have often wondered who they were and what they were up to.

I rather hoped that the elderly Customs officer would sting the Section Officer for her ill-gotten perfume, but he seemed to take the view that maybe British females deserved it. She, too, sailed out into the night. But I never wondered what happened to her. In the words of the story, I married her, chose civil flying as a career and lived happily ever after.

My first experience as a civil passenger came six months later. Equipped now with my airline pilot's licence and Navigator's ticket, I wrote in my diary, 'I woke up thinking, well, here I start a new career.' My state of mind was exactly the same as Winston Churchill's, who had written in his diary four and a half years previously about his first Atlantic flight, 'I woke up uncommonly early with the conviction that I should certainly not go to sleep again. I must confess I felt rather frightened.'

It was my first Atlantic flight, too. I was going to Montreal to join BOAC. But first I had to fly to Prestwick to board an Atlantic Division Liberator.

London civil aerodromes after the war resembled the bivouacs of the Crimea. Tents, marquees, ancient pieces of equipment. Lunch of a stale cheese sandwich turned up at 14.30 along with a decrepit Dakota.

'The pilot of the Dakota,' I wrote, 'elected to fly at 2,500 feet just under three-eighths cumulus and gave us a sickening bumpy ride. On the descent to Prestwick, he went straight into solid frontal cloud, and I was in fear and trembling that we were going into a mountain.'

13

We didn't, but since that day to date 604 civil airliners have hit high ground. The crossing of the Atlantic was long and cold. Then we were delayed in Labrador.

That trip has made me highly sympathetic to all civil air passengers. They have been just as much pioneers as the early airmen. Then they were coming to Heathrow in small bunches: 63,151 in 1946. In 1985 there were 29·9 million, up 10·7 per cent on 1984. A city now with almost as many employees as there were passengers in those early days, Heathrow grew out of small beginnings on the notorious Hounslow Heath.

The hamlet of Heathrow used to stand on the Terminal 3 site. Some say the name is a corruption of 'Hithero', which it is called on old maps. Some say it came from 'Row to the Heath', which is fitting, for from Hounslow Heath flew the first civil passenger. And fittingly, two-and-a-half-mile east-west runways parallel the Bath Road, along which passed the first mail coach ever – a service which afterwards built up to 400 a day. And emblazoned on the fuselage of some British Airways aircraft can be seen the same RM and hunting horn symbol of carriers of the Royal Mail.

For the mail coaches running along Hounslow Heath were the forerunners of civil aviation. Then, as now, the worst stage of the journey was getting from Central London. Now it is choked with traffic, but then it was the haunt of highwaymen, the less successful of whose bloody bodies hanging from gibbets punctuated the Bath Road from Brentford to Windsor, till the exhibition was discontinued in 1800 since it offended the eyes of the Royal Family on their way from St James's Palace to Windsor.

Now the village of Heathrow lies concreted under the airport, along with a Saxon Temple and an ancient British camp, to become an archaeological remain, like the skeleton of a hippopotamus dug up when the Great West Road was being excavated. Here was the gateway to the West in Roman times when Caesar pressed back the Britons.

The Heath was policed by Hounslow Barracks at the east end and by the Royal Guards at Windsor Castle at the west. Near Hounslow is the grave of Private White, flogged to death at the Barracks, after which there was such an outcry that flogging as a punishment was abolished in the British Army.

The Barracks are there and the Guards at Windsor are still very active. In July 1974 their tanks and armoured cars of the Blues, the Royals and the Irish Guards moved into Heathrow on an anti-terrorist operation. There were fears that terrorists would mount an anti-aircraft attack with missiles such as the SAM, which homes in on the heat of aircrafts' exhausts.

Guards were again in evidence in 1978 on the arrival of the Egyptian and Israeli foreign ministers. With the increase in terrorism, their presence became more frequent till in 1985, after the massacres at Rome and Vienna, extra protection was provided by tanks and British police patrols with machine guns. In the eighteenth century, extra protection was provided with Bow Street Runners patrolling the Heath, known as 'Robin Redbreasts' from their scarlet waistcoats. These days you won't see Robin Redbreasts, but on the tarmac Redcaps will be coordinating the details of your flight. They can be recognised by their red caps and their walkie-talkies. Especially in a delay, they are very much in evidence reorganising the flight.

The inns on the Bath Road are still there where the coaches stopped on their stages. The legs of an aircraft's flight are also called stages. Of course most of them these days are hotels made of concrete and glass and are christened with such aeronautical names as Ariel, Skyway and Skyline. But you will see near the main gate the Air Hostess pub, a few hundred yards away from the Three Magpies, where in 1798 a stagecoach passenger called Mr Mellish was brought after being robbed and shot in the head. The surgeon called to attend him was waylaid by

15

the same highwayman, and the passenger was dead when the doctor eventually arrived.

Further west is the Peggy Bedford, named after the famous landlady who was reputed to have regularly entertained Queen Victoria.

Two miles further west of Heathrow is the straggly village of Colnbrook – and yet it seems to belong to another country and another age. The main street looks like a film set – the picturesque White Hart, no longer an inn, the handsome Georgian façade of the George. Further down on the left leans a long, half-timbered daub-and-wattle and brick building straight out of a fairy story, with an arch in the middle of it that once led to the stables, but now leads to a large car park.

An old hand-painted sign of an ostrich creaks in the wind. A board proclaims *Ye old Ostrich Inn, circa 1106, Britain's third oldest hostelry*. The welcome is warm. The traveller is invited to try *Robustious Elizabethan Fayre in our Elizabethan Dyning Parlour*.

A couple of hundred years ago, it was rather different. The Ostrich was a favourite overnight stop for rich clothiers travelling with laden packhorses from the West to the London markets. Here a landlord and his wife called Jarman murdered sixty of them by dropping them out of their four-poster beds through a trapdoor into a vat of boiling oil in the cellar.

Now no longer does Colnbrook echo to the clatter of hooves or the thud of clothiers falling through trapdoors. And instead of the reek of boiling oil, there is only the sweet scent of kerosene as yet another Jumbo takes off on Runway 28 – so called because its direction is 280° magnetic. And instead of the rattle of wooden coach wheels, there is the thud of an aircraft undercarriage being retracted into the fuselage.

There are people who say Heathrow has a ghost. Perhaps it has, although I haven't seen it. What I have seen, though, are the same people as have always been
16

there, like actors and actresses coming in and out of a never-ending play – the soldiers, the thieves, the pedlars, the charlatans, even the warrior kings, though they call themselves other things like presidents and generals, the invalids, the monks, the clowns, the businessmen, the children, the painted ladies from Whitechapel, the hunters and the frightened passengers. Even dogs, cats and horses can be seen at a yellow brick building near the Cargo Terminal with a large Q on the top of it – the Animal Quarantine Station.

Just next door are the massive warehouses of the Cargo Terminal. Cargo can be considered the catalyst of civil aviation. For cargo in the form of mail was the generating force of all airlines. The Berlin Airlift of 1948/9 showed that besides passengers and mail, almost everything could be transported by air – even coal.

Cargo has rocketed from 7,500 tonnes in 1951 to 544,000 tonnes in 1985. Now Heathrow is the top British port, through which £9,890.9 million exports and £10,193.6 million imports passed in 1984, easily beating all seaports, even Dover.

Further east, maintenance men work a 24-hour shift system. In the central complex, immigration officers look out for illegal immigrants. Customs men watch for smugglers and drug pedlars. Policemen walk the modernistic beat.

In all, there are 43,880 people regularly employed here – 6,019 fewer than ten years ago. There are secretaries, traffic and operations staff, doctors, nurses, priests for the airport chapel, workmen working continuously somewhere on the airfield, air traffic controllers, administrators, loaders, drivers, barmen, waiters and waitresses, refuellers and shopkeepers.

Thousands of pilots, engineers, stewards and stewardesses form a floating population in and out, appearing only going off or returning from trips. The British Airways operating crews make six more appearances, twice to have their medicals at Queen's Building (the most usual cause of rejection is high blood pressure). In case they lose their flying licences, almost all are insured, but the premium can be as high as several hundred pounds annually. On the other occasions, pilots visit Cranebank, the Training Section at the far east end of the airport to do a two-hour session on the simulator, checked out by a Training Captain. Again, they can lose their licences here – but there have only been two or three cases in the past ten years.

Highwaymen there certainly are, and still very daring. Spectacular robberies have taken place. Hauls in bank notes and travellers' cheques regularly occur. In 1977, two men gained admission to the strong-room and stole £2 million in diamonds.

Industrial diamonds in the heels of shoes once used to be fashionable. Mail bags are still slit, luggage still stolen, drugs still smuggled in. But this should be looked at against a background of a billion pounds worth of cargo coming into Heathrow every year. The insurance on air cargo is still less than on ships.

And the highwaymen do not always disappear. Stephen Raymond got himself a job in Security. Posing as the manager, and with an accomplice and forged documents, he told strong-room staff that packets of currency had been wrongly labelled and got away with £2 million in 1976. At his trial two years later, the former girlfriend of his accomplice gave evidence of money carpeting the floor of her flat. He got a ten-year sentence.

In 1978, three warehousemen admitted stealing £157,582 worth of gold which had been sent to the cargo import warehouse instead of being locked in a strong-room. The judge said, 'It required incredible negligence and a series of deliberate breaks of regulations to make this theft possible.'

Guns turn up – usually at the Security Check. Everyone ducked there when a small boy produced a toy pistol and fired caps off into the air. But in September 1978, a wooden box split open and five hundred machine guns were discovered with eighteen drums of ammunition. They were listed as agricultural machinery, and were on their way to Mogadishu, scene of the successful rescue of a hijacked Lufthansa aircraft a year before.

Blood was found running out of a grille in the summer of 1978. The body of a man with a Canadian passport and travellers' cheques was found at the bottom of a forty-foot airduct. The incident was investigated by a unit of the Middlesex police.

In 1983 came the huge Brinks-Mat robbery at Heathrow. The gang got away with £26 million in gold bullion, platinum, diamonds and travellers' cheques. And though £2 million reward for the recovery of the haul has been offered by insurance investigators in the city, and though two men have been sentenced to twenty-five years imprisonment, no one has talked, and there are still few clues to its whereabouts. A very disturbing feature of the robbery was that the raid was obviously planned with inside information from a security guard, and petrol was poured over the guards on duty to terrify them into submission. An MP has called for private security firms to be licensed, and demanded that scrutiny of such firms' employees should be made compulsory.

In November 1984, the crime was for £2 million worth of heroin, and again at Heathrow. Undercover officers in the Customs Investigation Branch (part of Operation Fisherman, launched by Customs in 1981 to smash smuggling rings) kept watch on the employees of a certain cleaning company working at Terminal 3, the interconti-nental terminal. As a result, four men were convicted at Reading Crown Court of smuggling 17.1 kilograms of heroin, worth £2,177,000. The method was simple. A courier arriving aboard an Air India flight from Delhi carried a holdall containing the heroin. As he walked along a connecting pier from the aircraft, he was met by another of the gang who guided him to an emergency exit where an employee of the cleaning company waited. The holdall was pushed into a rubbish sack and then into the waiting cleaning company van.

This method had been used successfully to bring in illegal immigrants. An employee of the same cleaning company would hang around the tarmac waiting for the aircraft, usually from India, to land. As soon as it did so and the illegal immigrant disembarked, he would be handed overall and broom and would literally sweep himself into the country.

But Heathrow doesn't improve. In December 1985, as Judge Michael Argyle QC gaoled four men for stealing and using more than £1 million worth of travellers' cheques, he said Heathrow Airport is 'rife with corruption.'

'The clearest evidence in this trial is that the security system leaks like a sieve,' he said, when Heathrow should be '. . . a jewel in the crown.'

Millions of cheques were stolen from planes before take-off. These were cashed in Europe and the UK. Consignments of cheques for South Africa and Hong Kong were passed to members of an international syndicate who used false passports to cash them.

A police search of employees' lockers at Heathrow revealed a huge quantity of stolen property, obtained from slit bags, boots of cars, missing luggage. So much of it, in fact, that it was put on display to try to trace the owners.

On 10 January 1986, fifteen British Airways baggage handlers at Terminal 3 were gaoled for a total of 53½ years after hidden police video cameras filmed them stealing from passengers' luggage. Judge Lawrence Verney said the level of dishonesty at Heathrow was appalling. 'A message must go from this court to those others behaving like you that when they are caught, the sentence of the courts is likely to be severe.'

Baggage theft may be reduced by science. At O'Hara airport, Chicago, the baggage handlers simply call out the destination of the bag when they fling it on the conveyor belt. Not only can computers speak, they can now listen and respond. The computer takes the bag to the correct aircraft without further human attention.

Theft by employees, however, is only the tiny tip of the iceberg. Crime at airports is world-wide, and drug trafficking one of the most lucrative and ruthless rackets. It is part of a huge international business and a fast growing one. Up to fifty employees of America's Eastern Airlines, mainly baggage handlers and mechanics, are about to be charged with operating a giant smuggling ring, using mainly John F. Kennedy Airport and Miami Airport. The airline itself asked the drug agency to investigate after cocaine had been found in August 1985 in the air-conditioning compartments of two Eastern Airlines jets arriving from Colombia. That discovery followed consignments of heroin seized in April 1984 in the electronics panel under the cockpit of an incoming Eastern 727. The airline had tried using sniffer dogs in Colombia where the consignments appear to originate, but very soon the dogs were found poisoned.

In Britain, Heathrow has become known as Britain's biggest smuggling depot. Young girl couriers, usually unemployed, are being recruited, especially those whose background enables them to pose as bona fide holiday-makers. BA flight 262 from Jamaica is called in some quarters the 'Pot Special'. Some women with young children have been known to bring in drugs packets strapped to their infants' bodies or in their baby food. Prostitutes are being drawn in with the promise of a handsome reward for a successful 'run' and a fortnight in one of the glamorous drug headquarters like Miami or Jamaica or Rio.

Customs officers have been helped recently by a sophis-ticated computer record system known as CEDRIC –

Customs and Excise Departmental Reference and Information Computer. Terminals are installed at Heathrow. In its memory bank are records of 170,000 people.

But main reliance is still on the observation and sixth sense of the four hundred Customs officers, plus the occasional tip-off. Last year at London's airports Customs men discovered drugs to the street value of £35 million.

Then there is the ticket fraud, now reckoned to total £200 million a year. The International Air Transport Association, the umbrella organisation for world airlines, has a scheme whereby all their members share the costs of ticket fraud. A blacklist of stolen tickets is circulated to airlines and updated weekly. Tickets are transferable between airlines, and at present an airline honours a blacklisted ticket as though it were good currency.

British Airways says that this gives no incentive to crackdown on crime and is proposing to leave IATA's scheme and introduce fraud-proof tickets with machine-readable magnetic strips to tighten security.

Naturally, with such a rich field for stories, reporters are at Heathrow. In the old days, it wasn't so much crime stories they were after, for flying itself was news.

Most passengers were GI brides or much decorated servicemen. And there was always the possibility of a crash, for the air passenger fatality rate was thirty times what it is today.

In fact, there have been very few deaths from crashes at Heathrow. A Vanguard stalled on Runway 28 Right, killing all on board after the flaps had been selected up too early on an overshoot in fog twenty-one years ago. The Captain was on my squadron and I taught the first officer at the Hamble College of Air Training. The engine of a 707 failed on take-off in 1968. The crew were half-way through the items of the engine failure check-list when it caught fire. They changed to the engine fire check-list, and because it was identical till half-way down with the engine failure check-list started half-way down.
22

Unfortunately, in the changeover the most important item – cut off the fuel supply – was missed. A skilful landing back at Heathrow was made, but the fire had caught and five people died.

The biggest crash was a Trident at Staines in 1972 when 118 were killed. Even including this one, which happened several miles from the airport, crashes at Heathrow have been remarkably few. The same is true of Gatwick, where the last fatal crash was in 1968 when an Afghan 727 ploughed into a house during an attempt to land.

It is certainly a favourite aerodrome for pilots – flat approaches, excellent landing aids, and British Air Traffic Control is certainly the best in the world. In spite of ever-increasing aircraft movements – there were 274,184 in 1985 – there has never been an air collision, a record few big airports can match.

One of the reasons for this is that light private aircraft are discouraged, and if a military aircraft enters the zone, it is *one* RAF Controller's sole responsibility to look after and keep it away from airliners. Around four big civil airliners collide every year – most of them in America, which has more light aircraft than the rest of the world put together. Seventy per cent involve a small aircraft, either a fighter or a light aeroplane, as in the San Diego 1978 crash, and eighty per cent occur in the vicinity of the airport. Air miss reports are increasing all over the world, and after unintelligible or hectically delivered instructions along their routes, pilots hear with relief the calm, clear voices of the London Controllers. The further east, the worse airports become, except for Australia and South Africa. Landing facilities such as Instrument Landing Systems and radio beacons become fewer. Control becomes worse. Hills become higher.

Heathrow's runways were built for the RAF in their traditional triangular pattern. The idea was originally to make it a combined land and marine base. Flying boats were to land on the surrounding reservoirs. None arrived. Only the perennial mist settles on the water in October and drifts over its inadequate 2,958 acres. The buildings are imprisoned by the runways in the centre, and twelve million vehicles a year struggle through the main entrance tunnel to emerge like moles up amongst Terminal 1 (domestic traffic and Europeans, mainly Aer Lingus and British Airways), Terminal 2 (twenty-nine non-UK airlines operating European services and handling six million passengers annually) and Terminal 3, from which thirty-five longhaul airlines transport ten million passengers a year.

Heathrow's capacity is now being approached, which is why the £200 million Terminal 4, giving direct access to sixteen wide-bodied aircraft stalls, has now been constructed as 'an airport within an airport'. It is well away from the other terminals, with its own underground station, car parks and road access to the M25 motorway. This satellite is designed for eight million long- and short-haul passengers, but due to the fact that arriving and departing passengers are segregated on different floors, it won't have the 'milling-mass-look' which is a feature of other Heathrow Terminals.

But it is unlikely that there will be a Terminal 5. For contained within the western perimeter of the airfield stands the gigantic Perry Oaks sewage treatment works, effectively blocking further expansion.

At present, seven piers stretch like spiders' legs to aircraft stands from the three central terminals. At peak times, like early morning or evening, thirty Jumbos can be cheek by jowl in this central complex.

In the middle of the complex, like a periscope, sticks the Tower, its glass-sided top where take-offs and landings are controlled looking over a jigsaw of numbered pieces of concrete. Should an incident occur, the exact position, like a kind of grid reference, can be passed to the police or rescue service.

24

Over to the east are the big British Airways maintenance hangars, with wall-enclosed hard standings with
special metal mufflers where aircraft engines are run-up
and tested.

To the south, with the new Terminal 4 as its neighbour,
Air Cargo has its own terminal with its own piers and
twenty-eight docking positions and its own tunnel to the
central area. Tucked just to the east of it is the luxury
suite for Very Important People – like the Queen. There
are forty-one categories of VIPs, ranging from Heads of
State and the boss of IMF to church dignatories. MPs
and pop stars are not included.

The next most important people are CIPs or Commercially Important People who are the big spenders on
airline travel and are given free drinks and personal
attention on British Caledonian's Chieftain Club or Pan
American's Clipper Club. British Airways Travellers'
Club members are entertained in Heathrow's Monarch
Lounge. There is now even a Diners' Club, lodged in the
Queen's Building. But there is no special treatment for
the bulk of the flying public – the ordinary man and
woman in the street and their families who are taking to
the air in ever-increasing numbers.

Passenger traffic is estimated to increase annually by 10
per cent. Like Heathrow, airports are trying to expand to
cope with the travel boom.

The problem of London's third airport has at last been
resolved. The Eyre Report has designated Stansted, and
work has begun on the expansion.

But who owns the airports?

Airports by tradition are local. Especially in America,
they are owned by cities such as Newark, Chicago or
Kansas City. The same used to be true of Britain, where
almost anyone with a piece of land could get it approved,
buy a £10 licence and be in business. In the 1950s the
government encouraged local authorities like Manchester
and Birmingham to have their own airports. The result

was the emergence of such anomalies as airports at Teeside and Newcastle, very close to one another and in competition for minimal business. Big cities such as Manchester, Bristol, Luton, Cardiff, Birmingham, East Midlands, Newcastle and Southampton still hang on to their own municipal airports, and there are also the independent airports of Belfast, Isle of Man, Guernsey and Jersey.

Eight aerodromes in the Scottish islands and highlands are owned by the Civil Aviation Authority. They were put up for sale in 1984, but attracted no bidders. So a Company has been formed which will be sustained by government grants.

The British Airports Authority (BAA) owns seven airports – Heathrow, Gatwick, Stansted, Glasgow, Edinburgh, Prestwick and Aberdeen – from which 174 different airlines operate. BAA is a government body set up in 1966, composed of airport professionals, business people, union representatives and private individuals. It is self-supporting, financing its programme of maintaining the airports and improving and enlarging facilities by the sale of concessions to duty free shops and restaurants, the renting of land on which the airlines build their hangars, and landing and handling fees.

At Gatwick, these landing fees can be as much as £2,000 for a Jumbo at peak periods, and as low as £20 for an executive jet. They are 20 per cent less than at Heathrow. There are reductions in certain cases, the most valuable of which is a 20 per cent reduction for aircraft with the latest 'quiet' jets.

Stansted and Prestwick made small losses in 1985, but the overall BAA trading profit for that year was £73 million. The seven BAA airports are due to be sold in the near future as part of the government's privatisation plan.

A huge price is expected, for BAA is now a highly successful organisation. And of all BAA's airports, by far the most profitable and most rapidly expanding is Gatwick.

If London Heathrow is a microcosm of metropolis history, London Gatwick is its rural counterpart. It is sited thirty miles south of London in the county of West Sussex, between the North and South Downs.

A hundred million years ago, the area was a vast lake, till the rivers that fed it brought sufficient mud and clay for the ground to emerge and forests to grow. Fifteen hundred years ago, drawn by the iron ore, the Saxons built the manor of Charlwood and the sub-manor of Gatewyk. Then came the Normans, who built the churches, and in 1304 John de Gatwicke was granted two acres 'for his fealty and sixteen shillings in silver, and a yearly rent of sixteen pence'. The Gatwickes prospered and expanded, John's daughter marrying Thomas de Cobham. The Cobham family then held the land through the ravages of the Black Death till it was sold to John Jordan in 1495.

In that family it remained through the Civil War and the Industrial Revolution, till the now large Jordan estate was divided between two sisters, and Philippa Sharp inherited Charlwood and Gatwick. The Sharp family erected a new mansion near the Reigate-Crawley road which was called Timberham from its vicinity 'to a bridge anciently styled Kill-man Bridge, now corrupted to Kilberham or Timberham Bridge, near where there was a great slaughter of the Danes by the inhabitants of Surrey and Sussex, who fell on the rear of their forces and gave them an entire defeat'.

The Sharps sold out to Alexander Fraser, who in 1890 sold to the Gatwick Race Course Company. A one-and-a-half-mile railway in the grounds was dismantled, and a vast grandstand (now the site of the passenger terminal) was put up in its place.

Here Lester Piggott's grandfather won the Grand

National in 1918. Then an astute businessman called Ronald Waters realised in 1930, with the growth of the then tiny civil aviation industry, that Gatwick was directly opposite the gap in the North Downs through which aircraft could slip when London's main airport of Croydon was fogbound. And he built a small private airfield.

Officials reportedly did not bother to reply to his idea of a big airport and he sold out. The famous beehive terminal was then constructed in 1936 – forerunner of Pan American's Worldport and the new Gatwick satellite – as well as a railway station to which the terminal was connected by a tunnel.

Independent airlines began operating in competition with the quasi-government Imperial Airways. A year later, the drains broke down and the place became a useless quagmire till it was repaired just in time for the war.

On 18 May 1946, I made my last flight in the RAF from Gatwick, the starboard outer engine of the Liberator failing on the way to Oakington, where we landed on three.

For years after that, it was simply a flying club, till 1952 and enter the Air Tourist, propelled by Pan American's insistence on mass travel cheap fares.

At a cost of £7.8 million, the one runway was strengthened and extended. One pier for aircraft boarding gates and a passenger terminal were opened in 1958.

At last, out of the mists of history, Gatwick came into its own.

Its rise has been phenomenal. Terminal buildings, hangars, car parks were built at a cost of £100 million – BAA's money, not the taxpayers'. With the runway now 10,150 feet, further passenger facilities, 77 aircraft stands, 12,000 public car-park spaces and 380 trains a day, in the last ten years its passengers have almost trebled to 14,227,954 in 1985.

In comparison, Heathrow only increased by a third over the same period.

Gatwick is now the busiest single-runway airport, is the fastest growing and the fifth biggest of the one thousand international airports in the world (the other four are Heathrow, Kennedy, Frankfurt and Charles de Gaulle, in that order). There were 159,722 aircraft movements in 1985 and 156,561 tonnes of cargo and mail were handled.

Essentially, Gatwick has stayed true to its origins of being the 'private enterprise' airport, where non-government airlines like Dan-Air, Air Europe and British Caledonian – the largest independent airline in Europe – operate. But now, in all, 30 airlines fly out to 116 cities. Fuel for their aircraft comes to Gatwick by rail, thence to a tank farm north of the field. From there it is piped through hydrants on the tarmac or is taken by tanker to the aircraft.

Like a huge white circular memorial, now an office block itself marooned in a small sea of other offices, still stands the prophetic 'beehive' terminal. To the north, hiving off the main terminal, is its larger white circular grandson, known as the 'satellite', opened in 1983 and built to up Gatwick's passenger capacity from 12½ million to 16 million.

If your aircraft is departing from one of the satellite's eight gates, you go to a 'station' where a train (part of a £3 million automatic system) awaits you. The low door shuts. A metallic voice calls, 'Hold tight!' Then you are off on your 44-second trip at 22 miles an hour.

Below the big front window is your 'driver' – a computer. More a bus than a railway, it runs on rubber tyres. Horizontal wheels grip a central rail through which comes both the power and the computer information.

'You are approaching the satellite,' the metallic voice warns you. 'Gates 31 to 38.'

The car stops. The door opens. The other car is just leaving the 'station' for the main terminal. You go up into a wheel surrounded by glass, from which the eight gates and their 'jetties', along which you walk to your aircraft, stick out like elongated spokes. On a busy day, you will see the whale-like noses of eight Jumbos nuzzling the glass outside.

The passenger seating is colour-coded with the lights and the carpets below – red for Gates 37 and 38, purple for 35 and 36, blue for 33 and 34, green for 31 and 32. There is a pavement complete with globular street lamps in the hub, where there are buffet bars and a duty-free shop. In its own way, it is like your own private VIP lounge.

The satellite lounge has increased Gatwick's passenger capacity, but the tourist boom brings still more passengers.

And Gatwick is a popular airport, both with passengers and the people who work there. It has a friendly atmosphere and is surrounded by countryside. Grass and trees and shrubs and flowers are planted between office blocks and terminals. A spur from the M23 motorway brings the motorist directly into the airport. In 1936 Gatwick was the first airport in the world to have a direct rail link to the city of London, and now has a regular express service at fifteen-minute intervals.

On arrival by car, bus or train, straight away you are channelled into the departure hall. It is decorated in brown and beige – relaxing colours – and the lighting is reduced. The decor is purposely arranged to have the maximum calming effect. The arrival hall, on the other hand, is coloured a cheerful yellow and bright green.

Here is everything you want for the time being, information desk, check-in counters, post office, banks, car hire, telephones, left luggage, arrival and departure board, children's rendezvous points, Customs and Immigration. Note that though you appear to come in at ground level, this is the floor above. So if you go in a lift, it's 3 you want.

Seven boxes await passengers' comments at Gatwick. Usually strike delays are tolerated better than weather, though delays like those caused by the 1978 French air traffic controllers' strike increased the number of complaints from 40 to 280 a year.

Over all, complaints about the seven BAA airports have decreased dramatically from a peak of 11,997 in 1979/80. Complaints per 100,000 passengers have fallen from 23·5 in 1980 to 8·3 in 1985 at Heathrow, and are down to 5·9 per 100,000 at Gatwick. The complaints are usually about catering, or about baggage – availability of porters or trolleys (though 2,500 of these are provided at Gatwick, and Heathrow has 4,500, more than any other airport in the world). Other complaints are about cleanliness, comfort and convenience of buildings, car parks and roads.

On the fourth floor are restaurants, buffets, most non-duty-free shops, rest-rooms, a medical centre and a chapel. St George's Chapel at Heathrow is an underground crypt, surrounded by a pavement lined by flower beds that is dominated by a sixteen-foot cross, but here it is on the fourth floor amongst the shops and restaurants, in what is called 'Gatwick Village'. On the brown carpet is the altar, behind which is a slightly garish silver curtain. There are Church of England and Catholic padres. A copy of the Koran is available. Roman Catholic Mass is held on Saturdays at 12.00 and 14.30, and on Sundays at 08.00, 09.30 and 10.30 (May to September). Members of other faiths should contact the information desks for advice.

On the outside chapel wall in a glass case is a core of concrete, 'which Pope Paul II kissed on May 28th, 1982, the first time a reigning Pope has visited Britain'.

Just down the corridor is another reminder of history. Under a huge cracked-open fruit called 'The Big Orange', a girl dispenses real orange juice at 50 pence a glass, commemorating Braniff's Big Orange, an orange-coloured 747 from Dallas which used to fly over my house at nine o'clock prompt every morning – now vanished into

the shades of time with the racecourse and the Grandstand and the Sharps' elegant mansion – killed by the
bankruptcy of the Braniff airline in the cut-throat struggle
for aviation survival in 1983.

In that particular battle, Gatwick has shown itself well
up front. With the collapse of Laker and his cheap walk-
on service, a decline in the airport could have been
expected instead of its spectacular advance. But the
airport is still expanding. Now coming up fast in reserve
is the new North Terminal, being built at a cost of £200
million.

On paper, it looked impossible. The River Mole went
right through the middle of the proposed site. As if that
wasn't bad enough, a little further south, so did the
perimeter road to the cargo area. The important A23
would have to be closed for weeks to build a 1,200-metre
railway line, similar to the satellite connection from the
mainline Gatwick station to the new Terminal. Then,
water will not drain away through concrete and disappear
like it does through soil, and twenty-nine acres of concrete
were being laid.

But David H. Williams, who is in charge of the project,
was not daunted. Between May and October 1983, the
River Mole was diverted northwards. The earth from
that excavation was arranged in a gigantic shield against
noise for the Gatwick Post Hotel and the inhabitants of
houses nearby. This has been landscaped with shrubs and
trees, as have the banks of the Mole, and a balancing
pond has been built to take care of excess water.

When the North Terminal is opened in 1987 it will
increase Gatwick's passenger-handling capacity to twenty-
five million annually.

But will that be enough to cope with the air-passenger
boom?

As a result of the Eyre Report, the Airports Bill
was passed through Parliament on 16–17 January 1986,
naming Stansted as the third London Airport, thus bring-

ing to an end a heated and expensive controversy that has lasted for many years.

Thirty-four miles north-east of London, with nice flat approaches and originally built in 1942 to accommodate American bombers, Stansted handled a record 547,000 passengers in 1985. Now a railway station is to be built beside a new terminal, together with an hotel alongside. Cargo provision – it is already noted for transporting racehorses for Newmarket – is to be dramatically increased.

Drama of a less desirable nature happened when an attempt was made to kidnap a Nigerian diplomat, Mr Biko, who was found at Stansted, drugged and bound in a packing case labelled for Lagos. On arrival, apparently the intention was that he should stand trial for misappropriation.

In Scotland, aircraft movements have also been increasing, particularly in Aberdeen, with its North Sea oil connections, though there has been a lessening of its North Atlantic traffic. Now the oil crisis has hit it.

All in all, with the BAA, CAA and municipal airports added together, there does appear now to be ample good airport provision in the UK for the rest of the century.

Facilities for handicapped and sick passengers

Large airports and some airlines provide special services for the sick and handicapped, so long as they are notified. The airline's travelling agent will arrange for someone to help providing they know in advance. At Gatwick a disabled passenger will be met by the rail air hostess and escorted to the check-in. For those in wheelchairs, ramps, lifts, special parking and toilets, permitting access to standard wheelchairs, are provided. There are facilities for the deaf (indicated by an ear symbol), and some staff at the Information Desk are proficient in finger spelling. Passengers who could experience difficulty in reading

33

signs and information displays should notify their handling agent.

Each airline is handled by one of these agents:

Gatwick Handling	– (0293) 28822 Ext. 2596
British Caledonian	– (0293) 27890 Ext. 2099
British Airways	– (0293) 28822 Ext. 2485

The disabled air passenger particularly should make sure which of them is handling his flight.

Special electric cars are ready to transport those who have difficulty walking.

In 1981, Gatwick received a British Tourist Authority award in recognition for their facilities for disabled visitors.

British Caledonian Medical Liaison Unit liaises for stretcher-cases, wheelchairs (700 are provided each month) and other medical and surgical requirements. They arrange ambulances and see that oxygen is available.

No charge is made for wheelchairs or oxygen. A charge is made for stretchers on the aircraft – 50 per cent of each seat displaced. If an attendant travels too, they are charged half of a one-way fare.

The Unit also arranges for babies in incubators. In one case an incubator had to be specially fitted to a British Caledonian aircraft. Then the aircraft had to be flown out to Dublin with an engineer and two nurses. On arrival in England, the baby was taken to Great Ormond Street Hospital.

A first-class medical service, run by British Caledonian, is at the airport to deal with emergencies. Passengers who haven't brought their pills, who suddenly feel ill, are treated immediately. A surgery with two sickrooms attached is manned by nursing sisters twenty-four hours a day.

The facilities provided are so good that now and again attempts are made by passengers to use a normal scheduled flight as an air ambulance, usually by those with gunshot wounds obtained in Africa. One passenger with a minor gunshot graze on his ankle collapsed in a car on his way to the airport. The driver opened his shirt to massage his heart and found a gunshot wound in his chest.

There is a form which should be filled in for incapacitated passengers by the agent, the second part of which must be completed by the attending physician. For heart and respiratory complaints, patients should be able to walk 100 metres if they wish to be accepted as passengers. Fractures should not travel for forty hours after application of plaster of Paris in case of swelling. Pregnancy is not generally acceptable after the thirty-sixth week for European journeys and the thirty-fourth for Transcontinental trips.

In the aircraft, it would be expected that the seats with the most room would be reserved for the disabled. Unfortunately, these are almost always by emergency exits – and it is essential to have able-bodied people there to open them and help, for there are no standardised ways of opening them. Left turns, right turns, pull up, pull down – each type of aircraft seems to have its individual open sesame, and this chaotic state of affairs is certainly a safety hazard.

Lost Property

There is a Lost Property Office at all main airports. At Gatwick it is down in the basement and open seven days a week, 08.30 – 16.00. They deal with property lost at the airport only. For property lost on an aircraft, the passenger must apply to the airline.

Where do the passengers lose their property? Usually any place where their train of thought is interrupted. Immigration, while they look for their passports. Inside and outside toilets. By bookstalls. False teeth have even been handed in from the restaurant. You can always tell what the weather was like by the number of mackintoshes handed in during the month.

In August 1983, 922 items were handed in. The inventory for November 1982 reads like a shop's stocktaking: 48 cameras (19 of them Kodak, 1 Pentax, 3 lenses, 1 flashgun – all contained in a hand case), 5 hairdryers, 7 radios, 5 clocks, 3 calculators, 2 video games, a cine camera, torches, microscope, 2 electric razors, binoculars, 2 stereo systems, 34 bottles of alcohol (mainly whisky), 207 pieces of luggage, ranging from rucksacks and briefcases to suitcases, 111 purses, 88 luggage wheels, 19 bottles of perfume and 4,280 cigarettes (Benson and Hedges easily the favourite).

Sometimes a passport is handed in. As the more recent ones have the next of kin's address, if the owner can't be found, the next of kin is contacted.

If there is an address on the item, it is contacted. Sixty per cent of the property is returned to the owners, the department doing a fair bit of detective work to find them. Library books are returned to their respective libraries.

People in general on British airports are reasonably honest and bring in items they have found. It has to be explained to them that under a 1972 regulation they will not be given to the finder if unclaimed. When they hear this, some finders try to snatch the stuff back.

If the items are not claimed within six months, they are auctioned at Haywards Heath. There are two auction sales a year, which bring in £3,000–4,000. This is used to help defray the office expenses.

On the shelves lie rows of watches, cameras, coats, skis, a couple of rubber tyres, a bicycle, a pair of crutches, innumerable pieces of Spanish and Portuguese pottery, a tennis racquet, a box of Californian peaches – all neatly labelled with the date when they were found.

People do strange things. Faced with having to pay excess for overweight luggage, they leave the bag behind.

An insurance claim might be tried if it was lost. If it goes to Lost Property, the airline might be talked into tucking it into a spare corner of a plane going to the passenger's destination free of charge.

Even stranger was the woman who locked her dog in a ladies' toilet, boarded her plane and flew off. Presumably plans or hopes of taking it with her had been dashed. Hours later, Lost Property had a frantic phone call from abroad. The woman had failed to contact her husband to tell him to collect it – and now asked Lost Property to oblige instead.

And of course Lost Property called the police.

The Airport Police

On the left-hand side of the North Perimeter road at Gatwick going southwards is an unobtrusive red brick building that resembles a small office block, except for what looks like a quaint blue lighthouse standing outside – Gatwick police station with antique police telephone alarm worth £4,000.

Inside, it is the same as any other police station of a medium-sized town: cells, offices, lecture rooms and stores. Its duties are also much the same – mainly law-enforcement over the whole area, air-side and ground-side. That means patrolling beats in the terminals, cargo warehouses, aircraft parking areas, car parks, roads and perimeter tracks. But its complement is likely to be larger because of one important additional duty.

Originally, during the Second World War, aerodrome police were under the Ministry of Defence. Then the British Airports Authority had its own police on the airports it owned, while the CAA and the municipal authorities employed their police for the airports belonging to them.

In 1975, the policing of most large airports was put under the local forces – in Gatwick's case, the Sussex

Police. In addition, airlines such as British Caledonian employed their own security men for their own areas.

These police salaries are paid mainly from part of the passenger levy (now added to the aircraft landing charge), partly by the central government and partly by the local authority.

One duty that occurs more often on an airport than in a town is the policing of the arrivals of VIPs, such as the Pope and Heads of State. There is likely to be a band, a red carpet and a guard of honour as well as a Minister to welcome them. As soon as the dignatory's feet touch British soil, a signal is sent by radio for a 21-gun salute to be fired, usually in Hyde Park. The visiting party is then accommodated at one of two Gatwick VIP Suites – the North Gate or the Churchill Suite, to which is attached a Press Conference room – before leaving for London escorted by motorcycle outriders.

In contrast, when the Queen arrives at Gatwick, it is likely to be a low-key affair and she slips away quietly.

Thefts, break-ins, fires, losses, casualties, cars illegally parked – these are the usual offences on an airport as in a town, though with 12,000 cars parked at the height of the season, the stealing of vehicles occurs more frequently. A dead man, apparently murdered, was found in a car boot at Gatwick in 1985. Luggage disappears, but with containerisation less than previously. Unattended bays and luggage are watched, and if too long a time elapses without the luggage being claimed, are investigated. The police have equipment to do so, but really suspicious articles are left for the Bomb Squad to deal with.

What makes the task of the airport police more difficult than outside is the prevalence of 'airportitis'. Everyone who is going on a flight is to some degree tensed up. People will be more liable to leave valuables in toilets, lose their tickets, their passports, their relatives and their way. There are 50,000 notices in Gatwick giving out information and indicating where to go. But people get tunnel vision and walk straight past, staring anxiously ahead.

As a result, people tend to drink more than they would otherwise. That makes them more forgetful, more childish and inclined to be obstreperous. A high degree of understanding has to be exercised by the airport police in handling them.

And that important additional duty that is always in the minds of airport police is their anti-terrorist role. Once every year at Gatwick flying is cancelled and the procedure for a full-scale emergency is practised. Watched over by inspectors, unless it is well handled, no licence is granted to the airport. It is a measure of the efficiency of the airport security and safety forces that a licence has never been withheld. And so far, unlike Heathrow, tanks are not seen on the Gatwick perimeter track and the police rarely carry machine guns.

But the air transport industry remains particularly vulnerable to terrorist attacks which increased to horrific proportions in 1985. Though there has been a lot of inter-government talk, very little high level agreement on how to cope with them has been reached.

Reliance is therefore put on each country's police and security forces to maintain constant vigilance – a task certainly carried out to the letter on British airports.

Weather and Maintenance

All European main airports have a fog problem with the exception of Prestwick, which is remarkably fog-free. Particularly in the autumn, mist forms on Heathrow's reservoirs and drifts over the field. The bends of the River Mole do the same thing for Gatwick.

In 1982/3, the number of hours that the Runway Visual Range (the visibility near touchdown electronically assessed continually by an instrument called a transmissometer that measures the loss of light from a source

39

projected from a standard distance to Air Traffic Control) fell below 800 metres and/or cloud base of less than 200 feet were 122 at Heathrow, 232 at Gatwick, 418 at Stansted, 87 at Glasgow, 63 at Edinburgh, 9 at Prestwick and 41 at Aberdeen.

Most of that time, aircraft would have been able to land on Category I Instrument Landing System. But many modern jets are now equipped to land on Category III ILS automatically in virtually nil visibility. It is once they are on the ground, taxiing to the stands, that their problems really start.

Crosswinds remain a problem, particularly at Gatwick where there is only the one 08/26 runway – and no possibility of another. However, as the number of hours in a year when the crosswind component was more than 20 knots was only 20 hours in 1982/3, there is no real call for another. In any case, there is now a signed undertaking with Surrey County Council *not* to build one. The number of passengers that Gatwick can take is therefore limited by the aircraft movements (take-offs and landings) that the runway can cope with. However, the authorities are confident that more wider-bodied aircraft will be landing, able to bring in a greater number of passengers per landing.

That runway nevertheless has to be carefully watched and maintained. Major operations are let out to contractors on a three-year basis, but three gangs are under the supervision of the BAA engineers for smaller jobs. The maintenance of the hangars is attended to by the airlines which lease them.

The cost is phenomenal. The simple repairing of a bay is likely to be around £140,000. When the runway has to be attended to, because closure is so expensive, the whole operation is done at night and is organised with split-second timing by Operations. Lorries, vans and cars – all engines running – assemble on the south side of the runway under a concourse of floodlights, waiting for the
40

'off' from Operations as though at Le Mans. Immediately the runway is closed, the contractors take over, working at full tilt throughout the night. Routine runway maintenance is carried out for a fortnight in March and November, when the runway is closed from 23.45 to 07.45.

Sometimes improvements have to be carried out, like the fitting of an ice alert – three sensor heads on the runway – one at ambient temperature, one cooler, one heated. These three compare notes electronically through a computer, which decides when ice will form and transmits the alarm to Operations.

The men wear luminous reflector jackets which show up well. Working often in cold temperatures, they have to use blow torches to get the concrete to harden in repairs.

British and American airports are carefully looked after, and excellent modern aids provided. This is not the case with others, particularly in Africa, Asia and South America and indeed some European airports. It is a pity that the airport 'rating' is not highly publicised, since it is one way the responsible authorities can be persuaded to improve their facilities. It could be shown on signs as stars, as in the hotel business. And people could ask what rating their departure and arrival airports have before booking.

Most international airports are named either geographically, as in Britain, or after famous people like Kennedy, La Guardia, Charles de Gaulle. Canada's new Mirabel on the other hand is named after a farmer's two daughters, Miriam and Isabel. His farm is now sunk in the middle of the airport's 88,000 acres. It has excellent flat approaches free from fog, but it has the disadvantage of being 14 miles from downtown Montreal.

On the other hand, you can't miss it. The airport highway will take you there and nowhere else. That's quite unlike British airports which can be hard to find.

And when you do find them, you can promptly lose yourself again in their complexity.

Getting to the airport and through its various hurdles is the worst part of the trip.

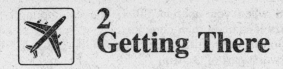

2
Getting There

Getting to an airport – particularly Heathrow – can be hell. It isn't just you. Everybody has the same difficulty. The time before you settle into your seat on the aircraft is the most uncomfortable and the most dangerous part of your flight.

The phenomenal success of civil flying is the real culprit. Nobody had any idea that the baby they inherited after the Second World War would grow into such a gargantuan giant. Four thousand passengers could cross the Atlantic annually by air, said the planners, crossing their fingers and thinking themselves terribly daring. The actuality is now four million to Heathrow alone. And in 1985, 31.1 million passengers used that airport, by far the busiest international airport in the world.

As a result, airports had to grow, inevitably in a makeshift pattern. They can also be difficult to find, and when you do find them, there may be further difficulties, particularly at Heathrow, threading your way through the maze till you reach your aircraft seat.

So here are plans of the main British airports and how to get there.

First of all, the London airports.

Heathrow

How to Travel to Heathrow Airport

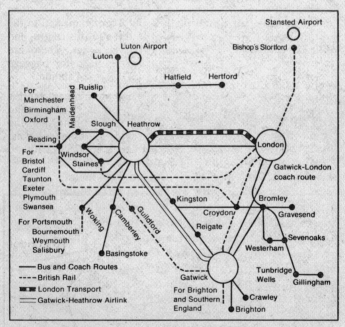

Heathrow, Gatwick and Stansted are well served by public transport – bus and coach, rail and underground from London to Heathrow. The helicopter airlink between Heathrow and Gatwick operated by British Airways is not now to be operated by British Caledonian. Green Line 727 serves Heathrow, Gatwick and Luton. Connections can be made at Watford with British Rail services to and from the Midlands and the North West.

Underground: Heathrow is linked to the entire Greater London area by the capital's underground railway network. The airport has two separate stations on the Piccadilly Line, one serving Terminals 1, 2 and 3, the other serving Terminal 4. They link the airport with London's West End and City by inter-changing with all the London termini of British Rail. Total journey time to Piccadilly Circus is 47 minutes, to King's Cross 55 minutes, to Liverpool Street (change at Holborn) 61 minutes. Trains run every 3 minutes at peak times and 8–10 minutes off-peak and Sundays. First train for Central London leaves Heathrow at 04.59 (Sunday 05.52) and the last at approximately 23.41 (Sundays 23.43).

Pedestrian subways: Terminals 1, 2 and 3 are connected to the Piccadilly Line underground station in the airport's centre, and to each other, by enclosed pedestrian subways. There are moving walkways in the subways, wide enough for baggage trolleys. There is no subway link to the Terminal 4 station.

Train and Express Coach: British Rail operate frequent express coaches connecting Heathrow with trains at Reading and Woking stations. The Reading link takes 55 minutes and the Woking link 45 minutes. The coaches call at all three terminals. First/last coach from Heathrow to Reading is at 06.55/23.10.

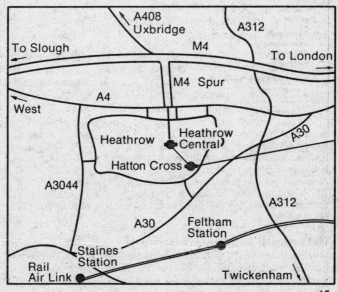

Bus

Airbus – Express London Bus: London Transport operate two express bus links between Heathrow and London. Airbus calls at all four terminals and has ample space for passengers' baggage.

Single fare: £3.00 (children £1.50).

A1: To and from Victoria station.

Frequency – about every 20 minutes.

A2: To and from Euston station.

Frequency – about every 30 minutes.

London Transport buses – 105, 111, 140, 202, 223, 285, N97* – service the surrounding areas of the airport and all stop at Heathrow Central bus station. (*Nights only)

Greenline Jetlink 747: Daily except Christmas Day. Non-stop Gatwick Airport with onward connections to Brighton. Costs £4 rising to £8.

Greenline Flightline 767: Set-down and pick-up at each Terminal and at Central bus station, Stop L. Takes 70 minutes. Every half-hour. Non-stop to London's Victoria coach station with onward connections to all parts of the country. First/last bus from Heathrow 05.15/22.15, Victoria 06.25/23.25.

Greenline: 701 Maidenhead and Slough, 726 Sutton and Dartford, 727 Watford and Luton, 733 Hitchin, 790 High Wycombe and Oxford.

Taxi: Taxis are available for hire at the authorised ranks outside each terminal. Drivers are licensed to operate in the Metropolitan Police District which covers all of inner London and a major part of the Greater London area. If your destination is less than 20 miles, and within this area, taxi drivers may not charge you for their return journey – you need only pay the fare shown on the meter. Average fare from Heathrow to Central London (15 miles) is about £12–£15. If you wish to travel outside the Metropolitan Police District you must agree the fare with the driver before starting your journey.

Air taxis are also available. Information (0428) 4804. Remember busiest times are Fridays, Saturdays and Sundays between 07.00 and 13.00.

ARAVCO (01) 897 3406

BRYAN (01) 759 3001

Car: Remember that 45,000 people work at Heathrow. Avoid 08.30–10.00 and 16.30–18.00. Access roads are anyway inadequate and likely to be crowded. Access to Terminals 1, 2 and 3 is through the tunnel from the M4 motorway spur or the A4 (Bath) road. Heathrow is 15 miles from Central London.

There is direct access to Terminal 4 from the A30 from Staines, access is left on to the Stanwell road and then via the southern perimeter road. Travelling south-west from London, access is left and over the flyover.

Passengers may alight and luggage may be unloaded outside the terminals, but no waiting is allowed. Short-term car parks adjacent to each terminal are intended for people visiting the airport for short periods. If you need to stay longer, you are strongly advised to use the cheaper long-term car park, signposted at the tunnel end of the M4 spur and the A4 airport entrance. Short-term car park prices are £1.20p for up to 2 hours and 60p per hour for each subsequent hour.

If you are planning to leave your car for more than 4 hours, you will find it more economical to park in the long-term car park, costing £2.00 for up to 12 hours. A regular coach service will take you and your baggage to the passenger terminal free of charge and back to your car when you return. Pre-booking is not required. You can make enquiries on (01) 759 7160.

TAKE CARE NOT TO LEAVE YOUR CAR UNATTENDED OUTSIDE THE TERMINALS, AS IT MAY BE REMOVED BY THE POLICE ((01) 897 7373). A CHARGE OF £57 IS MADE FOR RECOVERY.

Facilities

Information: There are Information Desks in each Terminal.

Terminal 1	(01) 745 7702/3/4
Terminal 2	(01) 745 7115/6/7
Terminal 3 (Arrivals)	(01) 745 7412/3/4
Terminal 3 (Departures)	(01) 745 7067
Terminal 4	(01) 745 7139

Banks: Are situated in all terminals. Barclays at Terminal 3 Arrivals is open seven days a week, 24 hours a day.

Restaurants, buffets and bars: At all terminals.

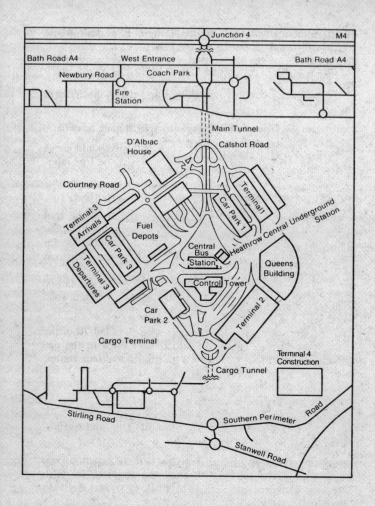

Left luggage: At all terminals. Charge 60p per item for first 24 hours, £1.00 for each subsequent 24 hours. Open 06.45–22.00.

Lost property: Is on the ground floor of Car Park 2 at the Exit end, opposite Terminal 2. Open seven days a week from 09.00 to 16.00. Tel. (01) 745 7727. Airlines should be contacted over anything left on aircraft or airline buses.

48

Hotel reservations: At each terminal there is a desk where accommodation can be booked in the UK.

Post Offices: Terminals 1 and 2. Open every day 08.30–18.00, except Sunday.

There are public coin-box telephones and stamp machines in all terminals.

Nursing mothers: Free facilities are provided at each terminal.

Transfer passengers: Passengers changing planes should check at their airline transfer desk where details about the free inter-terminal bus service will be given, if necessary.

Hotels: There are numerous hotels close to the airport.

Spectators: Visitors may watch airport activity from the roof gardens of the Queen's Building, where there is a buffet, bar and children's playground. Admission 60p for adults, 20p for children. Open 10.00 to dusk, the whole year except Christmas and Boxing Days.

During the summer a special bus runs between the spectators' car park on the north of the airport just off the A4 Bath road and the Queen's Building.

Flight enquiries and operational services: More than 70 of the world's international airlines use Heathrow. Each of the airport's four terminals is mainly designated for certain routes, i.e.:

Terminal 1 – serving UK and Irish airlines
Terminal 2 – serving European airlines
Terminal 3 – serving intercontinental airlines
Terminal 4 – British Airways intercontinental, Paris and Amsterdam, KLM, Air Malta.

CHECK YOUR AIRLINE TICKET TO CONFIRM WHICH TERMINAL YOU SHOULD USE. In the following section the terminal for each airline is given in brackets – i.e. (T1), (T2), (T3), and the flight prefix follows.
Note:
British Airways flights numbered BA 294 to BA 999 (European, Miami and Chicago) and all British Airways UK flights – use Terminal 1.
British Airways flights numbered BA 001 to BA 293 (Intercontinental) – use Terminal 4.

Aer Lingus (T1) EI   (01) 745 7017
Aeroflot (T2) SU   (01) 759 2525
Air Algerie (T2) AH   (01) 759 5642
Air Canada (T3) AC(01) 759 France (T2) AF   (01) 759 2311
Air India (T3) AI   (01) 897 6311
Air Jamaica (T3) JM   (01) 759 2525
Air Malta (T4) KM   (01) 745 4133
Air UK (T1) UK   (01) 745 7017
Alia, Royal Jordanian Airlines (T3) RJ   (01) 745 7031
Alitalia (T2) AZ   (01) 759 1198
Austrian Airlines (T2) OS   (01) 745 7179
Balkan-Bulgarian Airlines (T2) LZ   (01) 759 2525
Bangladesh Bimar (T3) BG   (01) 759 2525
British Airways
– UK, Shuttle, and Europe (not Paris,
Amsterdam)
– Intercontinental flights (including
Concorde, Paris and Amsterdam flights) (T4)   (01) 759 2525
British Midland Airways (T1) BD   (01) 745 7321
British West Indian Airways (T3) BW   (01) 759 2331
Brymon Airways (T1) BC   (01) 759 2525
Cyprus Airways (T2) CY   (01) 759 2525
Czechoslovak Airlines (T2) OK   (01) 759 2525
Dan Air (T1) DA   (01) 759 2525
Egyptair (T3) MS   (01) 759 1520
El Al (T1) LY   (01) 759 9771
Ethiopian Airlines (T3) ET   (01) 759 2525
Finnair (T2) AY   (01) 745 7534
Genair (T1) En   (01) 759 7017
Ghana Airways (T3) GH   (01) 759 2525
Gulf Air (T3) GF   (01) 897 0402
Iberia Airlines (T2) IB   (01) 759 4321 Ext. 5527
Icelandair (T2) F1   (01) 759 2525
Iranair (T3) IR   (01) 745 7222
Iraqi Airways (T3) IA   (01) 759 2525
Japan Air Lines (T3) JL   (01) 759 9880
Jugoslav Airlines (T2) JU   (01) 759 2525
Kenya Airways (T3) KQ   (01) 745 7362
KLM Royal Dutch Airlines (T4) KL   (01) 568 9144
Kuwait Airways (T3) KU   (01) 745 7774
Libyan Arab Airlines (T2) LN   (01) 759 2311
LOT – Polish Airlines (T2) LO   (01) 759 2525

Lufthansa German Airlines (T2) LH	(01) 759 5642
Luxair (T2) LG	(01) 759 2311
Malaysian Airlines System (T3) MH	(01) 759 2595
Malev Hungarian Airlines (T2) MA	(01) 759 2525
Manx Airlines (T1) JE	(01) 745 7321
Middle East Airlines (T3) ME	(01) 759 9211
Nigeria Airways (T3) WT	(01) 759 2525
NLM City Hopper (T4) HN	(01) 568 9144
Olympic Airways (T2) OA	(01) 745 7253
Pan American World Airways (T3) PA	(01) 759 2595
PIA Pakistan International Airlines (T3) PK	(01) 759 2544
QANTAS (T3) QF	(01) 759 2331
Royal Air Maroc (T2) AT	(01) 759 2311
Sabena, Belgian Airlines (T1) SN	(01) 745 7292
SAS Scandinavian Airlines System (T2) SK	(01) 745 7576
Saudia-Arabia Airlines (T3) SV	(01) 745 4373
Singapore Airlines (T3) SQ	(01) 759 2525
South African Airways (T1) SA	(01) 897 3645
Sudan Airways (T3) SD	(01) 759 2525
Swissair (T2) SR	(01) 759 7191
Syrian Arab Airlines (T3) RB	(01) 759 2525
TAP Air Portugal (T2) TP	(01) 759 2525
TAROM – Romanian Airlines (T2) RO	(01) 759 2525
Thai International (T3) TG	(01) 759 2331
Trans World Airlines (T3) TW	(01) 759 5352
Tunis Air (T2) TU	(01) 759 2311
Turkish Airlines (T2) TK	(01) 759 2525
Varig – Brazilian Airlines (T3) RG	(01) 759 1179
VIASA – Venezuelan Airlines (T3) VA	(01) 759 2331
Zambia Airways (T3) QZ	(01) 897 0470

Cargo Facilities

The Cargo Terminal on the south side of the airport covers 65 hectares (160 acres), and 16 airlines are transit shed holders together with about 130 freight agents in 120,000 square metres of accommodation.

For information, ring BAA's London-Air Cargo Gateway to the World – Tel. (0293) 599145.

Gatwick

How to travel to Gatwick

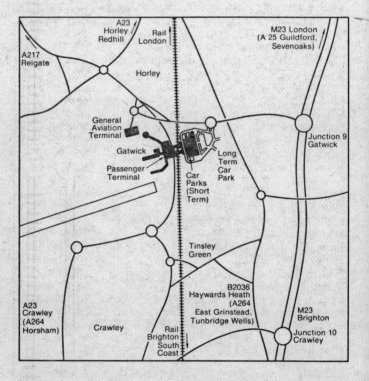

Airlink: The ten flight-a-day helicopter link between Heathrow and Gatwick has unfortunately been discontinued (June 1986).

Train: At fifteen-minute intervals, the Gatwick Express runs to and from Victoria throughout the day and hourly throughout the night, taking only 30 minutes. If travelling British Caledonian, luggage can be checked in at the air terminal in Victoria station and the airline will take care of it till final destination.

Car: Via the A23 or the M23 motorway. Open-air car park £2.00 per day (7,500 spaces), free bus service connects to terminal.

3,000 spaces in multi-storey park, connected to terminal by walkways. 40p for first hour to £3.60 for 24 hours.

No need to reserve spaces. Enquiries: Gatwick (0293) 28822, Ext. 2395.

Caution: car parks are divided into zones Make a note of which park it is in, zone, row, etc Take your ticket with you. You will have to pay at the terminal on your return.

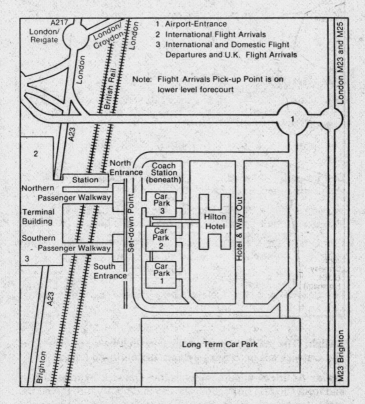

Bus: Express coaches from many parts of Britain. Main services are the Flightline 777 to and from London's Victoria coach station (half a mile from Victoria rail station). Runs at thirty-minute intervals, 06.30–21.00, then hourly to 23.00 from Gatwick. From London same interval but at ten and forty minutes past the hour. Takes 70 minutes. £2.00 single, £3.50 period return.

Flightline 747 and Jetlink to and from Heathrow. (£3.50 single, double between midnight and 05.30)

Flightline 727 to Heathrow with alternate buses continuing on to Luton.

Coaches stop outside passenger terminal building (upper level).

Frequent local buses to Crawley and Horley.

Facilities

Information: Desk is in the international arrivals hall. Telephone Gatwick (0293) 28822, Ext. 3600. For flight enquiries ring the airline.

Left luggage: Can be left at the arrivals hall, open 24 hours a day.

Lost property: Down the stairs by the British Caledonian check-in. Information Desk may be able to help.

Nursing mothers: Three free nursing mothers' rooms. Two in the international arrivals hall, the other in the departure lounge.

Post Office: On the international arrivals concourse. Numerous coin-boxes throughout.

Banks: Open 24 hours.

Restaurants and bars: Next floor above the international arrivals hall.

Hotels: There are numerous local hotels in the area. The Gatwick Hilton is next door to the terminal building.

Transfer passengers: Check at your airline transfer desk.

Air taxis: Three companies operate. Ring their Association: Haslemere (0428) 4804.

Flight enquiries: To check on arrival or departure, ring the appropriate number below, quoting the flight number – usually two letters followed by three digits, e.g. BA 656.

Aer Lingus	(0293) 502074
Air Europe	(0293) 502060
Air Zimbabwe	(0293) 518033
American Airlines	(0293) 502078
Britannia	(0293) 502075
British Airtours	(0293) 518033
British Airways	(0293) 518033
British Caledonian Airways	(0293) 25555
CP Air	(0293) 518033
Cathay Pacific	(0293) 518033
Dan Air Services	(0293) 502068
Delta Airlines	(0293) 502113
Garuda Indonesian	(0293) 502025
NLM City Hopper	(0293) 502070
North West Orient	(0293) 502079
People Express	(0293) 502061
Philippine Airlines	(0293) 518033
SAS Scandinavian	Gatwick (0293) 518033
Virgin Atlantic	(0293) 502060
Wardair Canada	(0293) 33161/502123
World Airways	(0293) 502073
Other airlines	**(0293) 31299**

Spectators: Gallery on the roof of the arrivals hall, access by lifts. Has a buffet and toilets. Admission 35p, children 15p.

Stansted

Now designated London's third airport. It handled a record 547,000 passengers in 1984/5. Britain's fastest growing airport for the third year in succession.

How to travel to Stansted

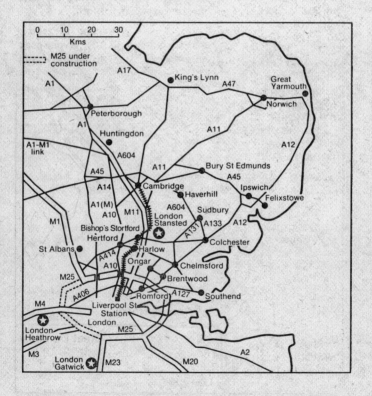

Train: Express from Liverpool Street station to Bishop's Stortford, which is approximately four miles from Stansted airport, in just over half an hour (taxi or bus to airport). Trains run about three times an hour. For details, ring (01) 283 7171. Do not book to Stansted station.

Coach: Route 799 links the airport with Cambridge, Harlow and London Victoria coach station. Single fare from London £2.00. For times of coaches, ring (01) 730 0202.

Bus: Eastern National Highwayman operates daily to and from Cambridge, Colchester, Ipswich, Norwich, Basildon, Chelmsford, Southend and Leigh-on-Sea. For details, ring (0245) 56151. A local bus runs approximately every hour during the day, Monday to Saturday, to and from Bishop's Stortford.

Car: Open car park near terminal. No booking necessary. Charge 60p for up to 72 hours. Thereafter £1.00. Avoid peak hours of 08.00–10.00 and 16.00–20.00 if possible. The M11 and M25 motorways provide fast access.

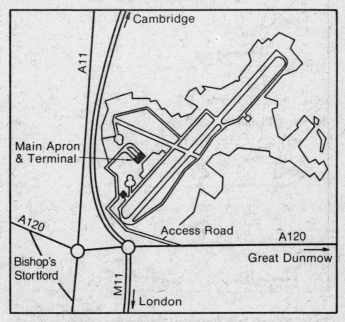

Taxis and car hire: Available from Aircars Taxi Service, whose office is in the terminal building. Telephone Bishop's Stortford

(0279) 815816. The fare from the airport to Bishop's Stortford station is about £3.00.

Air taxis: Blades Helicopters (Helicopter hire)   (0279) 815050
Kondair (Aircraft charter)   0279 813501
TAL-AIR (Aircraft charter and handling services)
                                                        (0279) 815027

Facilities

Numerous European and UK scheduled services operate from Stansted. An increasing number of tour operators are also using it.

Restaurants, bars and buffets at the Terminal, self-service buffet in the main lounge. For international passengers, a 24-hour buffet and bar through passport control.

There are numerous hotels nearby.

Information: (0279) 502379/502520. Airport Duty Officer (0279) 502387

Emergency medical service: Contact the Duty Officer through any member of staff. The Fire Service is trained to treat minor ailments.

Banks: There is a Barclays Bank at the terminal.

Lost property: Contact the Airport Duty Officer or your airline.

Nursing mothers: There is a room provided free at the terminal.

Disabled travellers: The terminal is fitted with ramps and specially designed toilets. You are advised to inform your airline if you need special help.

Spectators: An enclosure next to the terminal is open free, 09.00 to dusk during the summer.

Flight enquiries: Telephone Bishop's Stortford (0279) 502387 or appropriate airline below:
Air UK   (0279) 506301. Telex 97264.
Jersey European   (0279) 815151. Telex 817632.
Thurston International Aviation   (0279) 815027. Telex 817842.
Universal Airways   (0279) 814632. Telex 817102.
For further information and all other airlines contact:
Servisair   (0279) 57641 or 502388.
                                              Telex 81475

Luton

Britain's third largest airport in terms of international charter flights. It is growing in line with government policy from 2 million to 5 million passengers a year, and employs 4,000 people within the airport boundary. Impressive new airport buildings.

How to travel to Luton

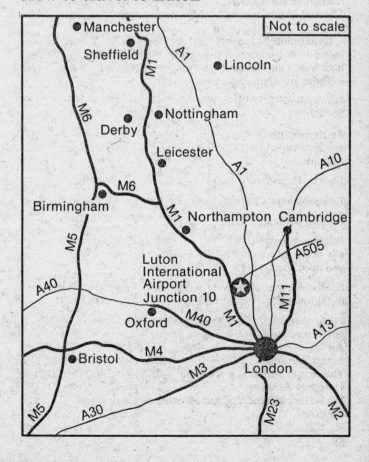

Train: Luton station is on the main line to the Midlands and the North from St Pancras. Midland Electric trains from Moorgate, Midland City from King's Cross.

Coach: Frequent services in Flightline 757 from London (Finchley Road, Marble Arch, Victoria, Battersea Bridge – daily every half-hour, Monday–Saturday. Hourly, evenings and Sundays).

Green Line 707 and 717, also an hourly service from London.

Green Line 727 links Luton with Heathrow and Gatwick. Hourly.

Jetlink 747 to Gatwick and Heathrow now extended to Luton.

National Express and Scottish Express offer frequent services to many parts of the country.

Local bus 32 runs each weekday between the airport and the town centre bus station from 06.00 till 18.45 every 15 minutes, thereafter at 58 minutes past each hour till 22.58. Hourly service on Sunday.

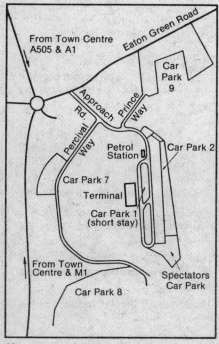

Flights Coach Travel Ltd operate between Luton and Birmingham seven times daily. Telephone (021) 554 5232.

Eastlander runs a daily service, eastbound to Ipswich, and west to Oxford.

There is an undercover coach lane with weather-protected set-down and pick-up points, only a few yards from the check-in areas.

Car: The airport is about 2 miles from the M1. Leave M1 at Junction 10. The route to the airport is well signposted. The southern section of the East Circular Road provides a link from M1 – (Junction 10A to airport).

Car Park charges: £1.50 per day. Less than 12 hours, 60p.

10,000 car parking spaces. Can book in advance – request booking form from Airport Director, Luton International Airport, Luton LU2 9CY. Telephone Luton (0582) 36061.

Facilities

Information: In terminal building. Ring (0582) 36061.

Nursing mothers: Room in the terminal building.

Porters and trolleys: Porters are available to carry your baggage free of charge. There are also trolleys distributed through the terminal building.

Car hire
Airport Mini-Cars	(0582) 25692/32585
Avis Rent-a-Car	(0582) 36537/8/9
Central Car Storage	(0582) 26189

Bank: Barclays Bank. Open Summer weekdays Mon, Fri, Sat, Sun. 07.00 to midnight. Tues, Wed, Thurs 07.00–20.00. Winter hours somewhat shorter.

Lost property: If on the aircraft, contact airline. If in the terminal, enquire at the Information Desk.

Restaurant/buffet/bars: Open 24 hours. Restaurant serves breakfast, lunch and dinner. For advance bookings telephone (0582) 33641.

Shop: Open 24 hours in the terminal. Similar facilities in the departure lounge.

Telephones: Public coin-box telephones in the terminal.

Spectators: Custom-built building for spectators, with bar and buffet. Charges: January–March 30p, April–December 40p.

Flight enquiries: Contact Information Desk or appropriate airline.

Medical centre: In the terminal building.

Facilities for the disabled: Open air parking within the airport boundary. Unaccompanied disabled drivers should write to the Airport Director if special arrangements are required. Written permission to use the car park opposite the terminal building will be given. There are wide spaces in this car park. Short-term parking (less than 12 hours) free, if badge is displayed.

How to travel to Manchester

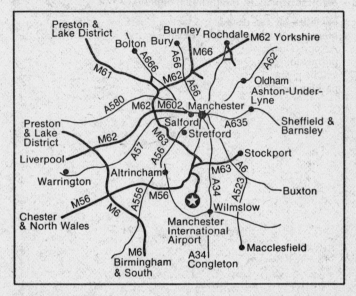

Train: Nearest station is Heald Green (2 miles), linked to airport by 44 and 369 bus. Wilmslow station (4 miles) is on London–Manchester main line and served by 300 bus from the airport. Manchester Piccadilly and Victoria railway stations are about ten miles away.

Bus and coach: From Manchester Piccadilly bus station 100, 104, 44, 118. Manchester Piccadilly rail station 200. Manchester Victoria rail station 200. Thirty-minute frequency. One-way fare is £1.00. Airport has its own bus station outside the arrivals hall. Frequent coach services from London and the Midlands.

Car: Ten miles south of Manchester and linked to the M56. A spur from the M56 runs right to the main terminal building.

Parking is multi-storey car park adjacent to the terminal (now bookable). Charges up to 30 minutes free, one hour 50p, going up progressively to £3.20 for 24 hours in summer, £2.70 in winter. The same rates apply to Surface Park B (maximum stay 4 hours). Surface Park C (not bookable): rates up to 12 hours £2.20 (summer), 80p winter; one day £2.20 (summer), £1.90 (winter). Surface Park G available April–November. Advance booking for 7 days and over. Up to 12 hours 80p, one day £1.90, seven days £13.30. Advance bookings, telephone (061) 489 3723 and (061) 489 3000. Advisable to consult Manchester airports free car parking leaflet.

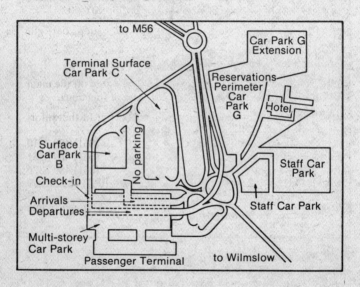

Facilities

Information: Desk in the terminal. Tel (061) 437 5233. Main concourse and the international arrivals hall.

Banks: Available. Branch of Midland Bank available on main concourse.

Post Office: Open during working hours.

Car hire: Available.

Children's nursery: Nursery in main concourse for babies and young children where they can be attended by parents.

Nursing mothers: Free service for nursing mothers.

Shops: A number of shops and a Gentlemen's Hairdresser.

Bars and restaurants: Bars, buffet, café and restaurant.

Taxis: A taxi rank is situated on the ground floor level of the multi-storey car park between the international and domestic arrivals halls. Fare to central Manchester is about £6.50.

Spectators: Viewing terrace with fish and chip shop, bar, gift shop.

Airport Health Unit: (061) 489 3344

Conference Facilities: The Brabazon Suite, situated off the main concourse available for conferences and special functions.

Flight Enquiries: Ring the Information Desk. For further information, ring:

British Airways (scheduled flights)	(061) 489 2510
Dan Air arr.	(061) 489 3321
dep.	(061) 489 3326
British Caledonian	(061) 489 3238/9
For other airlines:	
Servisair	(061) 489 3238/9

Birmingham

The number of passengers using the new Birmingham airport rose by almost 10 per cent in 1984/5 to 1,752,746.

How to travel to Birmingham

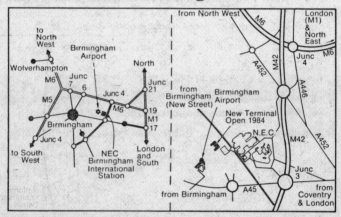

Train: MAGLEV shuttle train links the airport terminal and Birmingham International railway station in 90 seconds. The airport is a few minutes by road from Birmingham International station. There is a frequent bus service to the airport. Taxis can be obtained from the station taxi rank. Inter-City trains stop (Birmingham New Street 10 minutes, London Euston 75 minutes), as do frequent local trains. Passenger enquiries: (021) 643 2711 (08.00–22.00).

Bus and coach: 58 City–Airport terminal. Every 10 minutes; 20 minutes Saturday. Sunday no service.
159 City–Airport–International station (NEC)–Coventry. Every 30 minutes.
174 Airport–Hall Green. Every 30 minutes (one hour after 19.00).
199 Northbound Solihull Station–Castle Vale 30 minutes (one hour after 19.00). Southbound Airport–Solihull.
Enquiries: West Midlands Passenger Transport Executive (021) 236 8313.

Car: Recommended routes:

North-west: M6 to Junction 4, M42 to Junction 3, A45.

North-east: M1 Junction 21, M69, M6 north to Junction 4, M42 to Junction 3, A45.

South-east: M1, M6 Junction 4 then as north-east or M1, M45, A45.

South: A41/A34, M42 to Junction 3, A45.

South-west: M5, M6 south to Junction 4, then as north-west.

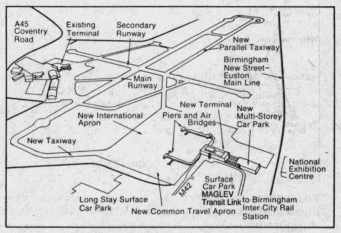

Birmingham, showing the MAGLEV passenger shuttle from the International station and the National Exhibition Centre.

Car parking available for 5,000 cars in multi-storey and 3 surface parks within a short stroll of the terminal building. No booking required. Fully computerised 'payment on foot' system reduces queues at the exit barriers.

National Car Parks (021) 767 7861

Facilities

Information: Desk open 07.00 to 23.00. Telephone (021) 767 7704/5.

Catering: Buffet, bars and restaurant.

Shop: Open 06.00 to 23.00.

Hotels: Freephone to hotels. Hotel list from Information Desk.

Banks: Open 06.30–21.30 (summer); 06.30–19.30 (winter).

Post Office: In working hours.

Telephones: Coin-box telephones available.

Car hire: Available.

Taxis: In rank in front of main terminal.
Control Room (021) 440 2201 (24 hours daily)
Airport Rank (021) 743 3744

Flight enquiries: Airport Information Desk (021) 767 5511

Disabled passengers: A unique passenger service vehicle specially designed for disabled passengers in operation. Invalid cabin lift is elevated from ground level to the door sills of the aircraft. Can accommodate both stretchers and wheelchairs. All terminal facilities are easily accessible on the ground floor or by lift to the first floor. Braille maps and cassette tapes (cost £2.00) available from the Airport Director.

Medical centre: There is 24-hour medical care at the centre in the terminal building.

National Exhibition Centre: A 90-second ride in the new MAGLEV transit link takes visitors to walkways and escalators leading into the National Exhibition Centre.

Spectators' viewing gallery: Access by lift on the ground floor outside the front of the terminal. Admission 30p. Spotters' shop and buffet.

East Midlands

How to travel to East Midlands

Train: The nearest railway stations are Loughborough (9 miles), Derby and Nottingham (each 15 miles) and Leicester (20 miles).

Bus and coach: Bus services to Derby, Leicester, Loughborough and Nottingham. Bus stop adjacent to terminal.

Car: The airport is two miles from junction 24 on the M1 motorway. 2,000 spaces in short- or long-stay car park. 2,000 further spaces in spectators' car park. No booking necessary.

Facilities

information: Desk open at all times when flights operating.

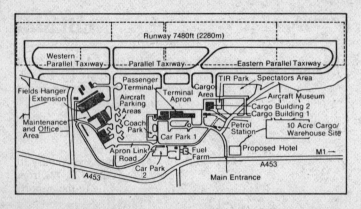

Messages for passengers can be left there. Telephone: Derby (0332) 810621.

Banks: In terminal and open normal banking hours.

Telephones: Coin-box telephones at various points.

Shop: There is a shop in the terminal.

Taxis: 24-hour service from front of the terminal.

Spectators: Spectators have their own viewing area where there is a refreshment kiosk. Free for pedestrians.

Air museum: Adjacent to the spectators' car park.

Lost property: Enquiries should be made at the Information Desk.

Bars and restaurant: Café, bar and restaurant.

Nursing mothers: There is a free nursing mothers' room in the terminal.

Air taxis: Available at the airport.

Car hire: Available.

Flight enquiries: Check with appropriate airline:
British Midland Airways	(0332) 810552
Britannia Airways	(0332) 810741
Orion Airways	(0332) 810741
Servisair	via airport switchboard

Bristol

The fastest growing charter airport in Europe began in 1929 as a flying club before developing as an airport for Bristol. Requisitioned by the Air Ministry at the outbreak of the war, it was the only civil airport in operation in the UK.

How to travel to Bristol

Train and bus: Frequent services from all over the country to Bristol Temple Meads station. By buses 120, 121, 122, 727 from the central bus station via Temple Meads station to the airport. Timetable from Bristol Airport (027 587) 4441.

Car: Bristol Airport is on the A38, 8 miles south of the city.
From the south – follow M5 to exit 22. Follow A38 towards Bristol.
From the north east – follow M5 to exit 18. Follow signs to the airport.

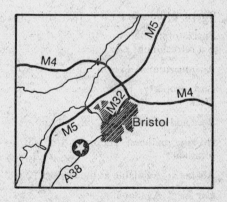

Ample parking next to terminal. Short-term (up to 5 hours) 50p. Coin-operated. Long-term 1 April–31 October £1.00 per day; 1 November–31 March free.

Facilities

Information: Desk in terminal.

Catering: Lounge and restaurant. 24-hour bar and soft drinks facility.

Nursing mothers: Room adjacent to the Security Search Area.

Disabled travellers: Car parking spaces allocated close to terminal building. Wheelchairs available. Special toilets, low-level telephones.

Car hire and taxis: Taxis can be pre-booked by telephoning the airport on Lulsgate (027 587) 4441 ext. 289
Car hire: Avis, Godfrey Davis, Hertz

Hotels: Well served at all ranges.

Flight enquiries: Telephone Lulsgate (027 587) 4441.

Cardiff

'We're big enough to cope, small enough to care.' The regional airport for South Wales and South West England was built for the RAF in 1942 and used as a training station for Spitfire pilots.

How to travel to Cardiff

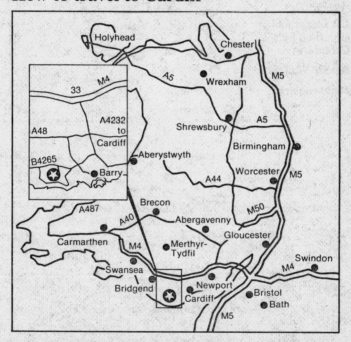

Train: Barry is the nearest station, 3½ miles away.

Bus and coach: Limited stop service 351 from Cardiff Central bus and rail station (12 miles away), about every hour, Mondays to Saturdays. Journey takes 30 minutes.

On Sundays 351/354 every hour, change at Romilly School, Barry to local service 350 – journey time 55 minutes.

Local service from Barry every hour.

Car: Access to the airport is by the A4226.
1,100 parking spaces adjacent to the terminal.
Charges: up to 1 hour 20p; up to 3 hours 40p; up to 12 hours 65p. 95p for 24 hours.

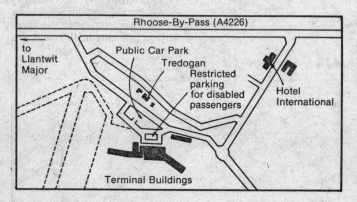

Facilities

Information: Rhoose (0446) 711211 Ext. 123.

Car hire
Avis   (0446) 710652
Hertz   (0446) 710837

Taxis: 24-hour taxi service available.
Panda Cabs   (0446) 710693

Bars, restaurants and buffet: In the terminal. Cafeteria, licensed bar, conference room.

Telephones: Coin-box telephones.

Shop: In the terminal.

Flight enquiries: Information Desk or from the airline.

Spectator terrace

Glasgow

Originally the home of the famous 602 (City of Glasgow) Squadron of the Royal Auxiliary Air Force, Abbotsinch was an RAF station in the war and was then transferred to the Fleet Air Arm. It became Glasgow Airport officially in 1966 and was opened by HM the Queen.

How to travel to Glasgow

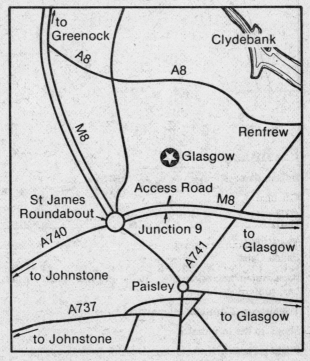

Train: Via Paisley Gilmour Street, a mile from the airport.

Bus: Service to Glasgow city centre leaves from the forecourt every 30 minutes weekdays and every 40 minutes on Sunday till

18.55, thereafter every hour. Local bus service to Paisley every 15 minutes and to Renfrew every 30 minutes.

Car: Via M8 motorway from Glasgow city centre to airport in 20 minutes. Parking for 1,200 cars opposite terminal building. Also a long-term car park for 800 cars to south-west of the terminal next to the Excelsior hotel. Charge £2.40 for 24 hours.

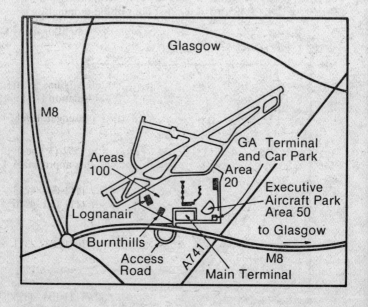

Taxis: Taxis can be hired from the rank at the western end of the terminal. Typical fare to Glasgow at present £6.80.

Car hire: Self-driven cars can be hired from desks in the domestic arrivals hall: Avis, Swan National, Hertz.

Facilities

Information: (041) 887 1111, Ext. 4552 (3 lines). Desk on the first floor of the main terminal.

Transfer passengers: Check with your airline.

76

Restaurants and bars: A full range is offered at the terminal. 24-hour bar and buffet in the International Departure lounge.

Post Office: On the first floor. Coin-box telephones in terminal.

Lost property: Office open 07.00–22.30, Monday–Friday. Telephone (041) 887 1111, Ext. 4558.

Meeting point: There is a sign entitled 'Rendezvous Point' hanging above the centre of the first floor of the terminal.

Air taxis: Air Charter, Burnthills Aviation, Kwikair, Loganair, McAlpine Helicopters.

Hotels: There are numerous hotels in the vicinity.

Emergency medical services: A State Registered Nurse is in attendance at all times. Contact through the Information Desk.

Disabled travellers: Access to terminal is at passenger level. Lifts, special toilets and telephones available.

Flight enquiries: Telephone (041) 887 1111, Ext. 552 (3 lines). For further information on airlines, contact the appropriate airlines:

Air Ecosse EC	(041) 887 1111 Ext. 4253
British Airways BA	(041) 887 1111 Ext. 4376
– Inter City AQ	
– LOT LO	
British Caledonian BR	(041) 887 2311
– Aeroflot SU	
– Guernsey Airlines	
– KLM KL	
British Midland Airways BD	(041) 887 1111 Ext. 4333
Burnthills Highland Helicopter Service KB	(041) 887 7733
Dan Air DA	(041) 887 1111 Ext. 4333
– Centreline EZ	
Loganair LC	(041) 887 1111 Ext. 4253
SAS Scandinavian Airlines SK	(041) 887 1111 Ext. 4239/4330
For other airlines contact:	
Servisair Ltd	(041) 887 1111 Ext. 4227

Prestwick

Scotland's transatlantic gateway is situated where it escapes
most of the bad weather. A freeport zone exists on its doorstep.
It was designated an international airport in 1945, when BOAC
began its London–Prestwick–Gander–New York service. Cel-
ebrated its Golden Jubilee in 1985.

How to travel to Prestwick

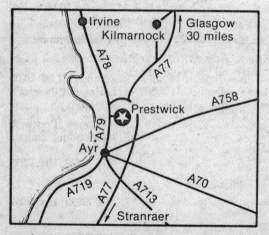

Train: Prestwick station is on the main Glasgow to Ayr line.
Trains run at half-hourly intervals, take about an hour, and
single fare to Glasgow is £2.15.

Coach: There is a coach service from Prestwick airport to
Glasgow city centre (Buchanan Street Bus Station). Also a daily
coach between Edinburgh and Prestwick airport. Courtesy coach
daily between airport and Prestwick station.

Bus: Local bus services to Prestwick, Ayr, Kilmarnock and
Glasgow approximately half-hourly.

Taxis: Call points in the terminal. Fare to Prestwick station
£1.50.

Facilities

Information: Information Desk in main concourse. Telephone Prestwick (0292) 79822, Ext. 5090/1. Open between 08.30 and 16.30. After that, phone Ext. 4058.

Banks: There is a Clydesdale Bank in the main terminal. Open Monday–Friday 08.00–17.00, Saturday and Sunday 08.00–14.30.

Lost property: Enquire at the Information Desk.

Nursing mothers: There is a free nursing mothers' room in the terminal.

Medical service: staffed by Nursing Sister 08.30–16.30 Mon–Fri. Also 08.30–16.30 Saturday and Sunday in summer.

Restaurants and bars: There is a buffet, bar and restaurant.

Transfer passengers: Contact your airline.

Spectators: A terrace on the second floor, open 07.00–18.00 summer, 07.00–17.00 winter. A lift is available, and there is a buffet and amusement arcade.

Flight enquiries: For flight enquiries, telephone Prestwick (0292) 79822, Ext. 5090/1. For further information, contact appropriate airline:

Air Canada AC	(0292) 79822, Ext. 2055
– Air Florida QH	
– Canadian Armed Forces SF	
British Caledonian Airways BR	(0292) 79822, Ext. 2057
– Air UK AQ	
– Arrowair JW	
– British Airways BY	
– British Midland Airways BD	
– Guernsey Airlines GE	
– KLM KL	
– Loganair LC	
– Pan American World Airways PA	
– Wardair WD	
– Worldways WB	
Northwest Orient Airlines NW	(0292) 79822, Ext. 2013
For other services:	
Scottish Express International	(0292) 79822, Ext. 2018

Air taxi
Scotia Safari Ltd(0292) 76511

Edinburgh

Edinburgh airport was originally Turnhouse Aerodrome, established by the Royal Flying Corps in World War I. It was a fighter station in the Second World War. Seven years ago the BAA spent £15 million making it a true capital gateway.

Train: Waverley Station connects to most parts of the UK. Thence by taxi or bus.

Bus and coach: Coach service from the terminus at Waverley Bridge in city centre at approximately 30-minute intervals. Takes about 25 minutes, the airport being six miles from the city centre.

Taxi: From city centre takes about 20 minutes and costs around £5.60.

Car: Adjacent to the junction between the M8 and M9. Road access to the terminal is via the two-level junction on the A8, Edinburgh–Glasgow road midway between Maybury and Newbridge roundabouts.

If approaching from Edinburgh and the east, join the A8 and proceed via the Maybury roundabout towards Glasgow. Just

80

before reaching the Royal Highland Showground, take the left-hand slip road and use the underpass beneath the dual carriageway to join the terminal approach road. Clear direction signs are provided.

From the north and west, join the A8 at the Newbridge roundabout and proceed towards Edinburgh. Just past the Royal Highland Showground, follow the directional signs and take the left-hand slip road which connects with the terminal approach road. A car park with 1,200 spaces for both short-term and long-term parking is provided in the terminal area. Most parking spaces are conveniently situated close to the terminal, and drivers are advised to proceed direct to the car park unless setting down or picking up passengers. Payment is made on exit from the car park.

Facilities

Information: Desk in the main hall, open 07.00–23.00. Staff will answer your queries, including flight enquiries, on (031) 344 3136.

Banks: Clydesdale Bank open 08.30–19.00 Monday to Friday, 09.00–16.30 Saturday, 11.00–17.30 Sunday. Some reduction in hours during winter.

Lost property: Enquire at Information Desk.

Disabled travellers: Wheelchairs, special toilets, lifts available.

Nursing mothers: There is a free nursing mothers' room on the ground floor of the terminal.

Emergency Medical Services: Qualified nurse usually on duty. Ask at the information desk or any of the airport or airline staff.

Restaurants and bars: Buffet, bars and restaurant. Drinks can now be served from 11.00 to 23.00.

Hotels: Numerous hotels in the vicinity.

Transfer passengers: Check with airline.

Spectators: Spectators' gallery, open during daylight hours, on second floor of the main terminal. Can be reached by lift and stairs.

Flight enquiries: For general flight enquiries, telephone the Information Desk (031) 344 3136.

For a specific airline, contact:

British Airways BA

Flight enquiries	(031) 344 3152
Sales and Reservations	(031) 225 2525

– British Airtours KT
– Lufthansa LH

British Caledonian Airways BR

Flight enquiries	(031) 344 3122
Sales and Reservations	(031) 344 3338

– Aeroflot SU
– KLM KL

Aer Lingus E1

Sales and Reservations	(031) 225 7392
Flight enquiries	(031) 344 3273

Air UK UK

Sales and Reservations	(031) 225 3978
Flight enquiries	(031) 344 3273

Air Ecosse EC

Sales and Reservations	(031) 447 9958
Flight enquiries	(031) 344 3273

British Midland BD

Sales and Reservations	(031) 447 1000
Flight enquiries	(031) 344 3282

Loganair LC

Sales and Reservations	(031) 344 3282
Flight enquiries	(031) 344 3247

For other airlines contact:

Servisair Scotland	(031) 344 3111

Aberdeen

This began at Dyce with the landing in 1931 of a tiny Blackburn Bluebird by Eric Gandar Dower. He formed his own company, Aberdeen Airways Ltd and in 1934 began flights to the Orkneys. It became a Fighter and then Coastal Command station in the Second World War. Now a new terminal has been built, capable of handling over one million passengers a year.

How to travel to Aberdeen

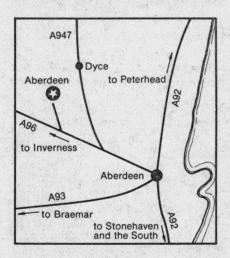

Train: Aberdeen station ((0224) 594222) in the city centre is the nearest rail station, 7 miles from the airport. Dyce station (2 miles) is connected by a bus service to the airport.

Bus: Grampian Scottish operate a half-hourly service (exact fare), Mondays–Saturdays, less frequently on Sundays, to and from the city centre. Also serves Bristow and British Airways heliports.

Taxis: Can be obtained from rank outside the terminal. Telephone: Aberdeen (0224) 725728.

Car: The bypass to the airport is signposted off the A96. There is a car park adjacent to the terminal.

Helicopter: Helicopter passengers should proceed to the airport via A96 and Dyce Drive. Access routes to Bristow and British Airways Helicopters are signposted. There is a longer term car park opposite Bristow Helicopters.

Facilities

Information: There is a desk in the check-in area of the terminal, open 06.15–22.15. Staff will help with general advice, tourist information and flight enquiries. Telephone (0224) 722331, Ext. 5312/3/4.

Banks: Open Mondays to Saturdays 06.30–18.15. Sundays closed.

Emergency medical services: Available in the main terminal building. Qualified nurses on duty at the Information Desk.

Lost property: Inform Information Desk.

Left luggage: Available adjacent to the Information Desk.

Nursing mothers: There is a free nursing mothers' room adjacent to the Information Desk.

Restaurants and bars: All catering services are in the passenger concourse, including buffet, bar and restaurant.

Disabled travellers: Access to the terminal from road level by dropped kerb to the entrance. Same level maintained through terminal to aircraft steps. Restaurant and self-catering buffet and bar are accessible to wheelchair travellers. Special low-level telephones, toilets etc. Telephone Management Duty Officer to make enquiries: (0224) 722331 Ext. 5111.

Hotels: There are a number of hotels within easy reach of the airport.

Transfer passengers: Check with your airline.

Air taxis: Available.

Flight enquiries: Phone Aberdeen (0224) 722331, Ext. 5312/3/4.

For further information, phone appropriate airline:

Air Ecosse EC	(0224) 725038
British Airways BA	(0224) 722331, Ext. 5122
British Caledonian Helicopters	(0224) 770195
Bristow Helicopters	(0224) 723151
British Airways Helicopters BV	(0224) 725059
Business Air Centre	(0224) 725566
Brymon Airways	(0224) 725703
Dan Air DA	(0224) 722331, Ext. 5124
Guernsey Airlines	(0224) 723090
Loganair LC	(0224) 725027
North Scottish Helicopters	(0224) 722331, Ext. 5350
For other airlines phone:	
Servisair	(0224) 722331, Ext. 5106
Scottish Express International	(0224) 722331, Ext. 5120

Now you've arrived, things don't look so strange. You go and check in at your airline counter with your ticket, joining the queue for your destination and your flight number, that most important Open Sesame that you must remember.

Your aircraft is likely to have returned from a trip to some other city or country. As soon as its arrival time is known, an early warning system is carried out by busy airports like Gatwick and Heathrow via Approach Control. The BAA at Terminal Control watch the aircraft by radar, listen to the landing instructions, and teletypes go out to airline, baggage, customs, catering, maintenance, refuelling, cleaners, steps and ground power – all of which converge on the chosen docking position.

The amount of concrete a Jumbo stands on when parked is just over an acre, and will have cost £400,000 to lay. There are at present eleven of them at Gatwick – soon to be almost doubled when the new North Terminal is completed – and over fifty at Heathrow, sixteen more now that the new Terminal 4 has been completed.

The service is no longer announced at Gatwick and other BAA airports. Instructions on the gate number and pier are given on the electronic board. Hand luggage is examined by Security, which used to be run by security firms like Securicor, but is now controlled by BAA. An electromagnetic beam searches out metal objects as the passengers proceed through an empty doorway. A high screech indicates a 'find' – after which the passenger is searched more closely by a 'torch' that also screeches. The 'find' is usually keys or loose change. But now with the increase in terrorism, extra precautions are naturally carried out. Special 'sniffers' locate ammunition or bombs. El Al have a special screening procedure for each passenger – a long process, but certainly effective as their first-class anti-terrorism record shows.

Some airlines have their own passenger terminals, such as Pan Am's Worldport at Kennedy. Aircraft are berthed right into jetties at many modern airports. From the new Gatwick satellites you walk down an elephant trunk of a movable corridor right into your aircraft in company with your fellow passengers.

They will all give the impression of being most experienced. But nevertheless, around 70 per cent of the world's population has still never flown. Even the experienced businessman – for the condition is universal – will have to some extent the peculiar butterflies-in-the-stomach condition which the northern British expressively call 'journey-proud' as he walks towards his Jumbo jet.

3
Taxiing Out

Close up, a Jumbo is a surprise.

A 747's 70-metre length, 60-metre wing-span and 160 tons empty weight – it carries its own weight in fuel and payload – does not look or sound particularly big. A DC2, grandmother of all modern airliners, would be needed to put beside a Jumbo DC10's 63-foot tail to appreciate its vastness and also the DC family likeness, for consecutively from 2 to 10, they are all unmistakably Douglases. In the benign whale-like body of the Boeing 747 can be seen the Boeing 319 flying boat, first commercial aircraft on the Atlantic run. Unlike Douglas, Boeing dotted all over the board with their design numbers, partly to confuse competition, partly because certain numbers (7 particularly – watch out for the Boeing 777) have a special appeal. Throughout aviation can be seen earlier history and evolution – for flying really is man evolving and developing in a new element.

A Pan American 747 will have Clipper in front of its name, for Juan Trippe, the airline's founder, named his aircraft after their true forerunners, those fast American sailing ships, a model of which will be seen in the passenger cabin. No name will be seen on a British Jumbo, although aircraft before the 707 were regularly named, usually after places. There will just be the registration letter G for British, D for Germany, F for France and so on, followed by two letters in sequence and a further two which are the aircraft's 'name'. British Caledonian 111s are named after Scottish burghs, their 707s after lochs and their DC10s after famous Scots. Aer

Lingus name most of their aircraft after saints, but not all. It's odd to see the Sir Reginald Purvis (who was he?) appearing in a fleet with St Andrew, St Magnus, St Elwyn and so on. Air Europe call their aircraft simply after girls – Joan, Kathy, Clare and so on.

Unlike sailors, aircrew have never called their aircraft by their names anyway. Nobody referred to the Constellation G-AHEM as *Balmoral*, but Easy Mike, remembering at the same time its slow take-off, for aircraft, like human beings, are different. One of its sisters was Easy Love, *Bangor II*, origin of much ribaldry on the flight deck.

Only the top half of a Jumbo fuselage will be painted – with 800 lb of polyurethane paint. The bottom half remains silver because of the extra paint weight involved. But the whole 1,690 square metres of the skin is polished with wax every twelve weeks, taking 180 man hours. This is not for appearance – polishing controls the oxidisation which corrodes the aluminium, and a high gloss adds ten knots to the speed. After every long-range trip, the salt and dirt collected is washed down by hoses, again to protect the metal.

On the wing-tips, the navigation lights, red on the left (port) and green on the right (starboard) are a reminder of aircrafts' early associations with ships. In the roof of each wing, there will be what look like car headlights – the landing lights, used mainly at night, but put on also by day round busy airports to advertise the aircraft's presence.

The old tailwheel of earlier aircraft disappeared during the war. On a 747, there are two nosewheels and sixteen mainwheels. The long, silvery pillars on which they are supported are the oleo legs, which move up and down on take-off and landing, acting basically as springs to cushion against jars. A thin wire used to trail down from each leg which was the first piece of the aircraft to touch the ground on landing, getting rid of the electricity that would

88

have built up in it at altitude at the same time. Now a special metal compound is added to the tyres to do the same thing. Eight tassels called static wicks used to hang on the trailing edge of the wing to prevent electricity building up in the air. This became mandatory on aircraft after a Boeing 707 without them was struck by lightning and exploded in 1963. Now a static pipe is fixed under each jumbo wing to do the same thing.

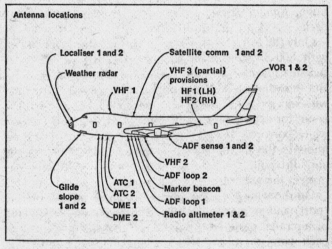

Antenna locations

Localiser 1 and 2
Weather radar
VHF 1
Satellite comm 1 and 2
VHF 3 (partial) provisions
HF1 (LH)
HF2 (RH)
VOR 1 & 2
ADF sense 1 and 2
VHF 2
ADF loop 2
Marker beacon
ADF loop 1
Radio altimeter 1 & 2
Glide slope 1 and 2
ATC 1
ATC 2
DME 1
DME 2

DME   Distance Measuring Equipment
HF   High Frequency
ATC   Air Traffic Control
LOCALISER or SLIDE SLOPE for Instrument Landing System
VOR   Very High Frequency Omnidirectional Range
ADF   Automatic Direction Finding
VHF   Very High Frequency Radio

The controls are the conventional aircraft ones, but as can be seen in the diagram on page 102 there are four ailerons and four elevators, instead of the usual two of each. A wing lifts when the aileron is depressed. The nose lifts when the elevator is raised. On each of these controls can be seen a cut-out, baby elevators or ailerons. These are the 'trimmers', designed to correct the controls themselves for nose or tail heaviness and wing-low, acting in the opposite sense to their bigger bodies.

The wing has a 37° sweepback which prevents air eddies building up at the tips and increases speed. Under the trailing edge of the wing are two sets of triple-segmented, triple-slotted flaps either side that increase lift and reduce the stalling speed.

The seventeen tiny protuberances and aerials on the fuselage are reminders that the aircraft has a powerful combined radio transmitting and receiving station all its own, licensed and certificated as such by the government. In the nose cone are located the weather radar aerials and the localiser for the Instrument Landing System.

Airlines never lose the opportunity for advertisement because of the frequency with which celebrities from the Queen downwards are photographed on them. Every step the passengers take upwards till they are seventeen feet above the ground is likely to be emblazoned with the airline's name.

At the door, they will be met by the Cabin Services Officer. There is also a Purser – a name inherited from ships, but the innovation here is that you may be greeted by a woman. Unlike the old days, there is now a career structure for stewardesses. Instead of being retired at thirty-five, they can now have fifteen or more other cabin staff (men and girls) under them. The stewardesses are dressed in a variety of uniforms – it used to be red, white and blue in British Airways with red or blue smocks for serving, a blue sweater and skirt with matching jacket and a French butcher's apron for serving in Pan American, kimonos in Japan, brightly coloured saris in Indian Airlines, and Highland tartans for British Caledonian. The smock for British Airways had no pockets. The steward-ess' pencil hung precariously on her lapel. All airlines appear to dress their girls in different uniforms every year or so, supposedly in line with fashion. With rare exceptions, the girls dislike the choices.

There is no cramped feeling of being in a thin tube as there was on earlier aircraft. Instead, the passengers seem to be in quite a nice-sized hall. Still lingering will be the smell of the slightly perfumed aerosol bomb. Soft music apparently coming out of the walls is likely to obliterate the slight noise of the 1,100 hp Auxiliary Power Unit – for the aircraft is also a power-station – serving the lights and air-conditioning.

The cabin decor varies but will often be blue and white for Pan Am and British Airways, red and white for American Airlines. The seat coverings are usually dark-coloured, blue or brown. Eventually it is hoped they will be made of fire-resistant material. At Orly 116 people died from asphyxiation after a fire that started in a 707's toilet, and in 1985 at Manchester there was another disaster.

Actual seat arrangements can be moved into a variety of combinations of first class and economy – or all-cargo with no seats at all.

The three operating crew would have reported one hour before departure. Twenty years ago, it would have been two and a half hours for a crew double the size for an aircraft one eighth as big.

They would have signed on, collected their mail, read the latest NOTAMs (notices to airmen) and proceeded to Operations to see the Flight Plan (made out by computer) and collect the weather briefing sheet. In the old days, there would have been a discussion with the Met. Officer. Not any longer. They will be there before the present weather at their destination changes very much.

The Captain would ask for a Flight Level of around 350 (a height of 35,000 feet), the best height for jets. This might not have been possible due to other aircraft, but provided the winds were reasonable, he would try to get as close to that altitude as possible and use the shortest route to his destination.

Meanwhile the Flight Engineer Officer would have gone out to the aircraft to start his checks, seeing that 51,000 gallons of kerosene were on board by means of a magnetic dipstick under the wing, reading the Technical Log, noting any previous faults and, if the aircraft is at Heathrow, setting 51° 28' North 00° 26' West (Heathrow's exact position) on the Inertial Navigation System. This will again be checked by the First Officer and the Captain. *All* checks are in fact done by two crew, and most by three.

When the Cabin Services Officer reports doors closed and passengers strapped in, the First Officer gets clearance to start engines, push back and to taxi out.

Number four engine (from tradition the engines are numbered from the port outer engine as number one to the starboard outer as number four) begins its start with a whine and ends it with a guffaw and a breath of brown smoke. Three, two and one follow in that order.

If it is in a dock, the aircraft is first pulled backwards by a tractor. Otherwise, the chocks will be pulled away and the 747 will begin moving forwards off the ramp and round the perimeter track.

The aircraft will taxi at between fifteen and twenty miles an hour. Sometimes the pilot has to get very close in to other aircraft or other obstructions. Seeing a 747's wingtips from his position is impossible, but with experience, the whole width and length of the 747 becomes an extension of his own body image.

Airways Clearance has been given by Heathrow Tower on 121.7. It will be a standard instrument departure, embodying Noise Abatement Procedure, in this case to keep clear of Windsor Castle, which was the first Noise Abatement Procedure ever to be enforced in civil aviation. Thirty-five years ago the clearance was a complicated affair that had to be reported back by the First Officer. Accidents due to getting clearance wrong were not uncommon. The standardisation of clearances as far as possible was another step forward.

Propped on the console between the pilots will be the Take-off Data Sheet showing AUW (All Up Weight – maximum around 712,000 lb), temperature, crosswind, the effect of slush, head or tail wind, the necessary allowances made on runway limit. Landing weight is 564,000 lb and if a landing has to be made immediately after take-off, fuel has to be dumped. Dump rate is 2,000 gallons a minute and Air Traffic Control would relay a dumping area. The main precautions are not to fly in a circle into the fuel-impregnated air or dump in the vicinity of other aircraft.

Other calculations on the sheet will be VI, the speed before which the pilot must 'abort' – close the thrust levers and stop; VR – the speed at which the Captain 'rotates' the aircraft (lifts the nosewheel off the ground); and V2, the safe take-off and climb-out speed even if one engine fails. These three speeds will be put on the airspeed indicator by means of little white arrows called bugs.

As it taxis, the 747 weighs itself on sensors in its oleo legs. Though the load and trim sheet has been made up, this is an added safeguard against exceeding the allowable total weight. The height of the runway above sea level will be on the form – the higher the airfield, the thinner the air, the less the lift. The first to find out that high airfields needed a lot of runway were Van Ryneveld and Brand, who crashed at Bulawayo (4,350 feet) in 1920 on the first flight from the UK to South Africa. If that is the case, then the 747 will need a longer take-off run and a lot of runway will be used.

The view forward from the Captain's window is excellent. He looks up at the weather. Sudden lone squalls may occur on eastern airfields, reversing the direction of the wind (Kano, 36 killed), windshifts, towering storms and turbulence may quickly materialise, particularly in India and America (Memphis, 45 killed). Other aircraft

93

may be on the move too close for comfort (Tenerife, 582 killed, the worst air disaster ever).

All these incidents will be imprinted on his consciousness like terrible cautionary tales. Now the crew will check that all the switches and levers on the Before Take-off Check have been activated.

Check lists originated in the Second World War. When aircraft were simpler, mnemonics were used, like G (gills closed), F (flaps up), P (superchargers on). Any one of these items missed would mean the aircraft was unlikely to become airborne.

Since aircraft have become complicated, a check list has been introduced for every single action, including all emergencies. Memory is not relied on at all, and all three 747 crew monitor each other as the checks are done. But on the new technology aircraft the check lists have been replaced by computer screens in front of the pilots.

The crew also check that the levers have done their work – that the flaps *are* 10°, the droop flaps at the front *are* out (they were not at Nairobi in 1975, though the lever was down. The circuit breaker or fuse in the panel above the crew's heads had popped out. The leading edge flaps were not out. There was insufficient lift and the 747 crashed soon after take-off, killing 45 people).

They check that all the warning lights are out – the door warning lights, the fire warnings. They check all the failure flags. The Captain moves all the flying controls 'full travel'.

All instruments must be in the green sector. If any action is not completed and the aircraft is not ready for take-off, a horn blows.

This is particularly important in that local conditions may alter the carrying out of check lists. A 707 First Officer was restrained by his Captain from putting take-off flap down because of the stony surface of the taxi-track. Stones thrown up by the wheels might have damaged their surface. When it came to the take-off, this interruption was not remembered. Take-off flap was not put down, and the aircraft crashed.

The 747 moves along the taxi-way, and takes it position in the queue behind three 'new technology' aircraft – the Boeing 757, Boeing 767 and the Airbus 310. Not, you notice, at the *head* of the queue. The Boeing 747 is no longer the Queen of the Sky, in spite of the fact that they carry the bulk of the world's passengers on long range routes, and 600 are still operating.

The new technology aeroplanes ahead of her now are fitted with the latest computer technology that spun off space age exploration.

In comparison to the Jumbo, the three new technology planes are small and only have two engines.

The 757 can take 224 tourist class with 5–7 cabin attendants. There are two galleys, one toilet at the front and three to the rear. The range is 2,300 miles, and cruise speed Mach .80. Mach 1 is the speed of sound, named after a German scientist who related the angle of a bullet's shock wave to the velocity of sound, and is around 760 mph at sea level. The Mach number is the true airspeed of the aircraft divided by the speed of sound at its altitude. Mach .88, the speed at which a 747 cruises at 35,000 feet, is 580 mph (see also p. 312). Eastern and British Airways started the ball rolling with an order for forty.

The 767 carries 180–255 passengers, has five toilets – two centrally, two aft and one forward – and galleys fore and aft. Nearly a third heavier than its slim sister, it has two aisles with seating seven abreast and still plenty of room – the arrangement most preferred by passengers – while the engines have nearly a third more power.

The Airbus 320 is smaller than the 310, with 150/179 seats in a single aisle. Though at $34 million it is more expensive than the 767, it offers lower fuel consumption and seat mile costs than any other aircraft, and has a range of 3,110 miles. British Caledonian hope to start using them in 1988.

Not only are the new technology aircraft highly economical – the manufacturers claim that the 767 can fly at 600 mph round the world twelve times on the fuel it saves in a year – they are also less labour-intensive. Now the Flight Engineer has followed the radio officer and the Navigator into oblivion, and the two surviving aircrew are more systems managers than pilots. Gone too are those mesmerising banks of round-faced instruments that lined the walls of the Engineer's position in older aircraft.

Everything has been streamlined, even facts. No one wants to waste time watching, say, an oil pressure needle endlessly registering 70 lb psi. What you do need to know is when the oil pressure rises too high or drops too low. And in this new need-to-know philosophy, that is what the pilot will be told – in words on a screen, together with the dial if he selects it – together with any action he should take. Not only that, in the event of more than one emergency, the computer will arrange them in the order of the priority the pilot has to deal with them. The pilot's training will usually also be on those same need-to-know lines.

This small television-type screen is on the instrument panel between the two pilots and is called the Engine Indicational Crew Alerting System (EICAS). Other computers of the 140 on board run the engine thrust management system which controls the throttles to give maximum fuel economy in all conditions.

Slightly to the right of the 757 and 767 co-pilot is another screen called the Electronic Horizontal Situation Indicator (EHSI). On it is the green line of the aircraft's track and the round blobs of the beacons or radio stations where the computer will be turning on to another course. Up the screen a little aircraft crawls, while in the bottom left-hand corner is an arrow with the wind speed and direction and the ground speed. Any other information, such as the track and distance to another airport, can be selected. Another switch will turn the aircraft to go there.

All this is run by one or other of the dual Flight Management Computer Systems (FMCS) which provide automatic en route and terminal navigation capability. They control all flight profiles for maximum fuel efficiency, since they are linked into the automatic flight control and thrust management systems. The Inertial Reference System (IRS), the older mechanical gyroscopes replaced by larger gyroscopes, provides the speed and direction information for the Digital Air Data Computer (DADC).

If the pilot wants to check the terrain, he selects whatever range he wants (10, 20, 40, 80, 120 miles) on the radar and up on the EHSI comes a map of the land in green. If he wants to check the weather, he tilts the reflector up, and then instead of land are the rain clouds and cumulo-nimbus build-ups ahead in colour. In addition, there are seven digital communication, navigation and identification systems, a VOR marker beacon receiver, ILS receiver, radio altimeter, transponder, Distance Measuring Equipment (DME), Automatic Direction Finder (ADF), caution annunciator (a man's voice calls out warning of the approach of high ground), and triple digital flight control computers which control the *three* auto-pilots, one coming in automatically should the 'driver' fail.

Everything is geared to flexibility. Different seating arrangements can easily be made by the operator, providing more seats or more cargo room. One of the reasons that British Caledonian chose the Airbus rather than the Boeing was that they carried standard pallets for cargo and baggage – a valuable asset on a mixed fleet of aircraft. The 757 and 767 have identical flight decks, making conversion training simple.

These three – the 757, 767 and the Airbus – will be fighting it out on the world's air routes from the middle 1980s through the 1990s, just as the 747, Tristar and DC10 fought it out to the death in the seventies and early eighties. There are already plans for a 6,000-mile 767 – but for all their new technology, the Jumbo has something that none of them can possibly aspire to. It has four engines.

Engines still fail, albeit far less frequently. New technology aircraft have begun flying the North Atlantic – but only on some airlines. There will have to be further hard thinking and hard testing before the Jumbo totally concedes her supremacy on long over-water routes.

The Jumbo waits patiently while the three young bulls ahead in the queue charge up into the sky.

'Cleared to position.'

Advised by the air traffic controller in the Tower, the old 747 moves off the taxi-track on to the runway.

4
Taking Off

To become airborne, an aeroplane, like a bird, has to achieve sufficient air speed for its weight and the lifting capacity of its wings. The lighter the weight and the bigger and more efficient the wings, the less speed is necessary. By taking off always into the wind, a bonus of air speed is given away free.

A heavy eagle achieves flying speed by falling off a cliff. A swan flaps its huge wings for an interminable time. A 747 employs 200,000 lb of thrust from its four jet engines. For air has weight. Like water, it has substance and presses against everything it touches. Two hundred and fifty years ago, Bernoulli found that when air flows over a surface, its pressure is lowered and the faster the flow, the lower the pressure. Thus when the slipstream moves over a wing, it is the low pressure *above* the wing that keeps it airborne, as if it were sucking it up.

On an aeroplane, four forces are at work – two opposing each other on the horizontal and two opposing each other on the vertical plane.

When thrust and lift exceed gravity and drag, flight will be achieved. As Sir George Cayley said in 1809, 'The whole problem is confined within these limits, viz. – to make a surface support a given weight by the application of power to the resistance of air.'

The *shape* of the wing as well as its size was soon found most important – the proportion between its length and its breadth (aspect ratio), whether blunt or pointed tips, its camber or arching, whether horizontal or slightly V-shaped (dihedral angle), its thickness and sweep-back.

The greater the aspect ratio generally the bigger the lift. In the average bird, it is only 3 : 1, less than the 747, while in gliders it can be as high as 20 : 1. Slow birds and aircraft have deep cambers for easier take-off, while what little wing there is on fast fighters has no camber and is almost as thin as a sword. The 747's slight (7°) dihedral wing has a fair camber close to the fuselage, tapering off at the tips.

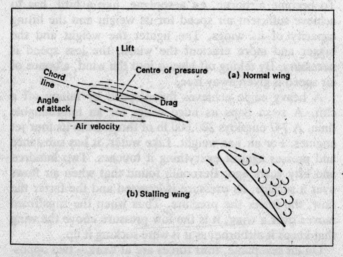

The most efficient design of an aircraft's wing is worked out using models in huge wind-tunnels powered by enormous engines that can produce a supersonic air flow if necessary. Experiments relating to air could be carried out in water, if that were possible, for the simple aeronautical law still applies that pressure varies in proportion to density and to the square of the speed.

The wing is streamlined, as is the fuselage, to minimise air resistance and eddies. As its angle of attack increases, so will its lift *but only up to a certain point*. If the angle of attack becomes too big, the airflow over the wing completely changes. Its lift stops increasing. Eddies and turbulent wakes are set up, vibration shudders through the aircraft, and the wing becomes *stalled*. The angle at which this occurs is called the *stalling incidence*, and the speed the *stalling speed*. The controls work sluggishly, if at all. If the aircraft is airborne, a wing usually drops. Recovery is through putting the nose down (less angle of attack) and increasing speed.

The controls steer the aircraft through its three axes of movement – 'yawing' (moving flat side-to-side) by the rudder, 'rolling' (wing lifting) by the ailerons and 'pitching' (moving up and down) by the elevators.

The Wright brothers found that they could move the wing up or down by twisting its tip. Ailerons, a kind of little wing, do this now. If the starboard aileron comes down, its angle of attack increases and it will lift up the right wing. If it goes up, the right wing drops. Rudders act just like a ship, but because most of a turn is done by the ailerons, on a large aircraft they are normally used very little. The elevators elevate *and* depress, and the Wrights put them in front of their aircraft. Like birds, these are now on the tailplane, and function in the same way as ailerons.

The 747 now moves into position on the runway. Although it is such a huge aircraft, it can operate from airfields used by much smaller aircraft, since what it needs to become airborne is the maximum area of an efficient wing.

The hydraulic pump sings out again, and from under the trailing edge will emerge the flaps that increase the wing area. The slots and flaps work in roughly the same way as the ten fingers on the 'hand' (outer wing) of a bird in controlling the airflow over it and the stalling speed.

At the same time from under the leading edge emerge the camber flaps which increase the camber of the wing. This increased 'camber' or wing edge from 'thin' to 'fat' guides the slipstream smoothly along the greater curvature path needed for increased lift. With all flaps down, wing area on the 747 is increased by 21 per cent and lift by nearly 90 per cent.

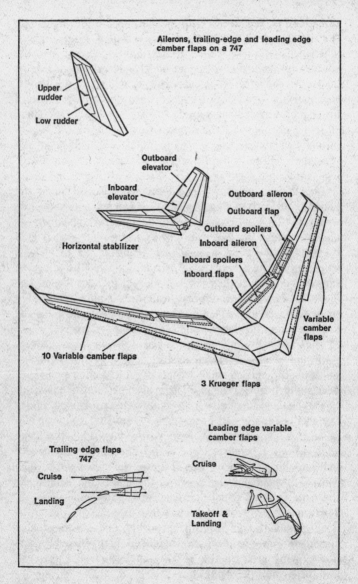

Ailerons, trailing-edge and leading edge camber flaps on a 747

Upper rudder

Low rudder

Outboard elevator

Inboard elevator

Horizontal stabilizer

Outboard aileron

Outboard flap

Outboard spoilers

Inboard aileron

Inboard spoilers

Inboard flaps

Variable camber flaps

10 Variable camber flaps

3 Krueger flaps

Leading edge variable camber flaps

Cruise

Trailing edge flaps 747

Cruise

Landing

Takeoff & Landing

Only 10 per cent of trailing edge flaps are used on take-off, since though lift is increased with further flap, so is air resistance. The full flap configuration is used only for landing, decreasing the aircraft's stalling speed so that it can land comparatively slowly. Big wings help take-off, but drag down speed. Fast aircraft need to look like darts. Variable geometry wings, whereby the wing shape is adjusted to the appropriate manoeuvre, were invented by Barnes Wallis and are now used in supersonic fighters.

The most efficient wing possible for the 747 to become airborne has now been produced. Power is next needed. Suddenly there will be a roar and a swirling of dust and movement of grass on the edge of the runway. A slight shuddering ripples down the fuselage as 200,000 lb of thrust is applied. Very slowly, the Jumbo begins to move.

Now the mind of the Captain will be filled with a series of instructions, memories and the actions which in certain events he may have to carry out very quickly.

His eyes scan the surface of the runway. Though highly unlikely at London, Paris and American airports, all sorts of things may be on or near runways. Steamrollers (fifty-one killed at Rome, thirty at Las Palmas), sheep (Latin American fields), a hydraulic jack (at Addis Ababa, forty-two killed).

In the winter, he looks out for slush. When the Elizabethan carrying the Manchester United footballers crashed at Munich, it was not understood that even a small amount of watery slush could slow the acceleration of the wheels so much that an aircraft could not become airborne. Pilot error was judged the cause of the accident, until the Captain's wife, by a long series of chemical experiments, showed that this could happen and the Captain was cleared by the British. Water on the runway can cause hydroplaning when the wheels are 'cushioned' by a film of water, making stopping after an abort or landing particularly difficult.

103

Ice on the runway can cause skidding and sliding. Salt is applied in icy conditions, and runways on big airports are usually 'grooved' to allow better tyre grip. If all is checked and the aircraft is ready for take-off, the Captain releases the brakes. He puts his left hand on the nosewheel steering, his right on the four thrust levers (American for throttles) and moves them forward. In his position, the Engineer also has his right hand on the thrust levers. The First Officer holds the control column.

The 747 accelerates very slowly. Dust comes up. From the jets some dark smoke is emitted. On the edge of the runway, the grass swirls outwards.

There is no tendency to swing. In propeller-driven aircraft, if the propellers rotate anti-clockwise, the aircraft would swing to port on take-off, sometimes violently. The Beaufighter II with Merlin engines killed dozens of pilots in this way during the war.

The Captain keeps his eyes on the runway. The Flight Engineer Officer watches the instruments on his panel. The First Officer's attention is focused mainly on the airspeed indicator.

Now at the top of the Captain's consciousness is what he will do if there is an emergency. He will immediately throttle back the engines and go into reverse thrust. If necessary, he will use the brakes as well.

The needle on the airspeed indicator creeps up. The First Officer calls, '80 knots!'

The Captain transfers his left hand from the nosewheel steering to the control column. The Flight Engineer Officer has already set all four engines to their predetermined take-off settings, but the Captain still keeps his right hand on the thrust levers.

The needle on the airspeed indicator creeps up to the white bug at 115 knots. The First Officer calls 'VI'.

The Captain puts both hands on the control column. At 'Rotate!' he gently eases back. Too roughly, and he might get the tail striking the ground. There is an attitude
104

warning system to stop him getting the nose too high. At around 6° nose up, the control column begins to shake. The tail scrape angle is 13°. The first civil jet accidents were caused by the nose getting up too high – there was no warning for the pilots then.

Just for a few seconds now there is a no-man's-land. Technically it is too late to abort if there is an emergency, too early to become airborne. Then comes lift-off.

'V2!'

All thoughts of aborting the take-off have left the Captain's mind. Now he concentrates on possible engine failure. In training exercises, this is where the instructor-checker would cut an outboard. Sometimes he would follow this up by another emergency: a fire warning on another engine. Some instructors became slap-happy, loading on the emergencies. Accidents became alarmingly common in the 1960s – almost all of them quite unnecessary and avoidable. Out of forty-eight major training accidents, thirty-one were caused by recklessness or carelessness. At Frankfurt, one instructor cut two engines on his pupil at lift-off – from evidence that materialised at the subsequent enquiry, a favourite habit of his. For some unknown reason, some civil pilots stop being fussy (which they should be) and become fighter boys when they check out colleagues.

So more accidents were caused by training pilots to cope with engine failure on take-off than by actual engine failure accidents in operational service. Engine failures are therefore no longer practised on training flights – only safely on the ground in the simulator. Costing only a fraction of the price of an airliner, simulators are cheap to operate and the instruments give a reasonable facsimile (except for the VSI) of what readings would be in the air. The chances of an engine failure on take-off are 300,000 : 1 against. A double engine failure occurs on landing once in a million flights.

The wider the engines are apart, the more swing if an

engine fails. A failure on a VC10, where all the engines are grouped together at the tail, causes no swing at all. An outboard going on a 707, on the other hand, is very hard to hold – the Captain's leg will be stiff holding the rudder against the swing.

The nose comes up like a lift as the Captain pulls further back to an angle of 9° for the climb. His eye level has risen from twenty-nine to forty-three feet. There is the slightest brushing sound as the wheels leave the ground. As the 747 inches up into the sky, the speed rapidly builds up to 185 knots.

The wheels come up with two thumps – a big one as the main wheels come into the nacelles and a smaller one for the nosewheels. The engine noise dies down – noise abatement procedure is being carried out.

Aircraft noise is unpleasant for those who live under it. Heathrow receives numerous letters a year complaining of it. Fifteen thousand homes round Heathrow have received double-glazing grants to try to help keep the noise out, and night flights out of Heathrow are strictly limited.

Aircraft noise in Britain is the responsibility of the Department of Transport which finances research and anti-noise protection. All noise complaints received by the airports are forwarded to the Department which talks to the airlines and deals with infringements. Complaints tend to die away. Huge demonstrations and hostile meetings opposed Concorde's entry to Kennedy. Now there is a regular service; opposition is decreasing even though the noise is increasing.

During the war, the worst noises that came down from the air were the scream of the air-raid sirens and the desynchronised engines of German bombers, intent in putting off the gun predictors. Some noises were pleasant – the sound of Spitfire engines, indeed the sounds of most propeller-driven aircraft. You could in fact recognise them by their different sounds.

106

Of course take-off noise was pretty wearing if you happened to live close to the end of the runway. But it wasn't till the jets came that it became excruciating.

The strange thing is that the weather seems to affect the noise. On a clear, calm day a jet at altitude makes a noise like a motorboat at the seaside. Cloak it in cloud and the noise becomes a growl or a whine.

Naturally complaints rose. People were becoming more sensitive to the contamination of their environment. And strenuous efforts were made by the authorities to lessen the nuisance.

A jet engine has what is called a noise footprint, because that is what it looks like on the ground. Measured in what are called 'perceived noise decibels' (PNdB), the contours are drawn round the areas of equal noise like isobars connect areas of equal pressure, from 120 (a 707 at two miles after take-off, equivalent to an unsilenced motorcycle) to a threshold level of 90. This noise is monitored at major aerodromes, and a maximum limit observed. Measurements at Heathrow come from thirteen microphones located at varying distances up to six miles from take-off. These are connected to a central automatic recording unit, and the approach of an aircraft switches on the microphones, recording noise, time and duration. Thus the BAA can identify any aircraft that infringes the limits, and the airline concerned is immediately notified. The limit at Heathrow is 110 PNdB, rather less than the noise of an electric train crossing a steel bridge. Concorde is excepted.

To bring the noise down to minimum, various operational measures have been introduced. Captains climb at the steepest safe angle, they follow minimum noise routes over areas that are less populated, avoiding Reigate, Horley, Crawley and East Grinstead from Gatwick and from Heathrow concentrating on mostly westerly departures (70 per cent of the time) over areas that are not so built-up. Whenever possible, 'straight-in approaches' to the runway are authorised, eliminating a circuit. Sometimes, in bad weather, aircraft have to be 'stacked' – that is, arranged at thousand-feet levels round a radio beacon (the four for Heathrow are Bovingdon, Lamborne, Ockham and Biggin Hill) from which they are picked in turn from the bottom to make their approach. The noise a 747 produces in a 'stack' is 85 PNdB, about the same as being inside a saloon car.

Houses in the worst hit areas may be eligible for government grants to cover insulation. A double-glazed window, for example, reduces the outside noise level by fifteen-sixteenths. Surveys are carried out to assess the impact of airport noise, particularly at night, and the Noise Advisory Council keeps the problem continually under review and advises the government.

On the technical side, considerable advances have been made. The noise problem for the jet is exacerbated by the fact that the source of the noise is the exhaust, which also provides the means of propulsion. Cut down the noise by silencers and you cut down the power.

Engineers initially concentrated on reducing the effect of the high-speed jet stream on the relatively still air, reducing the roar by splitting the main jet into a number of smaller ones.

Then came the development of the low-bypass-ratio (or fan) engine, which diverted some thrust to provide a cushion of slower air between the main jet and the surrounding air. This was succeeded by the high-bypass-ratio engine, whereby a very large diameter fan with a slower exhaust jet of greater volume produced the same thrust with less noise. But there is a tiresome by-product – the increased mechanised noise of the fan. So if you hear that awful whistle that sounds like metal grinding against metal, it's likely to be a jet with high-bypass-ratio engines on the landing approach. This whistle has now been reduced on the engines of more modern jets like the Boeing 757 and 767 and the Airbus. Even the earlier jets are considerably quieter than they used to be, the Tristar being much quieter than the Trident. The average jet today is two and a half times the size of its predecessors and its noise has been halved. The bigger-and-fewer philosophy will reduce noise even further.

Complaints of course still come in. These are entered on complaint forms and appropriate action taken. Complaints about low-flying aircraft should go to the airline, not the airport. And the airports are not responsible for noise complaints, which should really go to the Department of Transport. After all, it was the Head of the BAA who pointed out that: 'Airports aren't noisy. They just sit and shimmer quietly in the heat.'

It is aircraft that are noisy, particularly the old 707s and cargo aircraft. There has to be a Consultative Committee on British airports (at Gatwick there is also a Conservation Campaign) and there are financial penalties for noise infringement. But most countries are very cooperative, though if you want to make a complaint against an East European airline, forget it, because you'll never hear any more about it. The Americans are usually very apologetic and send back reports on all their investigations. The Germans are very efficient, since they have strict noise abatement rules in Germany. Many of their airports have a night curfew.

All sorts of complaints still come in, of course. At Gatwick during 1983 there were 607 complaints about noise, most of them about aircraft in flight. There were 47 complaints about the Heathrow-Gatwick helicopter service, 8 about smell – and that's strange because airports usually have a lovely old-fashioned scent like an oil lamp in a darkened room – and 24 others.

The sort of complaints airports receive include a woman who rings to say that the moment she puts on her bikini, the inter-airport helicopter comes and hovers overhead; the woman who reckons the airport blocks her drains; and the one who complains that the airport brings in illegal immigrants who flit around the streets at night and make shopping impossible because they've driven all the decent supermarkets away. One complainer declared that an aircraft was flying so low he could clearly see the faces of the terrified passengers pressed against the window.

Airports deal with other complaints too. While I was researching this book, I listened to a telephone conversation between an airport manager and a member of a family who had booked a holiday abroad. The manager was arranging for the family to be shown round an aircraft because the mother was frightened and the others wanted it demonstrated to her that airports weren't such bad places, after all. . . .

Suddenly the aircraft seems to sink. One of the commonest causes of accidents has been the selection of flap up at the wrong time. Selecting flaps instead of undercarriage up (thereby depriving the aircraft of lift area at low speeds and causing it to stall) has always been a major cause of aircraft accidents. The Trident that crashed near Staines lost its lift because the 'droop-snoot' (leading edge flaps) were retracted too soon. All sorts of warnings against doing things like this – lights, flags, stick-shakers and horns – are installed. It is at this time particularly that the crew watch each other to guard against inadvertent mis-selection. Sliding into the wing root can be seen 5° of flap, correctly selected up.

Now the speed is increasing all the time. Further flap is selected – first to 1°, then up. With a 'clean aeroplane' (undercarriage and flaps in) the aircraft climbs steeply away at 265 knots to its allotted altitude on the airway.

In cloud or at night, the Captain will be looking only at his instrument panel.

One instrument only remains unchanged on the 747 instrument panel from the beginnings of civil aviation nearly sixty years ago – then called the turn indicator but basically just a spirit level. There it is now under its
110

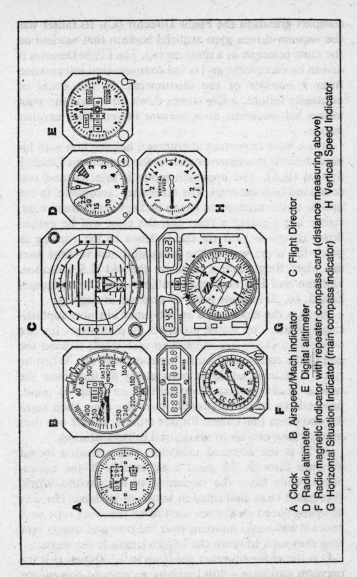

A Clock   B Airspeed/Mach indicator   C Flight Director

D Radio altimeter   E Digital altimeter

F Radio magnetic indicator with repeater compass card (distance measuring above)

G Horizontal Situation Indicator (main compass indicator)   H Vertical Speed Indicator

complex grandson the Flight Director (C). Its father was the vacuum-driven gyro artificial horizon that worked on the same principle as a spinning top. The Flight Director is driven by electricity, and is fed computerised information from a number of the instruments. In the event of electricity failure, a flag comes down on it, and the pilot moves his attention to a horizon driven from another source.

It is a most important instrument, helping him with his most difficult manoeuvres such as the Instrument Landing System (ILS). The approach mode is selected and two command bars descend. The stationary 'aeroplane' in the middle of the instrument has to be kept inside these bars, rather like sighting a rifle, and the pilot will be guided down the glide path on the localiser to the runway in much the same way as the horizontal and vertical lines did when they made a cross on the old ILS indicator. Horizon and ILS are here combined and the horizontal lines 5, 10, 20 indicate pitch up or down in degrees.

At A is the clock, also an old-timer but now sophisticated with a stop watch attached. A pilot times his run down wind (forty-five seconds in zero wind) beyond the end of the runway before he turns on base leg. When he is on a beacon let-down particularly he flies over the beacon in the reverse direction that he wants to point, proceeds to let-down (usually over the sea), then turns 45° and times that course for one minute. A rate one turn should bring him on to his desired runway heading.

At B is the airspeed indicator, still activated by air pressure through the pitot head outside in the atmosphere. Only since the beginning of the Second World War has it been calibrated in knots, as in ships. The way of telling speed on the sea used to be throwing rope with knots at measured intervals over the bow and timing how long they took to reach the known length to the stern.

D is the radio altimeter going up to 2,500 feet. E is the pressure altimeter – still basically an aneroid barometer.

112

The old one had three pointers – a large one for hundreds of feet, a smaller one for thousands and a tiny one for tens of thousands. So often was it misread that it was called the killer altimeter. A Viscount at Prestwick and a Britannia at Hurn mislaid 10,000 feet in this way. Another Britannia crashed in Yugoslavia, an Electra at La Guardia and there were many other incidents. The present one, with its one hundreds of feet pointer and its 'milometer'-type thousand presentation, is the result of learning from those accidents. The altimeter setting of the aerodrome in millibars or inches is passed to the pilots before landing and this is put on the instrument – QNH to give height above sea level, QFE to give height above the aerodrome (so that on landing the altimeter will read zero). There have been mix-ups with setting them. On many airlines, one of the altimeters (the co-pilot has an almost identical set of instruments on his side) is put on QFE and one on QNH and checks between the pilots are made. In addition (mandatory on many aircraft now), GPWSs (Ground Proximity Warning System) are fitted which warn the pilot that he is approaching high ground.

Above F is the Distance Measuring Equipment (DME) indicator which gives the pilot his distance from an omni-directional Range (VOR) station. F is the radio compass which will point at that range or a radio beacon when it is tuned to the right frequency. G is the gyro-compass repeater with the two 'lubber lines' right across it. If the needle is kept between these lines, the aircraft will be on the selected course or its reciprocal. What used to be called 'red-on-blue mistakes' are guarded against by heavily differentiating the north and south ends of the needle. There is also a simple magnetic compass. The big advantages of a gyro compass are that the needle does not swing all over the place on a turn as in the magnetic, and the compass itself is located well away from possible disturbances from metal and electrical circuits.

H is the vertical speed indicator (again on the aneroid

113

principle), which used to be called the rate of climb. It also shows dive and is a useful instrument. But like all the others with one exception, only more so, on occasion it can show wrong readings. This is particularly dangerous on an overshoot. When a Vanguard dived into the runway at Heathrow in 1965, the VSI's reliability had almost certainly been depended on too much and four seconds before impact had probably been showing a substantial rate of climb.

The one exception to the wrong reading rule is the artificial horizon either on its own or contained in the Flight Director. It always shows instantaneous right readings. In heavy turbulence particularly, the pilot will fly on his attitude indicator and regard all his other instruments suspiciously. In that he is taught to trust his instruments and not himself and his feelings of climbing or turning, this is another reversal that he has to learn, at the same time thanking his stars for the gyro.

But the Jumbo instruments are already old hat. The new instrumentation and engine control management are now totally computer orientated, a valuable spin-off from space exploration.

The instruments in the 757, 767 and Airbus 310 and 320 are basically similar, though they have different names.

The 'new technology' aircraft are worked by digital electronics which are smaller, lighter and more than twice as reliable as analogue electronics.

The flight instruments are electronic, and are presented on two colour cathode ray tubes, one above the other, directly in front of each pilot. The primary flight instruments screen is normally on top of the navigation display.

Only need-to-know information is presented in a logical, single-scan way, not concentrating it so much that it has a hypnotic effect, but saving the eyes from having to dart all over an instrument board to collect it. Crew workload is therefore considerably reduced.

114

The primary Flight Display replaces the Flight Director. As well as attitude information (in the old days given by the artificial horizon, one of which is still on the instrument panel, but displaced to the centre) it presents speed and speed limitations.

Below the Flight Display is the Flight Display screen (on the right in the A320) showing way points and flight plan, on which the weather indications radar map and track can be superimposed. Four modes can be selected (all delineated in white, blue, green, yellow and red). Plan mode is when the flight path is centred on a chosen point – with North uppermost.

Map mode presents an arc of compass rose on top and displays course and a plan view of the flight path, originating from the aircraft's present position. Ground speed and true air speed are in the top left-hand corner. The course and distance to the selected radio beacon is in the top right-hand corner. Wind speed and direction are shown in the bottom left-hand corner. Smaller concentric arcs show range in miles.

Arc mode is similar to map mode but without the flight plan data. Rose mode is an electronic copy of the electro-mechanical HSI.

The Navigation Display not only shows the pilot where he is and where he will be with checkpoints and radio beacons but also, if selected on one of three ranges (5–300 miles) three-colour radar maps and weather ahead when the scanner is tilted up.

Systems information and management are presented on two colour cathode ray tubes above the main pedestal by what is called the Electronic Centralised Aircraft Monitoring (ECAM) system. Between the two screens are the warning lights, while the control panel is just in front of the two throttles.

Sensors throughout the aircraft continuously monitor systems behaviour and report to the central computer. These trigger a simple abbreviated warning on the panel

– only what is necessary for the pilot to know. Further detail will be provided, either automatically as a situation develops or by manual selection if a pilot wants to check a system.

On cruise, the left-hand screen continuously displays fuel state, outside air temperature and memo items which might otherwise be overlooked or forgotten by the pilot. All the information he needs is either there or can be brought up immediately in front of him. There is no need to search all over the aircraft in a scan of masses of instruments. Any malfunction comes up in checklist form on the screen, with the necessary remedial action and any resulting operating limitations. The use of books and checklists for which there was never adequate stowage in previous aeroplanes and which used to clatter down on to the flight deck floor, is therefore eliminated.

The right-hand screen shows synoptic diagrams appropriate to the flight phase. In an emergency, the relevant systems diagram automatically appears, but at any time the crew can select manually any system they want to check. Not that it's necessary, as the ECAM is checking everything continuously and will report on the screen the first sign of abnormality well before a warning level is reached.

There are four modes, the first and most usual being the automatic flight mode. On the right screen automatically appears the appropriate display for each operating phase – pre-flight, take-off, climb, cruise, descent, approach and landing.

If anything goes wrong, there will be an immediate audio warning, a warning light flashes, while the lights for services or functions affected light up steady. In place of the flight phase on the left-hand screen up comes failure in plain language, together with corrective action. If it isn't serious, it will be in amber letters, otherwise in red. Corrective action will be in blue letters.

116

If there are other consequential failures or other separate failures these will also be shown arranged in the order they need to be dealt with.

Simultaneously with the blue remedial instructions, the appropriate push-button selector lights up on the overhead panel. All the crew have to do is to press each button. As each action is completed, the blue instructions turn white, and the synoptic diagram on the right-hand screen is altered accordingly.

Another press of the button and the aircraft status is shown. All sections operating normally are shown in green, while those not doing so are shown in amber. The pilot is warned to expect his landing distance to be longer.

Not only has minute care been taken with aircraft instrumentation to ensure minimum workload and guard against error, but equal attention has been paid to ergonomics to maximise crew comfort. The pressurisation provides 100 per cent fresh air to the crew. The right degree of lighting is provided to each flight deck activity – instrument monitoring, reading, note-taking. Cabin crew coming into a darkened cockpit are guided by floor lights so that instrument illumination remains constant. The pilots' chairs are electrically operated. Full adjustment of seat, backrest and armrest ensures the best posture for each differently built pilot.

The control column in the Airbus 320 has been removed so that a totally unrestricted view of the panel will be provided and the pilots will not be encumbered by its presence. Instead, there will be a tiny six-inch control on the side.

Since few pilots now wear gloves (the veteran O.P. Jones always used to wear silk ones), the control column and nose wheel steering tiller are covered in long-lasting, non-slip leather.

All in all, there has never been a better designed flight deck for a pilot than in the Airbus. Lufthansa and Swissair are now operating the Airbus 310 to a 97 per cent

117

technical dispatch reliability rate, and a daily utilisation that they are confident will reach eight hours. British Caledonian introduced their first 310 in 1984. The Airbus 320, when it goes into service, is likely to do even better.

Pilots are very enthusiastic, reporting a response as fast as a propeller aircraft (most jets have a lag which can be dangerous if an approach is allowed to get too low).

5
The Cruel Sky

Instinctively, man looks up at the sky. There for thousands of years he has tried to read his stars and find his future, little realising that there his future lies. A few saw further – artists like Leonardo da Vinci, poets, priests, writers, inventors. Taking off mentally, up on another wavelength, years before anyone else they saw the design of where man was going.

Three hundred and fifty years ago, of the inhabitants of *Atlantis*, Bacon wrote, 'We imitate the flight of birds . . . we have some degrees of flying in the air.' The three-thousand-year-old story of Icarus, who flew too close to the sun and melted the wax on his wings, can be taken as a warning, *not yet*: the sky was dangerous, much had still to be discovered.

The first human beings who were supposed to be able to fly were witches. At the trial of Jane Wenham, accused of witchcraft in 1712, the judge remarked, when it was alleged that the prisoner could fly, 'There is no law against flying.'

Sayings, legends, paintings, writings and plays could not only indicate to man what he is, but both encourage and dissuade him on courses of action years before they actually take place.

'I suppose we shall soon travel by air-vessels,' Byron said in 1822, 'make air instead of sea voyages: at length find our way to the moon, in spite of the want of atmosphere.'

H.G. Wells wrote of a world illuminated by beams that pierce cloud – clearly a reference to radar twenty-four years before it was invented. 'The Leak, the great Cloud-breaker of St David's Head, swings its unmistakable green beams forty-five degrees each way. There must be half a mile of fluff* in it in this weather but it does not affect the Leak,' he wrote of a transatlantic civil aircraft flight twenty-five years before one was accomplished. 'Our planet's overlighted if anything,' says Captain Purnell at the wheel. The transatlantic airliners of today cross the coast of St David's on Green One airway.

As regards men flying up into the sky, the vast majority of men repeatedly reiterated that it was impossible, and continued to say so even after it had been achieved.

Meanwhile, millions of other living things had preceded them millions of years before. Viruses, protozoa, algae, seeds. By the extraordinary processes of evolution, the maple's seeds eventually became weighted irregularly on one side so they could 'fly' a fair distance from their native tree.

Millions of years ago, the pterodactyl was flying – one huge eye in the middle of its huge forehead. With a wingspan of eighteen feet, it was the biggest living flyer ever built. How it ever became airborne and operated hundreds of miles out to sea is a mystery. The enigma was investigated by British aeronautical engineers with no positive conclusions. But pterodactyls were still flying when the bats and birds joined them millions of years later, though they disappeared for ever shortly afterwards.

Man made the sky the abode of his gods, and gave wings to angels, horses, lions and dragons. Zeus was originally the sky, Jupiter was a sky god, still commemorated in the planet. So was Janus, who had the added attribute of being the two-faced god, looking to the future and the past at the same time, so giving his name to the first month of the new year.

* Cloud.

The arch of sky is commemorated in the arches of churches and temples, and man imagined the tree of life as its central support lest the heavens fall, with its roots in the sky and its branches on earth.

The sky was a fearsome place in which the gods were always fighting. Rain fell when the rain god triumphed over the dry god, and winter came when the frost god was victorious. Flashes of lightning were the sparks in Thor's forge.

From down below, the sky looked a dangerous and difficult place for man, much more so than the ocean. The sky in any case by the movement of its air masses controls the weather on the ground and determines the dangers of the sea.

The sea has its huge waves, currents, whirlpools and tides, but so has the sky on a much grander scale. Its frequently empty and quiet appearance is deceptive. It is never empty and never quiet. There are a million molecules in every ounce of air banging and bouncing around, and there are five million billion tons of it in the atmosphere. The bland blue of the sky is deceptive. It is the product of violent action and the splitting up of the short-wave end of the spectrum, and blue over mountains often means hurricane force winds have torn the clouds to shreds.

Exploration was to confirm that it was an inhospitable place for man. At sea level, the pressure of this envelope of air bearing down on the earth weighs 14½ lb per square inch. Higher in the sky, there is less air, and naturally the pressure decreases. Its weight is only 7 lb at 16,000 feet, 3 lb at 38,000 and 1 lb at 60,000. Its density is half surface at 20,000, a quarter at 40,000 and one-eleventh at 60,000.

This atmospheric fact at high altitude was the big prize for man to stretch his arms towards. For if some flying object could be devised to reach that thin air, only a fraction of the surface power would be required to propel it because the barrier of drag would be so much less.

But man cannot possibly live in such air technically unaided. The temperature falls at around 1°F per 300 feet. At 10,000 feet, the average temperature is around −5° centigrade, at 35,000 −50° centigrade − warmer of course in the summer and in the tropics, colder in the winter and near the poles. Seven miles up in temperate zones, the atmosphere ends at the tropopause and the stratosphere begins. From there up, the temperature remains constant. At the equator, because of the higher ground temperatures, the tropopause goes up to eleven miles.

At these altitudes man could freeze to death, if he had not already passed out from lack of oxygen with 'bends' (bubbles in the blood-stream). Numerous experiments in decompression chambers have shown that the air above 10,000 feet is not enough. Unless he has been brought up at this altitude and developed bigger and stronger lungs, man feels breathless and he begins to think much more slowly. Higher up, and he cannot do simple arithmetic, his handwriting becomes illegible and he begins to behave irrationally, at the same time having the self-confidence of the drunk in his ability.

It is the differences in air temperature and pressure that cause weather. Warm, less dense air rises and dense, colder air comes in to replace it. The overall battle rages between the hot equatorial air and the cold polar air. Moisture and dust are scooped up by the moving air which now becomes wind, but its cold-to-warm direction is deflected 90° by the rotation of the earth, giving mainly westerlies except in the middle latitudes. Wind is said to 'veer' if it changes direction clockwise, 'back' if it goes anti-clockwise.

Winds can also be highly dangerous. Admiral Beaufort measured their strength in the early nineteenth century, giving his maximum Force 12 to a hurricane above 64 knots, 'which no canvas would withstand'. Above that figure ships capsized, trees blew down, houses were wrecked and towns devastated.

Even at sea level, winds could go up to 150 knots. In the sky, they could be higher. After the war, some airline pilots had a 'nose' for finding a strong tail wind from the pressure patterns on the meteorological charts, and would sometimes be assisted across the Atlantic in the winter at the rate of 300 knots.

There are westerly 'jet-streams' existing near the tropopause (two main ones in each hemisphere), caused by the big contrast in temperature when polar and equatorial air meet. The width of these fast-flowing rivers of air is small, rarely more than a couple of miles.

An added danger of wind is that it causes turbulence over mountains, producing tremendous down-draughts and forcing anything flying to the ground. The first flight over the Alps by Chavez in 1910 ended in disaster. 'It was horrible,' he said as he was pulled out of his plane, critically ill. It was not till 1925 that the German government decided to send a Dornier Komet over the Alps to mark 'German Day' at the Milan fair. On the return flight, wind caught it above the mountains round Lake Como and it had to go back to Milan.

Local winds can be violent: the Föhn off the Alps, the Haboub raising sand in Egypt, the Mistral funelling down the Rhône valley, the monsoons, the Roaring Forties round the capes of Africa and South America, the hot Sirocco off Africa bringing bad visibility and the Bora gusting down the mountains to the Adriatic.

The tight, round circles of hurricanes track west from the Caribbean and the Gulf of Mexico at a leisurely ten knots, then curve furiously round to the east off the coast of Florida. Typhoons spring up in the Indian Ocean, the China Seas and off the east and north coast of Australia. Sandstorms, waterspouts and line squalls are other variations of the disturbances that wind can whip up.

Tornadoes have picked up such huge loads as a railway

123

compartment full of passengers and lifted them eighty feet in the air. Poultry are sucked up to great heights, plucked clean for the oven and dropped again. Called expressively sea-trumpets in the Mediterranean, tornadoes lift deck-chairs and people hundreds of feet up into the air. Sandstorms can cause havoc to anything mechanical like an engine.

Storms in the sky are common – 50,000 every day, the majority in the East. Except for sandstorms, they are always accompanied by cloud, of which there are basically two sorts – layer cloud (stratus) and heap cloud (cumulus). A prefix in front gives cloud height – cirro (20,000–40,000), alto (6,000–20,000). Nimbo added in front of stratus and nimbus following cumulo means it is a rain cloud. In addition, there is cirrus, the feathery silk threads touching the tropopause.

Stratus cloud denotes steady air. Heap clouds look bumpy and are. The whiter the cloud, the fewer the bumps. Grey and black clouds mean that they are full of water vapour. But the only really dangerous cloud is the cumulo-nimbus – which can be white, grey, black, brown or a combination of all four. The completely brown ones are only found in the East and are the most dangerous. Before the high-flying jets came, flying through the monsoon could be very tricky. The Constellations used to go through either at 14,000 feet or attempt to go under the cloud. As many as eighty rivets could be shaken out of the fuselage on a Calcutta-Karachi trip.

Cumulo-nimbus is unmistakable. It rises like a huge tower from a base of dark ragged clouds, steaming and boiling, with loose untidy walls till the stabler cold air of the tropopause clean-cuts a flat anvil on its top which the high winds stream into an overhang. Initially composed of only one cell, it spawns four or five, so that a storm cloud of fifty miles in width may pack the punch of four atom bombs.

In the cumulo-nimbus interior, waterdrops are being

hurled upwards and downwards, the friction causing the electrical charge of the surrounding atmosphere to change from 150 volts per metre to 10,000. Lightning is the discharge of the electrical field which has thus developed, either from cloud to cloud or cloud to ground.

Waterdrops also cause ice. Hurled up beyond the freezing level, they do not freeze but become what is called super-cooled. Should something like an aircraft fuselage brush against them, the drop turns to ice on the object, spoiling the aerodynamic properties of wings and propellers and weighting down the aircraft.

It is clear ice clogging air-intakes and pitot-tubes, blocking carburettors and literally weighing an aircraft down that is the most dangerous.

Sometimes waterdrops freeze and become hail. Attracting more and more coatings of ice, they become too heavy even for the enormous upcurrents to keep them airborne, and they fall. Hailstones are usually around a fifth of an inch in diameter, but some the size of cricket balls and bigger have fallen, causing death and disaster. In the past, evil spirits were believed to be attacking the earth during a hailstorm, and church bells were rung and arrows shot up into the sky. The damage caused to anything flying could be lethal.

Snow is formed when the super-cooled moisture is too cold to bond together and the crystals remain small. Their shapes are beautifully symmetrical – needles, stars, flower forms and diamonds – the flakes are so light that five-sixths of the world's snow never falls. It blankets visibility at airports and makes aircraft wheels either skid or sink on landing. As much as nine feet can fall on a runway during one night.

Rain also affects visibility, but it is the freezing sort that is really dangerous to aircraft. Sometimes a layer of warm, wet air overlays colder air so that instead of dropping with altitude, the temperature will increase. That is called an 'inversion'. Rain falling from this layer is called freezing rain and can make an aircraft into a block of clear ice (like layers of glittering diamonds) in minutes. The aircraft becomes heavy, the aerodynamic properties of the wings become distorted, and the aircraft is no longer able to maintain level flying speed. Rain can also cause skids and slides on the runway.

Finally, there is fog – often simply low cloud mixed with smoke or dust. However, radiation fog occurs out of a clear cold winter night when the air is moist and when the ground cools by radiating off its heat.

Fog forms very quickly. Places like Gander in Newfoundland, the usual Atlantic refuelling stop before the long-range jets came in, were notorious. When the wind backed to the east, cold air would be brought from the cold Labrador current over the aerodrome, and the dewpoint (the temperature at which that air will vaporise) and the temperature would become the same. Fog would begin on the descent to the airfield, obliterating the runways in front of our eyes, necessitating a diversion to an alternative airfield.

Clearly anyone flying manually without an automatic landing system must see to land, and numerous crashes were caused by pilots trying to come in blind, usually undershooting. Take-off is much easier, and it is only necessary to see a few yards ahead. The pilot, like the motorist, can follow the white line or the cat's eyes in the middle of the runway.

During the First World War, Norwegian meteorologists produced their theory of warring cold and warm air masses divided by what they called 'fronts' after the Western Front. Since forecasting needed simultaneous actual readings a number of times a day, with the information immediately fed in centrally to be assessed, it was clear that a world-wide international meteorological network would be needed if the new science of weather forecasting was to be successful. There were then no sky routes explored, let alone mapped. All that had been discovered was that the earth looked very different from the sky, and it was easy to get lost.

Speed was absolutely essential to stay up in the sky. With piston-engines, power fell off with height, and superchargers were necessary. To produce that speed mechanically, fuel was necessary and would have to be carried aloft. Fuel was the aeroplane's life blood. No fuel meant no speed and an ignominious and dangerous descent to the ground became inevitable.

The difficulties that barred man's way up into the sky were immense – pressurisation, supercharging of engines, temperature and oxygen problems, turbulence, thunderstorms, lightning, rain, hail, ice, fog and finally night, when nothing could be seen anyway, and even the birds stayed on the ground.

The prize at the top of the sky was the very thin air that would make possible very fast flights with very little power. But first it was necessary to get up off the ground and into it.

After the craze for jumping off high towers to get flying speed had come to a sticky end, in 1500 Leonardo da Vinci designed what looked like an aerial sculling machine with wings instead of oars to be worked by the power of a man's arms and legs which in fact were totally inadequate. Then in 1650 came Father Francesco de Lana's boat that could not fly either, but it pointed the way towards ballooning.

In 1783, the brothers Montgolfier discovered that hot air rises and sent up a pig, a cow and a chicken in a hot air balloon. They appeared to enjoy the trip, so up to eighty-four feet went the first aeronaut, the Frenchman de Rozier, in a balloon cautiously tethered to the ground.

Then came the era of gliders and models. Sir George Cayley in the early nineteenth century designed a combination of helicopter and aeroplane. The first aero engine was made by William Henson and in 1848, powered by steam, the first model aeroplane was built by Henson and

Stringfellow. As was to prove the lot of all who made the first tentative steps to explore the new element, most other people laughed at them. Towards the end of the century, the German Lilienthal built a glider closely based on the results of his researches into bird flight and he carried out many successful flights till he crashed. His last words were, 'Sacrifices must be made.'

Then in 1901 came the trip round the Eiffel Tower in a powered airship by the Brazilian Santos-Dumont. And finally in 1903, lying flat on his stomach, Orville Wright flew a straight line in an aeroplane for twelve seconds.

As always in the march of progress, it was the individual who saw the way and worked towards the successful fulfilment. Most people and all governments, including the United States government which three times turned down the Wrights' offer to build aircraft for the army, still refused to believe in flight.

But now a new breed arrived on the scene – the original birdmen, not so much scientific as a cross between showmen, sportsmen and daredevils. Air meetings were held that were similar to horse-race meetings. Prizes were offered by newspaper proprietors, perfumiers, soft drink manufacturers and other firms for record flights. Natural selection and evolution invaded the new country of the sky: the aircraft which survived began to become stronger and faster and to fly higher and longer. Manufacturers began to build them.

But governments still remained disbelieving. 'Gentlemen,' said the British Under-Secretary for War in 1910, 'we are guardians of the public purse, and we do not consider that aeroplanes will be of any possible use for war purposes.'

Even so, Britain emerged from the subsequent Great War as the strongest air power in the world, bigger than France and Germany combined, and way ahead of the United States, whose air force at the 1918 Front operated only British DH4s with American engines.

Though British civil aviation began in 1911 when an aircraft flew from Hendon to Windsor with franked mail on the occasion of George V's coronation (the *Manchester Guardian* called it 'an amusing enough game for the silly season'), civil passenger flying basically evolved out of wartime flying. Two Handley-Page bombers plied between Boulogne and Lympne to return pilots who had ferried new aeroplanes to the Western Front. History repeated itself in the Second World War when pilots who had flown new American aircraft across the Atlantic to Prestwick in Scotland were flown back again in the Liberators of the Return Ferry Service – forerunners of the Atlantic passenger.

In the same way, those Royal Flying Corps pilots were then the forerunners of the cross-Channel air passenger. On 25 August 1919, an ex-RFC pilot in an ex-RFC bomber flew the first civil air passenger in the world from the aerodrome on Hounslow Heath to Paris. Wrapped up in an RFC leather coat, this passenger shared the two-and-a-half-hour trip with samples of leather goods, newspapers and mail, Devonshire cream and several brace of grouse. On the return trip that same evening, just before landing back at Hounslow, he was as sick as a dog into his hat. Not only had man got himself up into the sky, but the first airlines had started.

In 1919 1·6 million world schedule aircraft kilometres were flown. In 1977 the figure was 8,000 million. Today it is well over 12,000 million.

Civil flying is still in its infancy. It will go on expanding and become more and more profitable. After the setbacks of the oil crisis and the world recession, airlines in 1984/5 began to make profits. With the terrorist scare of 1986, income slumped, and once again there was cutthroat competition, especially on the Atlantic. But this will pass. In the long run, all the signs point to more passengers flying further and more often in faster and even more reliable aircraft.

6
Pilots

Originally there was only one man in the aeroplane, and he was Captain and crew combined. He was the man who set it all up, had the vision and the skill, the courage and the perseverance to continue in the teeth of the scorn of all governments and 99 per cent of the world's population in this first role – the intrepid explorer of a new element.

Came the First World War, governments took over the aeroplane they had laughed at, and pilots fought each other in mortal combat as the new Sir Galahads of the air.

Came the peace, and they were downgraded.

'Flying introduces no elements which are not in evidence in riding a motorcycle, game shooting, cricket or golf.'

So flying was described after the First World War in the Medical Research Council's *Medical Problems of Flying*.

The role of a pilot was that of a sportsman, a player of games, a horse-rider. It was right that the first civil pilots shared Hounslow Heath with the Remount Regiment. To this day, as with a horseman, a skilful pilot is described as 'having a good pair of hands'.

'An ideal pilot, with unlimited pluck, unfailingly good judgment, and what is equally to the point, an inexhaustible supply of good spirits.' So the navigator Lieutenant-Commander Mackenzie-Grieve described his pilot, Harry Hawker, with whom he tried to fly the Atlantic in 1919. Engine trouble forced them down halfway across, but they managed to find a boat before ditching.
130

Hawker was typical of the pioneer pilots and many others who followed him – an intuitive extrovert. Mackenzie-Grieve was typical of the navigator – a quiet introvert. Sometimes, as with Lindbergh, there was an 'occlusion' of the two.

War generates its own excitement which many ex-servicemen want continued. All the main trunk routes of the world – the North Atlantic, South Atlantic, Pacific, Australia, South Africa – were pioneered by military or ex-military pilots, usually in ex-military bombers, a spin-off from war that has never had its just recognition. They did the job for various reasons – money prizes, patriotism, but often just for the sheer fun of it.

The mail pilots who pioneered the route across America navigated by the cigar they lit before take-off. When it was burning their moustaches, it was time to come down!

The early explorers of the sky had something about them of wild-men-from-the-woods. The public regarded them affectionately as daredevils. Even the civil pilots, hedgehopping under the clouds from forced landing to forced landing, had that same quality. When the first enclosed cockpit was fitted to a British civil ex-bomber, the pilot got an axe and cut it off, saying he wouldn't be caged up. His leopard-skin helmet was all the protection he needed.

Rough and tough was the image they presented, and rough and tough treatment was what they got. When a pilot pleaded for the elimination of draughts in the open cockpit, the airline manager said, 'What do you want? A bathchair?'

The same manager, when in charge of pilots facing the fog, snow, ice, clouds and winds of the then unconquered North Atlantic winter, promised Churchill that 'not a single aircraft would make the crossing unless it contributed something to the war effort besides a joy-ride for the crew'.

The wild-men-from-the-woods gradually turned into
131

barons. Individual and independent, these new masters tamed the explored sky which other people could be forgiven for thinking that they owned. While ready at any time to strip off their coats and help in an engine change, they expected military efficiency on the ground.

Their word was Law. Nobody argued. A flying-boat captain an hour out turned back and landed again because the local station had forgotten to put the milk for his tea on board.

This concept of 'Master' (they were given the same title as in ships) was dangerous in that nobody dared question the Captain. Understandably, the airline Captain clung on to this God-concept. He signed for everything and everybody on numerous load-sheets, flight-plans and manifests before he took off. Therefore in the air, it was right that he should have absolute power.

This theory caused many accidents. A First Officer who warned his Captain he was 400 feet below the prescribed limits was told to keep quiet. Minutes later, the aircraft crashed twelve miles short of the runway. A DC3 crashed into an obstacle on approach which the co-pilot had been watching. Questioned on whether it was his responsibility to warn the pilot, he replied that he dared not interfere with the Captain's flying because he was only a co-pilot.

After the war, the barons regarded the new pilot intake suspiciously. These were the ex-bomber boys, all trained by several tours of military operations, many of them highly decorated. Regardless of experience, they had first to go back to being second pilots – the office boys in the right-hand seat. They had had to take their flying licences on sea navigation problems, tides and the lights on flying boats, often being tested by retired Master Mariners.

The barons expected trouble. They had surprisingly (and fortunately) become very safety-conscious. 'My job,' said BOAC's Atlantic Training Captain to the new boys, 'is to turn gallant young gentlemen into fussy old women.'

The baron and the office-boy concept took a long time to eliminate. The ex-bombers resented being pushed back into the right-hand seat, becoming merely the flap-lifters and the check-list-callers-out.

There were harsh words and cold silences on the flight deck. There were even fights over the controls, and misunderstandings. The First Officer's opinion of his Captain depended on whether or not he was allowed to do a landing. Flying is one of the few jobs where promotion will be accepted gladly without extra pay.

But the ex-bombers were a new lot again. War had got adventure out of their system. They were quieter and more tractable. Civil flying was becoming a job – a routine one at that – and colourful characters began to drop out of the caste.

Like most jobs, airline flying had its compensations and its disadvantages. On the debit side was the length of time away from home; there were few services and slow aircraft, so crews were strewn all over the globe on slip-stations – that is, they would bring an aircraft in and hand it over to a crew already there, while they themselves waited for the next aircraft (sometimes a week later) to arrive; at some fog-bound stations such as Gander in Newfoundland, crews could be stranded for weeks, continually being overflown.

It was particularly hard on the wives, left to cope with the home and the children. No effort was made by companies to check on how they were managing. Holidays on cheap fares, clothes and presents from all over the world were the assets.

Against that were the continual worries about checks and medicals (on either of which the husband could lose his job) and the short working life. Many pilots took up other jobs or set up businesses as contingencies for this inevitable eventuality.

The actual working pay in private companies is good: up to £35,000 a year for a 'wide-bodied' captain (of a 747 or DC10). First Officers get around £20,000. In America, the pay is considerably higher. In addition, there is flying pay of around £1.00 an hour (the Captain gets slightly more) for time spent away from home on the long range routes. Around $55 a day is provided for meals in America, much of which is saved as crew make do with brunch and sandwiches.

British Airways pay their pilots the same, irrespective of the aircraft they fly. This came about as a result of merging British Overseas Airways four-engined pilots and British European Airways twin-engined pilots to form British Airways in 1972. The 'stick' was difficult enough to achieve without pay differentials.

The ICAO current standard is that no one should act as Captain of an air transport aircraft beyond the age of sixty, with the further recommendation that no one should act as a co-pilot either above that age.

The thinking behind the standard is motivated by the fear of incapacitation in the air. The Trident crash at Staines in 1972 in which 117 were killed had a number of causes, one of which was the Captain's heart condition. On 6 December 1974, a Piper crashed taking off from the Leeds/Bradford airport, the eight occupants all being killed. In spite of a satisfactory electrocardiograph a month before at the pilot's medical, the post-mortem showed that he was suffering from coronary artery disease, and it was considered probable that he had had an acute attack in the air, during which he was unable to control the aircraft.

Incapacitation incidents are practised on most airlines now, and in the event of something occurring in the air, the other pilot should be able to cope. The Pilots' Associations have argued that there should not these days be an arbitrary cut-off of a pilot's career – retirement should depend on fitness, which varies between individuals.

For much of the actual 'work' of flying has been

radically reduced. A computer 'does' the flight-plan – either at the big British Airways computer or from as far away as Los Angeles. With better forecasting and speeds of 600 miles an hour, weather isn't the fearful bugbear it was. Even if an airport did totally close down in fog (the private fear of most piston-engined pilots), now many big airliners and airports have automatic landing whereby a landing can be made in nil visibility and the only problem is how to taxi to the ramp once you're down.

The 'learning curve' affects pilots as it does everyone else. A new and unfamiliar task, like learning to fly a new aeroplane, will inevitably result in initial difficulties. Mistakes are made, but through learning from them, these begin to disappear until a high level of competence results.

The high-tailed jets, the ones with the engines in the tail and the tail plane perched on top of them like the Boeing 727, are a case in point. Such aircraft have a tendency to 'deep-stall' (that is, getting into a steep, nose-down position from which recovery is very difficult). Pilots had to learn to be extremely careful not to descend too quickly.

One after the other, the three-engined 727s crashed – nine appalling accidents in the first three years of service. The 727 was labelled the 'killer aircraft' and attempts were made to scrap it. Then the pilots learned how to cope. The 727 became one of the safest and most popular aircraft ever built, notching up a record of over fifteen hundred sold, and an updated version is still selling.

The Comet started badly too. The pilots were unused to not having the slowing-up effect of idling propellers. The fuselage was so beautifully streamlined, it was difficult to stop. They were continually crashing by overshooting the runway. Then the jet take-off technique was different. It was not known that the delta wing could stall on the ground if the nose was raised too high – but there were then no stick-shakers or warnings to the pilot. Two

135

bad crashes, one at Rome and one at Karachi, resulted. In both enquiries the pilots alone were blamed.

In comparison, because of exhaustive testing, the initial in-service record of the 747 and the Concorde were remarkably accident-free. And the training is designed so the aircrew can perform correctly and quickly all the actions required of them. Now there is a concept of crew operation, each individual operating to the same standard.

When long-range civil flying first began in earnest after the Second World War, 24-hour duty schedules were common. We flew one homebound from Bermuda via the Azores and Lisbon, starting off at midnight. It was almost impossible to get any rest before take-off, but no one complained. We knew that if anyone did object, another slip would be put in. That would mean another three or four days en route on twice-weekly services. And everyone wanted to spend those three or four extra days at home on stand-off.

Though the Americans had Flight Time Limitations, none of the Europeans had. Then accidents started to happen. Two DC4s followed each other into the sea at Bahrein in 1950, the pilots of which had been on duty for almost 24 hours. A Constellation crashed at Singapore where the crew had been on duty for much the same time. Sometimes in accidents, the time on duty was longer and once it was 47 hours.

Flight Time Limitations were then introduced. But although long hours on duty are a thing of the past, fatigue still remains one of the biggest talking points with pilots after pay. But there is no agreement on how much rest pilots need, and there are no standardised regulations. There is also argument on what duty time is – up in the air or hanging around on the ground, which is more tiring?

In the USA the regulations average twelve hours for operational crew but are dependent on the type of duty.

The UK regulations were sixteen hours on duty. Now they must not exceed fourteen hours, but vary day/night. Switzerland has fourteen, Egypt sixteen, Canada fifteen, Belgium sixteen, Australia eleven. In the Netherlands, no detailed regulations are laid down – the operator draws up his own regulations, taking regard of route, temperature, weather and time of departure. All countries have variations for stress.

The Scandinavian countries had a formula where Facc is accumulated fatigue, F is Fatigue Level, N is the number of landings and T is the length of duty time minus horizontal rest for over one hour. The formula that decides whether or not a Scandinavian crew can continue a flight on a jet is determined by a Fatigue Level number above which they cannot go. The formula is $F = Facc + 6 (T + N)$. Facc need not be calculated if there has been a rest period of twenty-four hours or more.

Various devices have been tried by airlines in an effort to combat flying fatigue. Some have stationed crews halfway down the long Eastern route, so their rhythms are five hours ahead of the UK. Aeroflot stationed crews in Cuba, where they lived a life based entirely on Moscow time, no matter when people were eating and sleeping around them.

Most pilots prefer short-haul routes, where they fly to one place and return to sleep in their own beds. Long east-west, west-east routes produce fatigue that seems to accumulate in the body, so you continually feel tired.

Aircrew fatigue, which I have studied for years, is a most frustrating and difficult subject in that it can't really be separated from stress or normal diurnal tiredness. A row with his wife before leaving for the airport can cause the pilot more 'fatigue' than hours of sitting on the flight deck watching the automatic pilot fly the aircraft. Nobody can yet measure it and nobody can yet say what it is. All an airline can really do is to rely on the common sense of the individual and trust his assessment of his own condition.

Because Flight Time Limitation regulations differ so much and have in some cases become so complicated, they defeat their own object. Their very presence becomes a source of fatigue. A captain is given a 'slot' to fly his track to his destination by Control. If he is delayed, he runs the risk of missing his 'slot' and being further delayed. Then up comes the bogey of Flight Time Limitations. If, say, he is on a return trip to the Canaries and back, that will be eight hours. If the delay runs on, then the stand-by crew may have to be called out at a moment's notice, something no one likes to inflict or have inflicted on them. Then the cabin crew's regulations are often different from the aircrew, which complicates things further. All of which adds up, when you have hundreds of passengers on board, aching to get on with their holiday, to a most stressful pressure on the captain to go.

Certainly something like that must have contributed to the worst aircraft accident ever in which 582 people were killed. There had been an emergency at Las Palmas, which was temporarily closed, and a number of Jumbos, including a KLM and a Pan American one, had been diverted to Tenerife. It was the holiday season and the hotels were full. There was nowhere all these hundreds of passengers could go. As time went by, the KLM captain inevitably began worrying about Flight Time Regulations and phoned Holland. Just a few minutes before he would have *had* to stay on the ground, Las Palmas opened again. One can understand the impatience of the KLM captain to take off – but no adequate clearance had been given, and he hit the Pan American Jumbo crossing the runway.

Certainly, up in the air these days much of the burden is taken off the pilot's shoulders. In keeping with the high technology aircraft he is flying, he has changed his role yet again. These days he is more a systems manager than what in the old days could be called a pilot.

138

In those early days, the pilot had to be everything – Flight Engineer, ground mechanic, Navigator, radio man – and if anything went wrong on the ground, he had to be able to put it right. Then aeroplanes got bigger and more complicated and an engineer joined him. This Engineer used also to bring round the tea and biscuits to passengers, but he was soon replaced by the cabin boy, who graduated into a steward.

Aircraft flew further, and next on board were Radio Officers and Navigators, both, interestingly enough, belonging to the Merchant Navy Officers' Union which originated them. Then, because aircraft had more engines and further complications and flew further still, another Engineer arrived on the flight deck.

So on a 1946 Constellation flying the Atlantic, there would be two pilots, a Navigator (who would keep a very full log and draw the flight carefully on the Mercator Chart in dead-reckoning), two Engineers and a Radio Officer operating Morse, since the range of radio telephony (RT) was then only about a hundred miles – a total of six men.

A kind of six-green-bottles-hanging-on-a-wall act followed. But here there was no accidentally-fall, as in the old song. The range of RT increased dramatically. Pilots were talking to Control right across the Atlantic. So the Radio Officer fell – and then there were five. With the advent of fast trips and more reliable aircraft and engines, the Second Engineer officer went – and then there were four.

Next came new developments in computers and in navigation techniques. The Navigator fell – and then there were three.

Finally, on the new technology aircraft there were far fewer instruments and dozens of computers monitored them, so the Engineer fell – and then on the flight deck were just the two pilots in their new role of systems managers, each monitoring the other.

139

It's difficult to say whether they are now under more stress than earlier pilots. They have lost four crew. They are responsible for up to six times as many passengers. Machines can go wrong. But the mundane stuff is taken away from them. The flight plan is computer-completed. On a typical 757 trip to Lanzerote, for instance, with a ground distance of 1,567 miles and average wind component of +49 knots (a good tail wind), the captain will complete and sign the load and trim sheet. The navigation log will be handed to him 90 per cent completed. Once airborne, he will engage the auto-pilot with the flight management system. It will do everything else – take the aircraft up to its allotted altitude of Flight Level 350 (35,000 feet), fly it on track along the airway that has already been fed into the computer, turn at the correct beacons and other turning points. If they get too close to high ground, a mechanical male voice will shout 'Pull up!'

All the data is there: latitude and longitude, fuel remaining, forecast wind on every segment of the route. The pilots fill in the actual time they reach the various points. The computer makes all the necessary adjustments for the wind being different from forecast. Any information they want can be obtained from it. The wind speed and direction and the latitude and longitude is continuously presented.

The pilots must monitor the readings, of course. But the machine is almost never wrong – unless the right latitude and longitude of their starting point were not set up on the Inertial Navigation System. Then naturally the machine is always out by the amount of the initial error.

The oil pressures and temperatures are also presented on the screen to look at if the pilots want to – but if there is something wrong, it would be flashed on the screen of the Crew Alerting System, together with the remedial action necessary.

140

The Captain usually points out various points of inter-est, if they are visible. There are the usual requests for young passengers to come up front, and if it's possible, these are allowed.

Otherwise, there's not a great deal to do. The pilots talk to each other, read newspapers, have their meals (not the same as each other, since there has been the odd case of dual food poisoning).

If the destination airport has the necessary ground equipment, the pilots need not touch any of the controls. The triple auto-pilots – one doing the work, one monitor-ing, one spare – will be doing the flying for them exactly (the exact speed, the exact height) far more accurately than they could do. And then the plane will land, after which all the pilots will have to do is to disengage and taxi to the terminal building.

In addition, the computer runs the engines at their most economical. The airlines – particularly the independent companies – will do all they can to save fuel. Saving a few minutes in the air these days means saving hundreds of pounds.

If a manual landing is made, these days either the Captain or the First Officer does it, taking turns unless the weather is bad or there is some other added difficulty. First Officers have always been hungry for landings. Some Captains will sometimes give all the take-offs and landings to them in return for the First Officer taking the allowance of their favourite tobacco through customs.

During the long hours of the old days, both pilots have been know to fall asleep. This can still happen. Boredom is also stressful. And boredom can make people less alert and more likely to fail to monitor. There have been cases of aircraft being hundreds of miles off course. There may be a number of reasons for this – including wrongful setting up of the latitude and longitude of the starting point on the Flight Management System. Or the switch that connects the auto-pilots to that same system might not have been put on, in which case the auto-pilot, while maintaining speed and altitude, would wander off course.

In spite of the fact that little manual flying is required, the stresses are still there. Much of our psychological world is still unexplored.

Modern aircraft still make belly-landings because the pilots have forgotten to put down the undercarriage in spite of light and sound warnings. Idiotic? That's what people have said in the past and continue to say. But it is now a well-known psychological fact that in deep concentration, the living organism, be it man or cat or other animal, may not hear or see things not directly connected to the task in hand.

Not able to see a 12,000 foot mountain? The pilot must be blind! When an Air New Zealand DC10 crashed into Mount Erebus near the South Pole, the initial enquiry's probable cause was pilot error in that the Captain must have descended through cloud, not knowing exactly where he was. Further tests and enquiries revealed that conditions might have been clear at the time, but the Captain still might have been unable to see the mountain. There is a condition known as 'whiteout' in such snowy areas which causes a kind of blindness.

The stress still remains of possibly being blamed unfairly. The more passengers carried and the greater the tragedy, the more eager become the authorities to apportion the blame as far away as possible from themselves.

The first thing examined after a crash will be the 'black box' on which all relevant flight parameters are recorded on wire tape. Monitoring of the aircraft has now spread to the flight deck. Cockpit voice recorders register the pilots' conversation. In the event of a crash, it will be analysed for clues. There are some sad recorded exchanges among the crew that end in a terrible bang.

Pilots now are also asked to note any incidents and

near-miss accidents, even if they might be interpreted to be their fault. The authorities have said that no action will be taken on these voluntary submissions – which they regard as safety monitoring, enabling action to be taken to avoid a possible future accident. All very laudable, but can the authorities be trusted so to regard them? That is a difficult one, and it is to the pilots' credit that nevertheless they make such submissions. A further stress factor in these days of recession has been the bankruptcy of airlines and the scarcity of jobs.

The inhabitants on the modern flight deck have shrunk from six to two. Now computers do the work of the missing four. Will they eventually also take over from one – or both – of the pilots?

After a long struggle, women have at last made their way to the left-hand seat. They did sterling service in British Transport Auxiliary during the war, delivering the biggest bombers to RAF fields, after which, the reward they got was a shut-out.

One by one and slowly, however, women became civil pilots. I used to fly over the Atlantic with Captain Peacock, an ex-flying boat 'baron'. His daughter is now a Captain with British Midland. There was a woman captain in British Caledonian who left to have a baby and is now back flying again. After receiving about 400 applications for pilots' jobs in 1984, British Caledonian took on 30, of whom 2 were women. There is no reason whatever why women shouldn't be just as good pilots as men, though men have resisted the advance, as they have done every other form of women's equality with them.

The first woman Captain was on Dan Air, and it is said that the company asked her not to put four rings on her uniform sleeve initially, so that the passengers would think she was only the First Officer and not be frightened. She agreed. Dan Air now employs four women pilots. First Officer Lyn Barton became the first woman to fly the British Aerospace 146. And Maria Aburto was the first woman to fly 747s for Iberia.

Consideration for the passengers is more evident in a woman. One female pilot was being tested in a simulator, and the instructor gave her a fire in the cargo compartment and an engine failure. The first thing she did was to pick up her microphone and comfort the passengers. And they failed her for getting her priorities wrong!

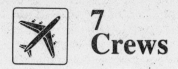

7
Crews

After the pilot, the second crew member to come on board British civil aircraft was the cabin boy. That was in 1922, and the boys were around fourteen years old, dressed in monkey-jackets and tight trousers. No food or drink was served and there was little for them to do. Not until two years later did Imperial Airways begin to employ stewards, similar to those employed on ships, whose job it was to look after sick passengers and hand out coffee and biscuits.

The Flight Engineers came with the introduction of flying boats, to all intents and purposes exactly like a ship's engineers, to whose union Flight Engineers still belong. They supervised refuelling and maintenance along the routes, often dishing out what crew rations there were when stewards weren't carried. Radio Officers – again just like ships' radio officers and belonging to the same union – made their appearance around the same time, closely followed by the Navigators.

When the flying-boats really started operating long-range routes, the stewards had much more to do, serving dinner in the restaurant on board and having the cabins and bar to look after.

The second member of the cabin staff, the stewardess, first made her appearance in 1930, against the wishes of the pilots, as a registered nurse to look after the air-sick on Boeing Air Transport, and she wore a nurse's white uniform. One of her jobs was to stop the passengers putting their heads out of the windows.

The opposition was not the first attempt to keep the

sky one-sexed. Two years before, Amelia Earhart had acted as one of the crew on an Atlantic crossing, to be subjected to such taunts about being simply ballast that she made the trip on her own two years later and became one of the world's most famous pioneer airwomen.

The carriage of stewardesses on the long-range airlines took a surprising time, considering that they were such a success on American internal lines. In 1941, Pan American still had none, giving the reason that 'the job has always been considered a little too strenuous for a young woman'. There were also problems of accommodation along the route, but two years later the company had changed its mind, claiming that the stewardesses' presence would relieve men for war duty. Their ideal stewardess was 'blue-eyed with brown hair, poised and self-possessed, slender, five feet three inches tall, weighs 115 lbs, is twenty-three years old, actively engaged in some participant sport, an expert swimmer, a high-school graduate, with business training – and attractive'.

The first eight put through training school did so well, winning their wings and the right to carry merchant seamen's papers (another hereditary relic from the sea), that further courses and regular recruitment were arranged. Their uniform was light blue with a white blouse.

BOAC emphasised that from a selling angle stewardesses must be employed on the North Atlantic route. There were 'just as good-looking girls in England and the difference in their ways and speech may be an asset'. Back in London, those against were still in evidence. Airline executives commented that stewardesses 'should be British – preferably lightweight', and they must be willing to undertake the duties of their task which should be described to them as similar to those of a domestic servant.

The emphasis on stewardesses' weight was an obsession with airlines. Selection procedures laid down – and still
146

do – weight and build. No other member of the crew was put on the scales as regularly as the stewardess. Even so, women were still keen to fly, and their fathers put pressure on the Chairman of BOAC. He visited the USA and found out about the Pan American girls. On his return, he gave instructions that stewardesses were to be recruited for the North Atlantic.

The reluctant Catering Department approved the uniform, which would 'consist of a replica of the stewards' uniforms – in other words, the same white Eton jacket with facings and, in lieu of blue trousers, a blue skirt'.

The appointments would be, for the time being, confined to the North Atlantic and the age limits were twenty-three to thirty years. The pay offered was hardly an inducement. Even three years after the war, Stewards Second Class only received £189 a year, plus £78 cost of living, and no tips were allowed, though they managed a considerable amount of perks.

Stewardesses were not to wear jewellery other than engagement or signet rings. The women would be required to undertake a ten-week course of training at the Catering Training School in the various aspects of their work, 'particularly as to the duties required of them as waitresses and elementary first aid'.

The training school was strictly disciplinarian. The exact height above the collar that stewardesses might wear their hair was demonstrated to them. One training school centre was held in an old convent school. After roll-call, hands and nails were held out and inspected for dirt or nicotine stains. Collars were checked for dandruff, stocking seams for a mathematical straightness. Trainee stewardesses waited at table, learned the theory of flight and the hierarchy of the company. Facilities were not good and classes were sometimes held in the open with the trainee catering crew waiting on their instructors, who sat incongruously at perfectly set tables positioned on the grass.

Eventually, in 1946, four stewardesses were posted to the North Atlantic run. BOAC issued press releases stressing that they were stewardesses, not air hostesses, wanting particularly to avoid 'glamour and frivolity'. It was not necessary. The women were on their feet nearly twenty-four hours on service, even if the aircraft were on schedule.

There remained the vexed question of whether the stewardess should be allowed in the galley and the crew compartment. It was discovered that 'the Standing Instructions for most of the American airlines are that entry into the cockpit is very emphatically laid down not to exceed thirty seconds'. The resultant British order stated that 'the stewardesses' duties do not require them to enter the galley or the crew compartment and they are to remain in the passenger compartment throughout the flight'.

A year later, the instruction had been modified – the stewardess was now allowed in the galley to prepare baby foods. However, the British Airline Pilots' Association had expressed dissatisfaction with the rule regarding entry into the crew compartment, and the Catering Department was asked to give sound reasons why the embargo should be maintained. Since none was forthcoming, stewardesses were at last allowed anywhere on board.

But stewardesses had to leave on marriage, and when they reached their middle thirties, ground jobs were suggested. Now there is a career structure for a stewardess working for British Airways. After three years she becomes a First Stewardess and further up the hierarchy there are girls who are Pursers, and they can reach Cabin Services Officer. There were no female air traffic controllers in the UK for many years. Now there are a dozen.

Though the Russian airline, Aeroflot, has had them for years, there are at last women civil pilots in Britain. Eight women out of fifty were amongst those selected from 10,000 applicants to fly for United.

In spite of the opposition, women still press to get up into the sky. When Pan Am started recruiting again in 1978, without advertising they got 10,000 applicants for 400 stewardess jobs. The UK pay is less than that of a trained teacher, but no academic qualifications are required – height, weight and the ability to get on with people appear more important. A foreign language and a knowledge of First Aid have also been dispensed with. The perks – holidays abroad at 10 per cent of full fare, overseas allowances, staying at good hotels in exotic places – still remain.

The glamour side of the stewardess is still overdone – particularly in airline advertising. The cabin crew and the operating crew are *one* crew and should be so regarded. There should be less emphasis on hairdos and make-up in training, and much more on safety. The cabin crew should be the real specialists on emergencies and what to do. In spite of enormous courage and resource on the part of stewards and stewardesses, one-third of all passenger casualties need not have happened.

The years just after the war were the romantic years of long-range flying. There was a taboo against marrying in the RAF and American air forces, for obvious reasons, and most of the ex-military pilots were unmarried. Stewardesses were now on board – one women in a crew with eight men. Because there were so few services and aircraft were comparatively slow, crews were together for between three and five weeks. Catering and operating crew used to stay at the same luxury hotels and resthouses in romantic places en route, and there was a fair amount of what a PAWA Captain called 'he-ing and she-ing'.

The trip to Santiago, for instance, took three weeks there and back. The crew could 'slip' (that is, get off the aircraft and change with crews waiting for the next schedule in) alternately every three or four days (for there were only two services a week) at the Azores, Bermuda and Panama. In Chile, they stayed in a luxury resthouse built in a garden of lemon trees right under the snow-covered Andes, drinking *pisco* (a highly potent liquor distilled from grape skins). Crew parties were the order of the day.

Those were the heydays for the stewardess. On one occasion, the First Officer and Engineer were fighting over the stewardess on the flight deck of a Constellation between Panama and Lima. Like so much in aviation, those days are over. The pilots now are largely staid married men. Slips are usually only twenty-four hours, and in any case the cabin crew normally stay in different hotels from the operating crew. The work is still hard. A small striped awning looking like a bathing tent shields four seats on the starboard side at the back. This is the stewardesses' rest position.

Up on the flight deck, the Radio Officer has gone, made redundant by long-range radio telephoning. Now pilots talk to the ground right the way across the Atlantic. The quiet Navigator has gone, too; his work is now done by a chattering machine – the Inertial Navigation System.

And finally, the ratio has changed. Now a 747 is likely to consist of three operating crew, four or five male cabin service staff, and twelve or thirteen stewardesses!

And will the cabin staff now follow the other members of the crew – Navigator, Radio Officer and Engineer Officer – off the aircraft? If such airlines as People Express and the new Virgin Atlantic across the Atlantic catch on, offering no-frills fares as low as £56, where you only get a sandwich or a cold meal which you pay for, will there be a reduction in numbers? This is unlikely to happen on airlines operating a First Class, where there will always be a demand for service. And in any airline, in the event of an emergency, a well-trained crew at the back is essential.

British Caledonian run a career structure for their cabin

staff that is fairly typical of most big airlines. They have no need to advertise for recruits, since they receive 20,000 unsolicited applications annually, mainly from girls, and have a special unit to deal with recruitment.

These 20,000 are reduced to 200, most of whom are interviewed but only 20 eventually selected. The girls must be over twenty-three and under thirty-five, over five foot three inches, with weight proportional to height. Too wide in the beam and they'd have trouble with the narrow aircraft aisles, say the airlines. They prefer people with experience of life, teaching, nursing or a service industry where they meet the public. The selectors are mainly looking for poise, charm and the ability to get on with people. They must have good eyesight – no glasses or contact lenses – and they must be able to swim. That they must be fit is obvious; bar canisters can be heavy and being on their feet for hours is tiring.

The Selection Board spend all day over 20 girls, eventually taking 4. There are tests on numeracy, literacy, handwriting, and a questionnaire, but most important is the interview. In British Airways there are eighty training staff, in British Caledonian only three permanent and four temporary. British Airways have a lengthy selection procedure, and send their girls off flying before they go to ground training school. Britannia Airways select by watching a group at a task together – similar to the Civil Service – watching for the over-pressing, the attentive and the too quiet.

If the girl is taken on, theoretically she has a job till she's sixty. Felicity Farquharson and Sheila Bruce used to fly the BOAC routes when I was on them, and they both went on to complete their careers to retirement. A new girl becomes a number three on six months' probation, and goes for a three-and-a-half week course at the Training Section. For the first two days she will be occupied in getting an American visa and being instructed in the company's history and policy. There are five days of

151

safety training, two days of First Aid, a day on hijacking and dangerous goods. Serving passengers is practised in a 111 mock-up, shortly to be joined by an Airbus and a DC10. All must pass service, safety and security examinations. She then goes out on an 111 as a supernumerary number three. She will sit in the centre of the cabin for take-off and landing. If the aircraft is full, she will sit up front on the flight deck with the number one, who will greet the passengers on the PA and stage manage the demonstration of the emergency drills, the number three acting as model. Number two is the bar girl and sits at the back.

At present there are 1,000 cabin staff at British Caledonian in the ratio of approximately six women to one man. All staff have a personal file and an annual assessment, and both seniority and efficiency are taken into consideration in promotion. There are now 100 Pursers in the company, both men and women. The first Purser retired in 1983, aged sixty.

As well as their basic starting pay of around £5,000, the cabin staff get flying allowances, stop-over and night-stop pay. In addition, they get commission on the tax-free goods they sell on board, some manufacturers giving them extra bonuses. There are also 10 per cent tickets for holidays abroad. Now, even when they're married, they can still fly. If they leave, they can apply to return for the busy summer months.

Wastage is around four a month, usually because some girls can't stand the strain. It has been as low as three and as high as seven. In the present oil and terrorist crises, however, redundancies have been introduced.

Once they are proficient on the 111, they are allowed to go on a familiarisation course on other aircraft, thus extending their licence to the 747, DC10 or Airbus.

First Class meals are cooked on board, and are served on china plates by a Purser and a number one. In the super-executive class, there is a bar girl and a number

152

one. The twos and threes are in the Economy, who get made-up trays and plastic plates.

The British Caledonian tartans are well known – it's part of their advertising, just as Singapore Girl is the symbol for Singapore Airlines. At one time, they had thirteen different tartans, now being reduced to four. The one the girls most like, the grey Monteith, is one that is being discarded. The red Macduff, disliked by most girls, is being retained, as the passengers, press and advertisers like it best.

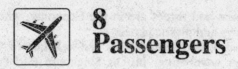

8
Passengers

The first aeroplane passengers were propelled into the sky by the same curiosity and pioneering spirit as the pilots themselves. They flew from ex-First World War aerodromes resembling the tented-and-hutted shambles of Heathrow after the Second World War.

'No palatial waiting rooms were there to lend us moral support,' wrote one of them on his first trip from Le Bourget to London, 'no cocktail bars or tea rooms, nothing but a row of wartime sheds, sandwiched in between a number of still heavily camouflaged hangars. To our astonishment, the big machine (one of our old friends the night bombers converted like ourselves to 'civvy' uses), was crowded, chiefly by Americans. So full was it, in fact, that there were no seats left for us in the saloon, and we had to be accommodated at the bottom of the ample cockpit, with the legs of the pilot and his second-in-command dangling above our heads. Two wide portholes, however, afforded us an excellent view, and the only drawbacks were the heat and the almost deafening noise, due to the fact that our seats lay exactly midway between the two giant engines.'

Women as well as men went off on those shorthaul trips. Booted and helmeted, they had taken to the air wearing exotically coloured quilted flying suits, earning the reputation of being fast in more senses than one. Now more soberly dressed in thick double-breasted leather coats over their long frocks, but still wearing helmets, they flew in open cockpits across the Channel, paying £25 (£720 in today's money value) for London-Paris return.

154

On that first airline network between the European capitals, the passengers' lot gradually improved. The aircraft were still ex-military ones, but now the cabins were converted to look like first-class railway compartments, with identical luggage racks, pelmeted curtains and a steward in a short white monkey-jacket. Certainly there was no heating and they shivered in their overcoats, but they had lunch-baskets with sandwiches and fruit.

So fierce was the competition, that the price of the flight rapidly came down to six guineas on the heavily subsidised French and Dutch airlines, putting the British airlines out of business until they were amalgamated with some government support in 1924 as Imperial Airways.

There were three big selling points to attract passengers on to aircraft – luxury, cheapness and speed. Those three cards have been juggled around by the world's airlines ever since. They were never really certain which was the ace. But in those early days, the safety of flying had still first to be proved.

Forced landings were frequent – the record was thirty-three between London and Paris. The accident rate was phenomenal. Not until 1928, when Imperial Airways began their Silver Wing service, did luxury come into the sky. Cold salmon salad and Chablis to Paris. French cream cakes and tea on return. Luxury was the first card the airlines played – in order to disguise the discomfort and the danger. They were acutely aware of the palatial comfort provided on the liners and in the airships. The *Graf Zeppelin* had a chef and a full-size restaurant. Only the rich could afford to travel – that was the belief. Flying was a new experience and people had to be enticed up into the sky.

As the comfort, regularity and safety of the European route began to improve, the airlines spread their wings further. The British Air Minister left in 1926 for India. He took his wife with him because 'we were both intent upon proving to a doubting world that flying was a normal

155

and dependable way of travelling for women as well as men, and no longer an adventure that only men could undertake'.

Now the successful air pattern that had been established over Europe began to be extended over the world. Juan Trippe started services with Pan American to the Caribbean then to South America. His financial backing came from the very flexible American airmail contract system which was far more effective than the British financial muddling with public and private money.

Unexpected hazards to passengers were still there. Finding a man lounging round in Croydon and believing him to be one of his pilots slacking, the Imperial Airways manager sacked him on the spot – only to discover that he was a passenger on a delayed flight to Paris.

Luxury and safety were achieved by the flying boats. It was natural for Britain, a maritime nation, to rely on civil flying boats for interconnecting their Empire with what they called the All-Red-Route (joining together all places coloured red on the map). It was as a political move rather than to help passengers that the British government sponsored the routes and the flying boats, but by 1932 there was a ten-and-a-half-day service over the 7,805-mile route from London to Cape Town.

There were problems in opening up the routes, one of which was blacking of flights across their territories by a number of countries, but particularly Turkey and India. Then the longer-range aircraft were even slower than the early 1919 ex-RAF ones. The big new Handley-Page 42 that looked so Victorian had a built-in headwind. To demonstrate its speed, it raced the Flying Scotsman to Edinburgh.

Air mail has always been more profitable than passengers. An Empire Air Mail scheme evolved in 1934 whereby a letter would be sent to anywhere in the British Empire for 1½d. To meet the huge demand expected (and fulfilled), the beautiful Empire flying boat was built

156

to operate the All-Red-Route. On the American side, this was matched in luxury by the Martin, which flew from San Francisco to Honolulu in twenty-two hours.

The flyingboat era was in its own way a little golden age for the air passenger, who loved them probably more than any other aeroplane. The British were particularly fond of them. Railways having made their contribution to aviation, now it was the turn of ships. The seamen have in fact helped the evolution of airmen enormously – giving them bearings and positions, navigation and other instruments (the gyro compass and the gyro automatic pilot were first used on liners), and spectacularly and bravely rescuing them from the sea when they fell in. It is quite right that behind the statue of Alcock and Brown standing outside the Control Tower at Heathrow, the sculptor has carved Neptune propping them up with his trident.

On the flying boats there were two decks, including a promenade deck. There were bunks and cabins. There was a bar and a restaurant. The Captain used to eat with the most important passengers at the Captain's table. The food and wine served by the stewards rivalled that of the first-class ships on the crack Atlantic run.

The pilots used to fly the boats across Africa, often very low to afford a unique view of elephant, giraffe, rhino, buffalo, lion and gazelle. The snow-covered heights of Kilimanjaro and Lake Victoria were leisurely inspected. The Empire flying boat was certainly the most wonderful way to see the Empire.

But there was one big gap in the All-Red-Route – the Atlantic, then and now the most important route in the world. Before the Second World War, it had never been flown in winter, and neither the British nor the Americans had an aircraft of sufficient range to fly it, though they were engaged in a race to be the first to do so. Actually, in exactly the same way as the French and the British

157

took off in their Concorde on the first commercial super-sonic flights in 1976, so did Pan American and Imperial Airways flying boats conquer the Atlantic in July 1937.

The British used their Empire boats, but all luxury had gone. The aircraft were stripped to the bone to pack in petrol. Irish officials who tried to hitch-hike a ride across, saying they realised that there was no cabin accommodation but they 'were quite prepared to stand up, or sit on the floor', were told peremptorily by Imperial Airways that there was no floor.

But it was the flying boat that led the way commercially over the Atlantic and in fact it was the most luxurious flying boat that ever flew for an airline, the Boeing 314. One look at it is enough to see it as the prototype of the Boeing Jumbo.

It was the biggest and most powerful aeroplane yet, weighing forty-two tons and carrying thirty-five passengers across the Atlantic. There was a private honeymoon suite in the rear (used by Winston Churchill on his first Atlantic crossing in 1942), berths, cabins, a fourteen-seat dining-room where seven-course meals were served with wine, a promenade deck and a big galley where the stewards prepared meals.

On the palatial flight deck were two pilots, a Navigator, a Radio Officer and an Engineer who could use a catwalk along the wings to attend to the engines in flight.

It was the *Dixie Clipper* Boeing 314 that carried the first fare-paying passengers from the US to the UK, via the Azores, at a rate of $375 single, on 28 June 1939, thus starting the first commercial Atlantic air service.

Then came the war, and it was back again to the pioneering days for the air passenger. Even the Boeing 314 passengers were rowed across to a bleak beach in Newfoundland for breakfast. Comfort in the converted bomber Liberators that did the trip was non-existent. The heating rarely worked. The lavatory was simply an Elsan in solitary and open splendour at the rear. There were
158

no seats. Passengers lay on the floor, shivering under inadequate blankets, or sat on a box. Often the aircraft had to go up to 20,000 feet, necessitating everyone on board putting on the nauseating rubber-smelling masks and sucking oxygen the whole way across. One man lost both his hands through frostbite.

Miserable and frozen, often unable to eat the spam sandwiches provided, the passengers would have been cheered if they had realised that they were in fact making history: it was in this way that the North Atlantic winter was conquered and a two-way, year-round North Atlantic route was established.

All the way through aviation history, most people were saying 'impossible': to the aeroplane itself, to carrying passengers, to flying the Atlantic. Most people said it couldn't be done, others underestimated. Only a very few have foreseen what flying could achieve.

Pan American got rid of its flying boats. Their hulls produced far too much drag and were too big to move easily through the air, though the British still clung to them and even built the biggest and most luxurious flying boat ever, the eight-engined *Princess*, which never flew commercially and which spent its days cocooned on Southampton Water.

Now aerodromes had sprung up everywhere, the faster streamlined aeroplane was the answer, and in the pressurised Constellation, with a speed of 330 mph, was found the first true long-range passenger-carrying aeroplane. The Captain used to go round and talk to the passengers. 'How many engines have you got?' passengers asked. 'And how many do you use at one time?' 'Is that a crack on the wing?' pointing to the ailerons. In the early hours of the morning during a Constellation crossing of the Atlantic, a Captain found that the only person awake was a little old lady looking wild-eyed and anxious. He said to her comfortingly, 'Only another five hours!'

'Five hours!' she almost screamed. Then grabbing his

arm, she whispered into his ear, 'Is there by any chance a lavatory on board?'

Passengers were usually very good about weather and mechanical delays in the days when those were frequent (the average Constellation delay into New York was four hours). But sometimes there would be an argument. One passenger complained bitterly when a night stop was called at Bermuda for an engine change, pointing out that three engines were working so why not proceed across the Atlantic on those?

Then there were the drunks, less common now than then. Fear is at the root of most excessive drinking and alcohol has twice the effect at altitude. The cabin crew take the brunt of most of this. One apt retort to a drunk was made by a British stewardess. To the man's belligerent question, 'You think I'm drunk, don't you?' she replied, 'Oh I do hope so, sir! I should hate to think there was any other reason!'

Pop stars are usually the biggest offenders and it isn't always drink that makes them high.

A Captain can close the bar on a tipsy passenger. This I once did on a VIP going to Nassau. We slipped (changed crews) at the Azores and I told the Captain what I'd done. The last I saw of this man was going into the bar at Santa Maria waving a wad of hundred-dollar bills saying he intended to drink the lot before he got on that damned aircraft again.

But the on-going Captain had a rather different idea. He let the man have as much to drink as he wanted, in the hope that unconsciousness would be achieved. However, this man was 100 per cent proof to the treatment. Halfway between the Azores and Bermuda, he began a striptease, finishing up naked racing down the aisle with the Captain pursuing him with an open blanket to preserve decency.

The same thing still happens these days. In 1978 a young woman who had been celebrating took off all her clothes and began to promenade the aisle. The American airline concerned wryly commented that they couldn't always guarantee this as part of the in-flight entertainment!

Blankets have also been used to cover amorous passengers and screen their activities from the rest of the cabin. Perhaps it's fear again, perhaps altitude, but strangers tend to become intimately acquainted with remarkable speed in aircraft. But perhaps the strangest use of a blanket was in 1939 in Kano. Hausa tribesmen had assembled at the airport to see one of their number off on a trip to Mecca, to the cost of which they had all contributed. Once this man saw what he was going off in (a DH86), he didn't want to go and began to panic. There were only two pilots and no cabin staff, and the Captain didn't want to take him.

However, after much talking, the tribesmen calmed him down and he went inside quite meekly. The station manager, who knew Hausa, reassured the captain, saying he was sure the man would be all right and wouldn't move a muscle. The tribesmen had told him that as soon as he was seated a blanket would be put over his head. He was placed well away from the cabin door, and a blanket put over his head. The First Officer kept an eye on him. At each stop, off came the blanket and he went with the other passengers to eat a meal or go to bed at a night stop until he arrived three days later at Mecca.

Sometimes there are awkward customers – usually the ones who say they have 'direct access to the Chairman'. They grumble about the coffee being too cold or the cabin being too hot. They complain about the Captain deliberately flying through turbulence every time a meal is served. They forcibly point out the connections they're going to miss when the plane runs late.

How far to try to explain mechanical things to passengers is a problem for airlines. When an aircraft piston engine failed, it was advertised by the fact that the propeller stopped and 'feathered' (its blades turned to

161

reduce drag). Since the passengers could see it clearly enough, they always asked questions, to which 'giving it a rest' was the usual answer. On Constellations it was invariably oil pressure trouble: the oil temperature would rise and the pressure would drop, and then the engineer had two minutes to feather it before it burst into flames. It was long enough. The Constellation on three engines was still a good aircraft, and it could cope on two.

Passengers often get worried about being shut in for long hours. Nearing Darwin after hours of going through continual thunderstorms, one passenger rushed to the main door and tried to open it. The heavy door on pressurised aircraft is like that on a safe. A sedative calmed him down. On some Russian aircraft, the emergency exits used to be firmly locked lest they be opened in the air.

Limited in their movements though they are, the passengers go about their lives as far as possible according to their routine on the ground. Several times at dawn, I have come into the cabin where many Moslems are facing east at their early devotion in the aisles. High over the Atlantic, the sound of 'Nearer, my God, to Thee' being enthusiastically sung could be heard one Sunday above the noise of the engines, coming from the passenger cabin. It was a charter flight for the Salvation Army, and this was the time they always held their services.

The airline managements still underestimated the capability of flying to attract passengers. In the guessing game of the total number of passengers that could ever be drawn away from the ships to the airlines, BOAC guessed a maximum of 40,000 annually, PAA 500,000 and TWA 575,000. The actuality now is nudging ten million.

The airlines were still playing the luxury card as ace. Just like their Silver Wing twenty-four years before, now in competition with Pan American's President, TWA's Ambassador and Air France's Parisienne services, BOAC launched the Monarch service on their American Stratocruiser, which had fourteen bunks (extra charge £8) and a bar downstairs reached by a winding turret staircase, of which the 747's staircase to the upper-deck luxury compartment is reminiscent.

The symbol of a gold crown was on all labels, menus and tickets. The passengers went under a detachable archway on which was blazoned *Welcome to New York* or *Welcome to London* on arrival. There was to be free perfume and free champagne. Free Monarch ties were provided for the men, Monarch luggage labels for the crew. The only thing missing in comparison to the President was an orchid for the ladies.

Of that successful first Monarch service, one enthusiastic journalist wrote that after the gourmet dinner bedtime came, 'and it really was bedtime for a number of the passengers. True, they paid extra for their beds, but they had the comfort of mattresses, pillows, blankets and crisp white linen sheets. The bunks pulled down from the side of the aircraft where in daytime they're hidden.'

The lowering of the bunks and the making up of the beds was arduous for the cabin crew – indeed if the flight wasn't non-stop, their work was. Then there was the serving of the elaborate meals, with one steward on duty all the time in the downstairs bar.

Over the years the luxury card lost value. Then the cheapness card began to come into its own. The ideal tourist plane had made its appearance – the DC6B, holding eighty-two passengers in five-abreast rows. On 1 May 1952, Pan Am's *Clipper Liberty Bell* flew the first tourist Atlantic service (cost $270 one way against the previous $395). The schedule westbound was round the houses via Keflavik and Gander and was sixteen hours. The tourist trips were highly successful. Loads across the Atlantic increased by 15 per cent every year.

Even so, it was not cheapness but speed that was the ace – naturally, since that is what flying is all about. Speed is why the *Queen Mary* is a tourist attraction at Palm Beach and the *America* rots beside the quay, why there is no longer a passenger ship service to South Africa and Australia, and why even the *Queen Elizabeth II* only operates the Atlantic during the summer. It has always been a maxim that when the North Atlantic could be flown in a normal working day and the round-about route via Iceland or Gander was a thing of the past, the ships would be 'sunk'. In fact, this is exactly what happened.

The British Comet was the first jet civil aircraft. It was a new development. And as with many new developments, it was costly in lives as well as money. There was much still to be learned about metal fatigue. One Comet exploded over the Mediterranean, then another one. A Comet had already been lost in turbulence over India and there were take-off accidents due to a ground stalling tendency. But after exhaustive tests, these troubles were eliminated and Comets have only recently been taken out of service. I had a smooth flight to Greece in one of the most ancient. It was packed to the gills with holidaymakers and one's nose brushed the back of the seat in front, but it flew beautifully.

In spite of its difficulties, the Comet was the first plane to fly over the Atlantic on 4 October 1958, although a stop had to be made at Gander. Soon the schedule London–New York in 707s was around eight hours.

In 1976, the passenger supersonic age started with the Concorde. After proving flights to Washington, despite protests on noise and pollution, the first Concorde New York–London service was established, with a schedule of three hours forty-five minutes. And now another new air era for the passenger is beginning. For there is nothing very different in supersonic flight – except speed, and speed always sells because it saves time.

Fast, cheap flights have finally made the aircraft supreme. The passengers flock on to aeroplanes in thousands. It has been a natural progress of evolution. And then, after travelling all over this world, they will begin travelling the universe.

But meanwhile, as the honeyed voice over the loud-speaker invites you to board at the appropriate gate, who are your fellow passengers likely to be these days?

Theoretically, the first aboard will be the VIPs, well wined, and the Queen's Messenger with the Diplomatic Bag. The Queen's Messenger is a frequent skytraveller, an unassuming civil servant carrying, if it's the British Diplomatic Bag, an unassuming grey canvas bag sealed according to its degree of secrecy and confidentiality. The Queen's Messenger has to take a special oath, carries a special passport, and the bag has a special seat of its own fully paid for by the British taxpayer. Besides secret letters, instructions and memos, the bag is used by the diplomatically immune citizens of most countries for an extraordinary variety of items. These are not necessarily dangerous ones like guns, weapons or drugs, for I know of one British Diplomatic Bag that was eagerly awaited across the world because it invariably contained Oxo cubes and gravy browning.

And from the first passenger aboard, to the most popular passenger. From Queen's Messenger to the Queen herself. The most popular but by no means the most pampered passenger in the world. She is reputedly easy to serve, modest and moderate in her requirements. She usually embarks, if she is flying British Airways, from the VVIP Suite. The aircraft is likely to be a Tristar which has been withdrawn from service and refitted and thoroughly checked for the flight. All staff working on it would have a special pass and stringent security is enforced. The seats will have been removed for her quarters. There is a red-carpeted lounge, a dining area, bedroom and dressing-rooms. The aircraft is equipped with special plates, decanters and cutlery. Menus are arranged beforehand by her household. But on many occasions when visiting friends, the Queen and members of the Royal family use aircraft of the Queen's Flight. This is stationed at RAF Benson, near Oxford, and the aircraft used to be ancient Westland Wessexes and Andovers.

There was no luxury on the Andover, but a certain pristine cleanliness. At RAF Benson there is what is called the 'E II R factor', which makes people work because they want to. It is said that there is difficulty making them go home.

Every aircraft was fully serviceable every morning. Unlike the computerised flight deck of the jets, the Andovers were still equipped with the old RAF item of a navigation station and chart table. The Wessex is a helicopter.

Sometimes the Royal Princes fly the aircraft of the Queen's Flight. Prince Philip, Prince Charles and Prince Andrew are also qualified helicopter pilots. But flights by the Queen in helicopters are frowned upon, after a bad crash in 1968. But in 1977, during her Jubilee visit to Northern Ireland, the Queen flew to the royal reception by helicopter, the danger of ambush being manifestly greater than that in the air.

Later that year the Queen ended her silver Jubilee year of travels appropriately by making her first flight in Concorde. She and Prince Philip flew from Barbados on a record-breaking flight of three hours fifty-nine minutes, which brought her home in time for the State opening of Parliament. Prince Philip was on the flight deck during take-off from Barbados. Commemorative covers were flown on Concorde from Barbados to London. The covers have a Barbados Royal Visit stamp affixed which was cancelled with a special one-day handstamp in use in Barbados. The covers were then flown on the Royal flight and backstamped on arrival at Heathrow.

When the Queen and Prince Philip travelled to Jordan for a state visit in 1984, they went in a Tristar with special anti-missile devices fitted to the wings. The Tristar was again used on their flight to Nepal in 1986.

On the Queen's Flight, the Andovers have now been

retired, and replaced by two British Aerospace four-engined 146/100s.

But what of less exalted passengers and occasions? On scheduled flights in the First Class section you will find most of the VIPs. Most, because a few prefer for reasons of anonymity or interest to travel Economy. So beyond that First Class curtain, sometimes enticingly glimpsed from the tightly packed Economy cabin, will be the film stars and the politicians, members of royal families, occasionally public relations officers, ambassadors, company directors and executives, columnists, producers, publishers, senior lecturers in every subject, service officers and civil servants of the rank of assistant secretary and above.

Up in First Class you will also find a sprinkling of people who regard it as a good investment for the contacts made over the free champagne cocktails and the seven-course meal. The con man, the salesman, the titled-husband seeker, the aspiring actress; address swopping on the back of menus is commonplace.

Businessmen and executives are very status conscious. They resent having to pay (or their companies having to pay) sometimes three times more for a seat than some of the other low category passengers. They also complain bitterly if a flight is downgraded to Economy, even though, if a flight is downgraded, the First Class passengers should have the difference refunded.

In the Economy section, though you're more cramped, it isn't quite so conducive to striking up friendships. There isn't the sense of belonging to the same exclusive club, of being vouched for because you've paid so much more than the others in the back, or your company has. But you get an even more interesting cross-section of humanity. In the Economy, you get lower ranks than those up front, the less high-powered salesmen, the executives a notch or two down. You get the people travelling either individually, or because they belong to one of the reunion clubs, to see

167

distant relatives, academics off to do research, artists, writers, students, brain drainers going down, or rather up, the drain. There is always a flowing tide of emigrants and immigrants, with all their hopes and aspirations, and their fears and anxieties for the extended families they have probably left behind.

On my last trip to Toronto, I sat next to a family from Bangladesh going to open a restaurant in Canada. They had been held up because their youngest daughter was mentally retarded. They told me something of the conditions in Bangladesh. But now the whole family was being admitted to Canada. Everything was marvellous. They wouldn't have complained if the aircraft had flown upside down.

Then of course there are the holidaymakers and the unaccompanied children. Sometimes holiday firms charter the whole aircraft, sometimes just a block of seats. The seats on package holidays tend to be more cramped, the service even less personal. But in general holidaymakers accept everything technical on the flight without question, even a loose seat, but raise hell on their return about the plastic ham and the polystyrene cheesecake, or a stewardess who hadn't deigned to answer their bell.

'We were delayed and they didn't feed us,' is, a travel agent told me, the commonest complaint about the flight. It's as if we all (as I think in a way we do) revert to being children when we fly.

But in any case, the chief grumble among package holidaymakers is either switched holidays or the hotel arrangements when they get there – the incomplete hotels in Spain, which hadn't got the water or the electricity switched on, overbooking, the courier who didn't know a thing, including English, queues for food, and its inedibility when they did get it.

One honeymoon couple were given a room which was no more than an annexe to a room shared by a couple of elderly spinster sisters. There was a large communicating
168

doorway between the two rooms, but, alas, no door. A clumsy attempt had been made to rectify this omission by nailing a discarded stair-carpet over part of the aperture. Neither the sisters nor the honeymoon couple found this adequate.

Another family couldn't eat any of the food at their Majorca hotel. They had to go out to almost every meal. The breakfast before their return flight consisted of such enormous stale and stony bread rolls that the mother decided to bring one home with which to confront and if necessary to crown the tour operator. She put it carefully with the pottery wine jars and other holiday souvenirs, hoping the millstone-like bread roll wouldn't break them, and savouring the tour operator's face when she presented it. Unfortunately for her good intentions, when she cast around for it at Gatwick customs, the youngest and most finicky of her children had found her appetite whetted in flight and had eaten it.

Unaccompanied children are big business for airlines. Children travelling to and from school, children of parents working overseas, and increasingly children of divorced parents spending their allotted time with one or the other.

Then why doesn't aviation woo the children? Is it because they don't actually hold the moneybags and pay for the tickets?

Practically all airlines' public relations effort and advertising is aimed at the businessman. One gets tired of the big seats he's offered, the food he gets, the drink he's bought, the stewardesses who smile at him. Yet the holiday companies know that it's the children who lead the parents to their choice of a holiday abroad. An airport is a fascinating microcosm of the top end of our highly sophisticated society. Children would much prefer to be shown round an airport than a museum. Why doesn't the BAA allow organised parties of schoolchildren round their airports? Why aren't continuous running films about airports and airlines shown in the terminals?

Some airports and airlines do make an effort. On the first floor of Gatwick airport (that's the floor you go into from Flight Departures set-down point), right at the back on the left near the lifts, you'll find the Children's Check-in. Here assemble children of expatriates, foreign families, children coming on visits, children of families split by divorce, handicapped children.

They all have two things in common. They are all unaccompanied. And they are here to meet 'Auntie'. Their ages range from six to twelve and they are classified 'unaccompanied minors' and their names and details about them will already have been filled in at the time of booking and circulated to all departments.

'Auntie' has been selected by British Caledonian from ex-teachers and nurses and ex-airline employees, who have themselves brought up a family and live within fifteen miles of the airport so they can be called on at very short notice. There is always a waiting list of applicants to be one, the airline actually recruiting about every three years. Their training consists of a four-day course on basic procedure, a trip 'shadowing' an operational escort with children, and a two-day course on safety procedure.

For a child below the age of six, a personal 'Auntie' will be provided at the cost of 50 per cent of the one-way fare (the same as the child). Beyond Europe, British Caledonian provide an 'Aunties' service for a group of ten or more free. Peak time is Christmas when the Check-in is full of unaccompanied minors carrying turkeys defrosting over the floor. Weather is the great bugbear. If there is a delay, the children are kept within the escort service, and parents and schools informed.

From the ages of twelve to sixteen, it is up to the parents as to whether an escort service is provided. Sometimes the children themselves are undecided whether to welcome it or not. A fourteen-year-old boy thought it altogether beneath him to be thus attached.

170

'I'll walk three paces behind you,' his 'Auntie' told him. 'Then nobody will know, but I'm there if you need me.'

The greatest number of children the 'Aunties' have had charge of was ninety on a flight to Hong Kong, and the Far East and Lusaka are the most frequent destinations for unaccompanied minors. Most children love flying, and on longhauls interest themselves in five Funpacks containing games and books. They also have the film and a special children's programme on the in-flight audio system, called 'The Sky High Kid Show'.

They can become members of the 'Lion Club', with which they get a badge, a magazine every four months and a log book which the captain signs for every flight they make. Once they've flown 60,000 miles, they get a certificate. At meal times they can have hamburgers, fish fingers, chicken, chips, trifle, jelly, fruit. And on overnight stops, 'Auntie' stays with them at the hotel. As far as possible, the same 'Auntie' is provided so that the children get to know her.

In addition to her own charges, 'Auntie' keeps an eye on mothers with young children, for whom the airline provides free packs of nappies, lotion and other useful items.

During 1983, British Caledonian 'Aunties' escorted 20,000 children all over the world, and they can have adventurous trips. On occasion, they take part in adoptions. One 'Auntie' became the legal guardian temporarily of children being brought to the UK to be adopted by their grandparents. Their father had disappeared and their mother had died.

One 'Auntie' had to take her charges up to a school in Scotland. Delayed by a snowstorm, she knocked on the door at three in the morning. The staff were none too pleased to take them in.

On one flight to Casablanca, the aircraft had to overfly because of bad weather and had to land at a tiny desert airfield in a sandstorm. 'Auntie' and children had to trek across the desert in an old taxi.

The children behave well on board, though now and again there are 'incidents'. Three once set fire to an aircraft seat. As far as possible, the airline doesn't make a fuss, but drops a word in the ear of parent or school that this is unacceptable behaviour.

A few other airlines have followed British Caledonian's example, but only a skeleton service is provided by British Airways, and this only on the ground.

There are odd sights at the Children's Check-in. Like the burly six-footer towering above a bunch of tiny tots, waving his arms and shouting 'Auntie, Auntie!'

It was an affectionate reunion. After all, in the past they'd travelled thousands of miles together.

Other airline travellers are pets, who often travel well. Some of the smaller ones used to be allowed in the cabin. Now, with the anti-rabies campaign, there are stringent regulations on most airlines even when animals are carried in specially designed IATA containers in the holds. What stories must lie behind total refusals such as British Caledonian's edict on dogs, 'Snub-nosed breeds will not be accepted for carriage irrespective of age', or British Airways', 'Mink will not be accepted for carriage on passenger aircraft'.

Animals come on board via the cargo department. BOAC, with its background of operating the Empire routes, realised that animals would be very profitable cargo. Thousands of monkeys were flown by Yorks into London from Delhi and Calcutta. Many were then sent on to America to be used for research into the fighting of polio and other medical experiments.

In 1951, the BOAC Commercial Director wrote to the Traffic Manager that 'in recent talks with the Sales Director we touched on developing monkey traffic over
172

the North Atlantic by means of a weekly freighter, estimated to earn $250,000 westbound.'

Fewer animals now appear at Heathrow. A million a year used to pass through in the late 1970s, when an RSPCA hostel with all modern facilities including an operating theatre was situated on the north side of the airport. Now the RSPCA maintain a presence in the Quarantine Station in a liaison capacity.

Numbers of animals reaching this country have gone down largely because of the efforts of conservationists throughout the world. The export of Rhesus monkeys is now banned from India. Tropical birds can no longer be brought in. Many species of animals – not just cats and dogs – have to undergo six months of quarantine in this country, and that is expensive. Strict IATA regulations lay down what leg and beak and tail room each animal should have, and the cage requirements, food and attendants are all specified. The behaviour patterns from aardvarks through dolphins, maggots, magpies and hippopotami to woolly monkeys and zebras are anticipated and catered for.

Then the cost of cleaning the aircraft and removing the smells – particularly of monkeys – was enormous. And sometimes they escaped, died or got out of hand in the air.

So except for racehorses attended by grooms, the movement of animals is down to a trickle compared to what it was. The Quarantine Station is run by the Corporation of London, because historically they were responsible for the Port of London, and Heathrow is a port. The up-to-date building with its modern hygienic cages both for outgoing animals and those waiting to be collected by commercially-run quarantine stations (or by zoos in the case of exotic animals) cost £750,000. The annual cost of running it is around £330,000. And that all comes from the rates of the City of London. Since the Quarantine Station performs a national service, not unnaturally the ratepayers consider this most unfair.

Before entering the quarantine section, protective

173

clothing and goggles have to be donned, and great care is taken to ensure against infection, particularly rabies. Inspections are also made of the conditions in which the animals travel, and any necessary action taken. The staff of the Station are primarily law enforcement officers, there to see that the 1981 Animal Health Act is strictly adhered to.

There are several categories of people who should not be on board. 'No go' lists for airline passengers include women seven months or more pregnant, those with wired jaws, contagious diseases, chest complaints and those liable to heart attacks. It is not advisable to travel with heavy colds. Earache becomes worse with changes in pressurisation. Boiled sweets to suck are still handed out on some airlines prior to take-off.

People do sleep on board, but it is difficult. They usually feel rather lacking in energy when they fly – and very tired when they land. This is now called jet lag. It was never heard of in propeller-driven aircraft, despite the fact that speed was half that of a jet and journeys twice as long. Basically it refers to that feeling of disorientation and fatigue after flying quickly across a number of zones of longitude. The time change is one hour per 15°, so that the time in New York is five hours behind London. It does not affect people flying north or south, when time remains the same. Time is something that is quite unrealistic on board an aircraft, since it is rapidly changing.

This means that anyone arriving in New York from London is pitched into a routine where bedtime and meal times are all put back five hours. His circadian rhythms have been upset, and he suffers from dysrhythmia.

Perhaps the slow propeller-driven aircraft gave time to its passengers to acclimatise themselves to these changes, as ships do. At any rate, there have been a number of studies on circadian rhythms.

Aircrews shuttling across the Atlantic are worst hit, as
174

no sooner have their 'time-clocks' adjusted to British time than they are subjected to American time. They never get much chance of settling into any rhythm. Undoubtedly this gives rise to accumulated fatigue.

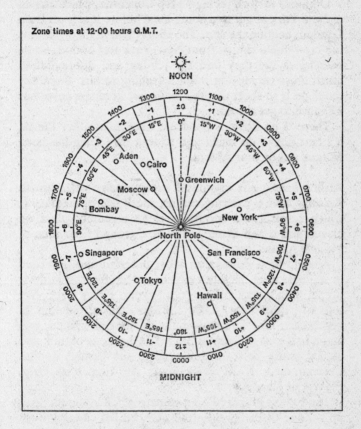

But it is the night departures that predictably contribute most to fatigue. Airlines believe that people do not like to waste a day; so Atlantic flights particularly are mostly scheduled to arrive at their destination in the early morning. This may mean not losing out where the action is, but it is very tiring. Recovery takes place within two days – some businesses lay down that important decisions are not to be taken during that time.

Opinions vary on jet lag on the Concorde, which arrives in New York about two hours local before it sets off from London, beating the sun. The short flight in theory means the crew could return from New York to London. Some passengers say they find the jet lag and disorientation much more exhausting when travelling so fast. Some say the flight is so short that the feeling of tiredness never has a chance to get a hold.

There is no obvious panacea. Like most other things, it's best not to do much and to wait till jet lag has been worked out of your system.

Airline catering is organised exceptionally well. British Airways have a catering centre, south site of Heathrow, which resembles a spotlessly clean assembly plant on eleven and a half acres and with a ground floor area of 145,000 square feet.

A huge food production area, panelled and furnished in stainless steel, includes kitchens, deep freezes, larders, preparation rooms and its own bakery. Every week, five tons of prime meat, 6,000 chicken breasts, ten tons of vegetables, nine hundredweight of smoked salmon, two and a half tons of fresh salmon, 1,000 gallons of milk and 50,000 butter pats are delivered to the Centre. Similar Centres serve KLM at Schipol, Air France at Orly, PAWA at Kennedy.

The food is prepared on a conveyor belt system to load up on one of the twenty-four six-wheeled catering hoist trucks, with bodies that rise hydraulically to eighteen feet, the door level of a 747. The package that is slid into the aircraft contains all meals (the Economy Class all ready on trays, with the exception of the hot main course – chicken pie or beef, but on Far East routes including fillet steak okaribayaki and medallion of pork with sweet and sour sauce, already cooked in silver foil topped packs), trays, cutlery, blankets, toiletries, newspapers and toys.

The hoist trucks take such packages to the 747s being turned round.

First Class food has an initial cooking. Steaks are browned, beef half roasted. These are finished off in the big First Class ovens, then cut from the roast when served.

There are ten galleys on board, fitted with refrigerators and ovens. The ovens in the Economy Class look like a multiple grill – thirty slots for thirty cooked main courses to be taken up to 300°F and then served on the trays already set out in the centre.

There used to be comment cards for passengers to fill in, but these have mostly gone – though American Airlines have a pre-paid comment card. Airlines found that people wrote on them for something to do. But passengers do write in. All letters are answered and the comments carefully scrutinised. Unknown to management and passengers, crew censorship used to intercept the worst comment cards.

British passengers have their own Air Transport Users Committee at 129 Kingsway, London WC2B 6NN, (01) 242 3882. The number of complaints has been rising, particularly against the travel trade which increased by 77 per cent in 1982/3. Many of these complaints were against 'bucket shops' dealing in discounted tickets. There are no statistics on the number sold, since they are illegal by the airlines' own rules, so the rise in complaints may be caused by the increase in sales. But it is clear that 'bucket shops' do fail to explain the handicaps and penalties of cheap fares, confuse the bookings or simply go out of business – the main subjects of complaint.

Unfortunately, some foreign airlines have now discontinued their own sales networks and rely on selling blocks of discounted tickets to middlemen, who dispose of them where they can. As a result, the airline may not have a complete list of passengers or their names until just before the flight. It is easy to see how the confusion reigns. But neither the airlines nor any regulating body appears willing to become involved in trying to control the market.

In the 1970s, approximately 25 per cent of the complaints were about cancellations or delays, 14 per cent about baggage, 13 per cent about overbooking. Only 3 per cent were about safety and 1 per cent about security.

In the 1980s, the picture has changed. Apart from the 'bucket shop' complaints, there were dramatic increases about late arrival of travel documents, delays in refunds, errors in the documentation and computer-generated mistakes in reservations during 1982/3. Complaints on overbooking, cancellations, delays and baggage-handling decreased, while complaints on inflight service remained steady. As the Air Transport Users Committee succinctly states, 'The passenger might therefore console him or herself that the worst is over once the aircraft steps are in sight.'

Not so the airlines. Tickets particularly are one of their major headaches. For airline tickets are better than banknotes for forging or for defrauding the airlines or others. Tickets to Paris or to other short distances are altered to places half-way round the world, then cashed in along the route at huge profits. Businesses mushroom up, then conveniently go bankrupt, defrauding both passengers and airlines. World airlines are defrauded of millions every year in these sorts of ways. It isn't only the passenger who gets a forged ticket.

One area that the ATUC is trying to improve concerns air passenger insurance liability limits. The Warsaw Convention places on the air carrier an absolute liability for death or injury to a passenger at 250,000 gold francs – long since obsolete, the sterling equivalent being
178

upgraded from time to time but standing at around £12,900 in the UK.

Outside Britain, there are a great variety of upper limits on airlines of different countries, ranging from £33,000 to £87,000. Every passenger should enquire of the airline he's travelling on what cover is in effect before he goes. The ATUC is trying to bring some order into this chaos, proposing a more universal upper limit of £87,000.

And when you have flown and had your holiday, what do you bring back? Liquor, cigarettes and perfume of course from the duty-free shop or on board. Fine embroidery from many countries, blouses, tablecloths, handkerchiefs, watches and clocks from Switzerland and also handmade chocolates, glass from Sweden, Kandyan silver from Ceylon, and their lovely dark sapphires, *plata*, the exquisitely wrought silver of Latin-American countries such as Ecuador and emeralds if you can afford them. If you can't, then ponchos made of goat hair up in the Andean villages, lace and carved wood animals. Wooden and leather goods again in Mexico, handmade wool blankets and wall hangings, dolls and basket work, Havana cigars from the Caribbean islands; smart cheap clothes from Canada, every sort of clever innovation for the home from the USA and from across the Pacific no one leaves Australia without their koala bears and Foster's beer. Thai silk, alabaster from Turkey, delicate Japanese ivories and embroidery, jewellery in Singapore and almost anything from anywhere in Hong Kong. I find that I'm always sorry for what I didn't buy. It seems to look rather touristy when you see it in its own country, but unique when you get it home. Besides, everyone loves a small present.

So my advice is, within reason, buy it. So long as you don't do as my wife did, and buy what she reckoned was a tremendous bargain, a very realistic four-foot furry toy camel for only a little over £1.00 in Cairo, just suitable

179

for our expected grandchild. Bringing it on board, she was told, sharply, that these camels were alive with fleas and were realistically stuffed with camel dung.

So what sort of airlines do people favour? There's always a solid core of passengers who choose their own national airlines. But increasing numbers of Americans favour British Airways, while Britons like to travel TWA, or the more exotic lines like Singapore Airlines or Japanese Airlines.

Saudi Airways is totally dry. Free drinks all round on Singapore Airlines. Even normally fairly abstemious passengers like to feel they could have a drink if they desperately needed it. And food and luxury still ostensibly attract people perhaps because they don't like to think about the rest of the flight.

Special diets of course are catered for by nearly every airline. If you regularly travel First Class you'll more than likely be settled into your seat by a steward or stewardess who'll remember your name and your little foibles – at least the nicer of them!

But despite cheaper and cheaper fares and despite the fact that millions fly, there is still a vast reserve of people who have never left the ground. It is estimated that in America 25 per cent of people have never flown. What keeps them back? The main cause is fear of flying.

'Fear – not fare – restricts the airborne market,' said the President of one of America's leading airlines. Around 70 per cent of the world's population has never flown. Even in air-conscious America, Pan Am consider that for one reason or another there are twenty-five million who are frightened of flying, a condition they call aviophobia. It's been called many other things in its short life – aviator's stomach, aeroneurosis, aviator's neurasthenia, *mal des aviateurs* and plain fear of flying. It has been coupled with fatigue, stress, shell-shock and cowardice. It was defined forty years ago as a chronic functional nervous
180

disorder characterised by gastric distress, nervous irritability, fatigue of the higher mental centres, insomnia and increased motor activity.

Trembling, dizziness, inability to think straight and vomiting are certainly some of the symptoms. Sometimes the mouth is dry, sometimes it is running with saliva or mucus. Certainly one of its origins is nausea from the Greek word for ship, 'naus', the physical side being motion sickness. The same effects can be even better produced by the roundabouts and big-dippers of the fairgrounds. Caesar was regularly sick when he travelled. So was Nelson, and Lawrence of Arabia even got sick on a camel!

It is something to do with upsets in the balancing mechanism of the inner ear. But in flying it's more than that. There is a definite difference between air-sickness and fear of flying – though many people fear flying because they are frightened of the embarrassment of being suddenly and publicly sick.

Noises are disturbing: once in a simulator, there was a sudden unexpected wail. Thinking that it was going to 'crash', an immediate evacuation was made. It was only a thirty-seater dinghy being deflated in the emergency equipment room next door.

On a 747, the main door gives a thump when it closes, and all the amber door lights on the engineer's panel are off. The engines start with a whine and a guffaw of smoke, the lights dim as the engineer checks that each generator can singly bear the electrical load.

On some aircraft, the hydraulic pump whines shrilly when the brakes are put on or the flaps or undercarriage are operated. On the 747, it is muted. If there is a beam wind, there is a buffeting noise against the fuselage while taxiing.

The engine noise on the runway reaches a crescendo. You can feel yourself pushed back in your seat by G. G is normal acceleration and it can especially be felt after

181

coarse movements of the elevator producing change in longitudinal attitude. It is called positive if the nose goes up, negative if the nose goes down. The 747 can take twice as much G as a man. How much he can take depends on the time element – six G for seconds, two G for minutes – and varies very much with his position and his general strength and fitness. On take-off, of course, the G felt is only a minute fraction of one and is not an unpleasant sensation at all and you almost immediately accommodate to it. Normal take-off is around fifty seconds. About 8,500 feet of runway will be used, less if there is a wind.

The aircraft sinks slightly as the flaps come up. There will be a sudden hush as the engines are throttled back for noise-abatement procedure.

At TOC (top of the climb), the engine noise will again decrease to a low hum. Descent occurs around a hundred miles from destination. Again the engine noise decreases. The flaps can be felt slowing the aircraft, and the undercarriage again thumps noisily down.

There is a hush as the aircraft is held off just above the runway, followed by a thud as the main wheels connect. Then the nose wheels drop.

A vast noise erupts. This is the engines at reverse thrust. 'Clam shells' close the normal jet exhaust path, and cascade vanes direct exhausts outward and forward so they slow up the aircraft. Too quick an application of brakes only would burn them out.

Once you *know*, such noises have no effect. The same is true about flying. Once you know what it's about and what's happening, you don't fear it, although some fear is perfectly normal. In varying degrees it will be found in practically everyone in the aircraft, including the crew. It is even necessary for alertness and motivation. Up in the air, everyone is in a suspense situation akin to readers being held by a suspense novel.

182

During a difficult landing it has been shown by electrodes attached to his chest and recorded in tape-recorders that an airline captain's heartbeat can go up to 165 a minute. The only difference between his condition and that of the fearful passenger is that his 'excitement' is understood, controlled and accepted.

It is the passenger's unnecessary lack of knowledge about it that is frightening. It is the fear of the fear. Passengers in this condition clutch the armrest with catatonic rigidity. When their hand lets go its hold, it shakes uncontrollably. Some drink large whiskies and some take pills.

Flying back from a holiday in Portugal, one lady who was thus afflicted was sitting next to my daughter, who was at that time somewhat afraid of flying herself. The lady began talking to her about it as though she was in the confessional. During the take-off, my daughter held her hand – it was similar to the short-sighted leading the totally blind. Once at altitude, the lady recovered perfectly.

'I don't mind being up. It's getting there that's the problem,' is a typical fear-of-flying state. Others fear claustrophobia, and begin shivering when the heavy pressurised door shuts like a safe.

Actual motion sickness as apart from fear of flying is five times rarer than it used to be. Bouncing around the middle of a violent cumulo-nimbus in mid-Atlantic, half the passenger cabin of a Constellation would be sick as dogs. The tail of a Stratocruiser used to wag like a pleased dog itself, invariably in turbulence-producing eruptions. The catering crew, as they were called, would produce what was bluntly called a 'sick-bag'. Now they are discreetly called by other names. It's the Hord-o-Pak in American Airlines, water-proof and air-tight 'for motion discomfort. After use, fold toward you.'

Even so, don't sit in the tail, even of a 747, if you have a tendency to motion sickness. It may be the safest place in the event of an accident, but because of the distance from the centre of gravity, like a see-saw you'll go up, down and sideways more in bumpy conditions.

Don't have parties a couple of days before you fly. Don't eat heavy meals on board or drink alcohol. Unlike British aircraft, American planes usually do not have humidifiers. This causes dryness in the air which should be relieved when necessary, preferably by plain water.

Don't sit in the smoking sections of the aircraft, and don't smoke yourself. In any case, nicotine (like alcohol) has double the effect at altitude.

Fear of flying sometimes starts with the activation of the mucous membrane, probably for psychological reasons. Phlegm pours down the back of the throat and causes actual physical sickness. Sometimes some actual earlier unpleasant experience of flying floods over people and makes them afraid. The same thing happens in hospitals, where memories of operations are activated by the smell of ether-meth, resulting in sweating and vomiting.

One of the best cures is success. A woman passenger who feared flying and was invariably sick accompanied her husband to South Africa with the expected results. While she was out there, she accompanied him on short business trips by air in which she was not sick and which she enjoyed. On the return trip home by Jumbo, she was not sick at all. Try a few short trips and build up your confidence.

Airlines gradually realised the need to educate passengers in flying. Quite apart from common humanity, commercial reasons alone dictate that such sealed markets should be tapped.

Air Canada held fear of flying lessons. British Airways produced a film on the subject featuring the female impersonator Danny La Rue, himself a chronic sufferer. Formed recently in the UK is the Society for the Conquest
184

of Flying Fear (SCOFF). Lectures and seminars are organised for members.

Pan Am used to have a course run by Slim Cummings, a retired 707 captain with many thousand flying hours. The cost was $100 and Pan Am claimed a 95 per cent success rate. There were seven two-hour classes in which flying was explained, and the class was exposed to the sounds and sights of aircraft. Everything about aeroplanes was discussed, including emergencies and accidents. In the middle of one course, the worst aircraft accident ever occurred – when two Jumbos collided on the ground in the Canaries. Only one person left the class.

There were also relaxation exercises, and instructions on how tension can be reduced. Most of those who attended the course were women, but only because, in Pan Am's opinion, women are more ready to admit being afraid. When things actually happen, they are usually calmer than men.

Flying high over the Atlantic, in the only air emergency my wife has had, there was a pressurisation failure. The aircraft went into a steep dive for the air with more oxygen content at 10,000 feet – the correct drill. Most of the men passengers got up and retreated to the back of the aircraft. The women stayed put.

Towards the end of the course, the class was shown round a big airport and finished up inside a 707. This taxied round, took up position on the runway, opened up its engines and began to take off – then throttled back, went back to the ramp, and the class got off.

The 'graduation day' was later. Then the class went into the 707 again, after being introduced to their volunteer crew.

As the engines were started, Cummings explained everything the crew did. He continued to explain while the aircraft taxied to the runway and stopped. There he told everyone to unbuckle, get up and stretch. When they sat down, the emphasis was on deep breathing to get

185

the alpha level of consciousness. This is a state of mind which reduces thinking but increases awareness, often unused and undeveloped in people.

On the flight, Cummings explained everything that was happening up front as the 707 came in on the approach and landed.

The course is no longer in operation, which is a pity, as there is a need for sympathetic and considerate instruction and treatment for air passengers.

British Airways have started Happy Hour Flights at Manchester and Birmingham. All the passengers have never flown before. Like Cummings, the Captain explains everything he does, tells them where they are, what to look out for, what to expect. These flights were an immediate success. All the passengers were surprised at how enjoyable flying is, and all fears were dispelled.

Flying does seem to affect people in sad and strange ways. On 24 January 1985, a passenger on a Bolivian 727 en route from La Paz to Miami locked himself in the lavatory and blew himself up. The cockpit and passenger cabin filled with smoke, but the crew brought the aircraft down to a safe landing, and no other passengers were injured.

On 9 April 1985, a trumpeter in the rock group Wham knifed himself on a flight from Peking to Canton. According to a member of the group, 'He went bananas. He went into the cockpit. The plane dived.'

The man was overpowered, and the plane returned to Peking, where he was taken to hospital.

A man on a flight from Washington to New York in January 1986 was told to put a cigar out, since the airline was one of those which forbade smoking on board. He did so, but shortly afterwards was found to have lit up again. The Captain told him to put the cigar out, explaining why it wasn't allowed. But within minutes, the passenger had entered the cockpit and began a fight with the
186

Captain, finally being restrained by the flight crew and another passenger.

On a TWA flight to Switzerland, a note was found by the stewardess to say that the aircraft was being hijacked and would be blown up unless a number of demands, including the release of Rudolf Hess, were met. The captain radioed ahead. The aircraft landed at Zurich, and was immediately surrounded by police and firemen. The passengers filed off the aircraft in an orderly fashion, including, presumably, the hijacker. For when the police cautiously went into the aircraft, they found it empty, and there was no sign of a bomb.

The 'hijacker' was never identified. TWA's comment was that they were sure 'he was a nut, but what sort of a nut we couldn't say.'

9
So You'd Rather Sit in the Left-hand Seat?

Well, it's certainly got the best view in the aeroplane.

But why *does* the Captain sit in the left-hand seat? After all, in a British car, we sit in the right-hand seat, even though almost all of the rest of the world sits in the left. And in the Vimy that first crossed the Atlantic in 1919, Alcock sat in the right-hand seat while Navigator Brown sat in the left. It was the same arrangement on most early bombers, such as the first Jumbo, the Handley-Page V1500.

The changeover is supposed to have come with the positioning of the throttles and other levers on a pedestal in the centre, coupled with the fact that 93 per cent of the population is right-handed. And yet the British have always managed to use the left hand to cope with the gear lever. . . .

Anyway, the left-hand seat is now the captain's throne throughout the world. And that's the ambition of many boys and these days lots of girls.

But how do you come to sit in it?

In the old days, at the beginning of the century, you built your own aeroplane, like the American, Samuel Franklin Cody, who in 1908 was the first man to fly one from British soil. He was illiterate and hardly calculated anything. Suck-it-and-see was how he learned to fly.

The flying schools mushroomed. The First World War gave flying a big push forward. The Second World War pushed it forward even further. But we had no tests of any sort – except medical and an interview – to qualify for pilot training in the RAF. The Americans gave tests

188

before entry into military flying schools in 1917, but 75 per cent failed their subsequent courses. Of one American intake of 575 in in the 1930s, only 42 graduated. Ground tests on people, apart from the health ones, still do not give any real pre-indication of whether or not they would make good pilots. Nevertheless, psychological selection tests still went on. When I was at the College of Air Training at Hamble, a 'tapping' test in a revolving circular maze combined with a visual attention test to produce a basically impossible task – supposed to test 'flappability'. Then the would-be students had to write an essay on why they wanted to be airline pilots. Afterwards they admitted that their main preoccupation was to avoid mentioning the large salary involved. In fact, they were judged on how many times they wrote 'flying' and similar connected words, with large scores supposed to indicate high motivation.

Even though some airlines and military flying authorities still do give aptitude tests, basically the pattern has continued. There *is* really no way of telling whether anyone will make a good pilot.

The first absolutely essential requirement is the ability to judge height above the ground. This is quite different from judging horizontal distance such as is employed in parking a car, and cannot be taught, though it is easily checked in a few initial flying periods. The second essential requirement is common sense, and that is more difficult to assess.

Few people are natural flyers. Even among professional pilots, the percentage is probably less than fifteen. The natural flyer shows his gift in the rhythmic handling of the aeroplane, flowing into the machine to such a degree that in some strange way he becomes part of it. The pilots who are 'made' are no less safe and no less competent and probably even more careful and conscientious. But even after thousands of flying hours, that 'join' between man and machine is visible in their flying.

189

Pilots are produced either by a national necessity – such as a war – or by very strong personal motivation. When the supply of military pilots dried up after the Second World War, airlines began to rely on flying schools. The Americans had big ones in Arizona (where Lufthansa pilots were also trained) and Los Angeles. The British government built up Hamble to supply pilots to their BOAC and BEA airlines, and the private Oxford flying school was also enlarged. A new generation of pilots emerged, quite different from any of the others.

But to get into these schools you had to be sponsored. Overseas governments in Africa and Asia sponsored and paid for their students at Oxford (cost at Oxford now £40,000 for a fifteen-month course), but the competition for a British student to get a place was formidable, literally hundreds applying for one place, and very high standards in such subjects as physics and mathematics and engineering were sought. British Caledonian had 1,500 applicants for 10 places at Hamble in 1978. So good was the experience and education of the applicants that they upped the intake to 12. Many would-be students had already learned to fly. The airlines sponsored the students of their choice, the cost often made up with an education grant.

The course at Hamble was tough, where aerodynamics, mechanics, navigation and engineering were taught. The cadets were almost invariably very keen and determined. The 'chop rate' (failure rate) was high, and there was a tendency to fail students more because there wasn't a place for them on the airlines than because of a deficiency in their flying ability. When 'chopped', the students used to run around like decapitated chickens, shattered. They had pinned all their ambitions on becoming pilots and could think of nothing else. Yet the Hamble boys that did survive and go into airlines were highly thought of. In getting a job, it was a great asset to have been at Hamble.

Those who failed were often victims of the fluctuating

demand rate for pilots, which is erratic and cyclical. It is very difficult for airlines to say how many pilots they will be needing in the years ahead. The airline business itself, like the oil business, is subject to the most horrible lurches, and survival is bound up with the terrifying swings of world politics and economics. Just as there always seems to be either a boom or a depression, so there always seems to be either a pilot glut or a pilot shortage.

As the present depression deepened, so did the pilot glut. Big airlines like Braniff and Laker went bust. Pilots were acting as stewards. Those who had struggled for years to get their Command Pilot's Licence could not find jobs. Hamble went into the hands of the Receiver. The flying school at Oxford had a very difficult time. Intakes in the full Command Pilot/Instrument Rating courses almost dried up during the second half of 1982/3, and were running at a half capacity rate of 100 students. Fortunately, their engineering courses were relatively unaffected.

In 1972, the total BOAC/BEA pilot workforce was around 3,400. Shrinkage began after they combined, and in early 1984 British Airways was down to 2,170. Part of this contraction is accounted for by the switch to bigger aircraft (747s taking over from 707s and VC10s, and Tristars and 757s from Tridents). Part is due to the fact that ten years ago, all the aeroplanes had three pilots plus a Flight Engineer. Now many have only two, and no Flight Engineer.

But now the pendulum appears to have swung again. British Airways and British Caledonian carried out a survey of pilot requirements and facilities and came to the conclusion that they would need to start training again in 1985/6.

Then came the oil price slump and the upsurge in terrorism, when Libyan students were sent home. Again the airline climate is uncertain. But airlines may sponsor students at Oxford, where there are new signs of increased

191

intakes from foreign governments. Not all of them will necessarily be young men. A number of individual students who have made a success in one career, for example as a garage proprietor or an estate agent, will decide to fulfil a life-long ambition and fly.

As has happened in the past, they will somehow get on a flying course, which they will be unlikely to fail, even though the failure rate at Oxford is around 15–20 per cent. Captain Jack Nicholl, who used to be BOAC General Manager Training and was for many years Principal at Oxford, says that the majority of failures occur as a result of poor aptitude as a pilot, with the student failing to go solo at all, and lack of motivation – neither of which will affect characters of this calibre.

Difficulties with coordination and judging height are among the main reasons for failure. Students also have difficulties in learning to ignore their bodily feelings and trust their instruments. This last is particularly difficult in that instruments they rely on – airspeed indicator, vertical speed indicator, compass, altimeter – for various reasons all have errors in them, of which the pilot must beware.

How do these brave individuals without sponsorship do it and what will it cost? First of all they have to have either a three-week Ground School course at around £500 for their Private Pilot's Licence. Or they might try a correspondence course at around £170.

They will need about 40 hours flying on single-engined aircraft at around £55 an hour, which will cost over £2,000. To bump up their Private Pilot's Licence to a Commercial Pilot's Licence they will need a course to get them through the examinations. This will cost around £700. On top of that they will have to take their radio telephony examination, and for each part the tuition will cost about £15.00.

On top of that – and here is the real rub – they will need around another 700 hours flying, which means at present flying rates tens of thousands of pounds.

So many aspiring commercial pilots then add a Flying Instructor's Course to their Private Pilot's Licence. This will need around a further 60 hours flying and with ground instruction, which will cost about £4,200. They then get an extremely poorly paid job at a club, but have the supreme advantage of their pupils picking up the cheque for their flying, reaching their 700 hours that way. They also get their Instrument Rating – showing their ability to fly 'blind' without reference to the horizon or anything outside the aircraft, being guided entirely by their instruments.

Once they get their Commercial Pilot's Licence and Instrument Rating, they become an interesting proposition to airlines for employment – always supposing, of course, that the airlines are looking for pilots – but they will be competing against seasoned pilots with thousands of hours' command time behind them.

They will also be competing with sponsored pilots who then are not taken on by their sponsors. British Airways found itself with too many newly qualified pilots in 1977, and British Caledonian took a number on as Second Officers because they needed pilots for their introduction of the DC10. These men were offered employment for three years with an option to return to British Airways, though none did. The Laker failure produced a lot of unemployed pilots, some of whom British Caledonian took on, some going overseas to Nigerian Airlines.

In 1984, British Caledonian held a Selection Board. The 111 Fleet Manager, the Chief Pilot, the Personnel Manager and the Company Medical Officer selected 30 from over 400 applicants.

On selection, the recruits go to the big Caledonian Training School for three to four weeks. At the same establishment, the pilots and ground crew of 45 other world airlines are trained on all sorts of courses from handling dangerous cargo to converting on to DC10 aircraft.

Initial pilot training is on the 117-seater 111 aircraft, and is rather different to American training which is done on a need-to-know basis. TWA claim to be forerunners here, first providing audio-visual courses geared to what psychologists call Specific Behavioural Objectives. If it is not necessary to actual operations, it is not taught.

In Britain, more is taught about aerodynamics, engines and systems, since it is considered that the students must have background knowledge and a good understanding of what they are doing and how it affects their aeroplane.

There are now more pilots' jobs, but not enough applicants with the right credentials. By the end of 1986, in spite of the crisis, many pilots' jobs will have to be filled.

France thinks it may suffer a pilot shortage as the older generation retire and air transport expands. Their Ecole Nationale de l'Aviation Civile (ENAC) turns out 25 newly qualified pilots a year. Airlines of developing countries, like Malaysian Airlines, now train their own nationals. British Airways have produced a pilot recruitment brochure to help young men and women at an early stage in their career. In 1987 they intend to sponsor students again through pilot school. Everything goes full circle.

Everything, that is, except individualism in aviation. That cannot be tolerated in an increasingly complicated aviation environment, particularly as crews do not fly together, and may not have seen each other before meeting for service.

Standardisation has now become not only intercompany, but international. With the arrival of the Jumbos and the new technology aircraft, far better communications have been established between aircraft manufacturers, airlines and administrations.

The use of audio-visual aids for training is now general. In rooms not unlike language laboratories, pilots not only learn but are tested while they learn. A whole course on the aeroplane and how to fly it is given audio-visually.

On the Fixed Base Simulator, they learn and practise normal and emergency drills, familiarising themselves with the dials, levers and switches. Then the routes are taught by coloured slides of the approach to airfields.

Audio-visual tutorials are provided by dual projectors connected to a tape recorder, so the student can learn in privacy and at his own pace. All background information is omitted. Everything heard, seen or read has to be remembered. On the instrument board in front of the pupil are all the buttons he needs: to start, to stop so that he can memorise the view or the instructions, to go back five seconds if he's missed something, or to repeat.

Up comes Rio on the screen – a beautiful photograph of the bay, the city, the mountains that make the landing tricky, and the airport on the island. To the sound of carnival music and drums, the route clearance presentation commences. A commentary continues on the let-down as the slides change. We are over the Outer Marker radio beacon and ahead in the water are poles on top of which are the lead-in lights. We are warned it is usually hazy. If we miss the approach we are told to climb ahead to 2,000 feet on to the 335 radial and then up higher.

Hong Kong is one of the trickiest airports in the world, surrounded by mountains up to 3,187 feet high within seven miles of the runway. The succession of pictures on the screen show the mountains and the high-rise buildings.

Quito is another airport surrounded by mountains, these up to 18,000 feet high. Its own elevation is 9,226 feet, and there is only one runway, which is hump-backed and slippery when wet.

Genoa is difficult. Coming in on runway 29, the terrain rises steeply just to the right of the radio beam.

Not only are pilots taught to find their way into and around airports in this way, but also around the aircraft itself. At Boeing, pilots new to the 757 and 767 first learn a glossary of abbreviations, then the need-to-know details of the aircraft.

195

The American 757 and DC10 courses begin with eleven days at AVT (Audio Visual Tutorials), progress tests and ten lessons in the FBS (Fixed Base Simulator). This is followed by three further days of 4-hour simulator sessions with the Flight Instructor. Emergencies may be practised on the aircraft itself before the pilot takes an aircraft on service.

In Britain, the students have to pass a CAA multiple-choice examination on the aircraft before they are allowed to put it on their licence. To neutralise the effect of guessing, minus marks are given for wrong answers.

To take the strain out of the examination, British Caledonian give their students (who come from many different cultures) a light-hearted 'CAA Commercial Pilot's Licence Irish examination', with such questions as: 'On the front of the VHF set is a switch marked ON and OFF. In which of these two positions can you expect the best reception?' And 'Name the odd man out: VC10/DC8/QE2.' And 'If an aeroplane has a lot of drag does it mean a) Pilots are dressed up as hostesses b) Resistance to airflow c) Being towed behind a tractor?' And 'How would you know you were flying along RED ONE Airway if you were colour-blind or at night?'

The real CAA papers are comprehensive, lasting from two to three hours on all aspects of the aircraft.

The American approach to training is different. The Federal Aviation Authority do not require a written examination. There is less content in ground instruction, the philosophy being that if you can't do anything about it going wrong in the air, you needn't know how it works. After ground school, the pilots go straight into the simulator.

This technique works in America largely because their airlines usually fly between big cities on the two American continents, where there will be ground engineers at the airport. But the British holiday airlines and British Caledonian often operate into airfields where there is not this
196

luxury. Pilots have to have the knowledge to spot what is wrong, and where possible to rectify it.

Similarly with spares, which on British Caledonian routes may be thousands of miles away. So they need a high level of base maintenance, since it will be expensive if anything goes wrong on the route.

The next step after passing the CAA examination is the big flying simulator, which replaced the early Link Trainer, the first of which was the Stratocruiser simulator. On this trainer, instrument flying ratings and emergency procedures were carried out regularly on all pilots.

Because every emergency could be simulated electronically, the checks became emergency-happy. No sooner had the checker settled in his seat than he got an engine fire, followed by hydraulic failure taxiing. Three-quarters down the runway he got an engine failure followed by another engine going as he lifted off. Staggering up to cruising altitude, he got an explosive decompression and a fuselage fire, and had to dive to 10,000 feet.

Only gradually was the simulator used properly to allow a full assessment of basic handling skill and crew coordination during normal operation, with a selective testing and training in emergency procedures.

With the arrival of digital simulators, every indication is given that the pilots are flying actual aircraft for an actual airport. Computers control the view from the windscreen to simulate actual conditions in making a sunny, foggy, snowy or night approach and landing on a lighted runway. The visibility, cloud base and weather can be altered at the instructor's wish.

So can the airfield. A view of London or New York may be brought up, and every little movement of the control, every change of speed or altitude correctly changes the picture ahead, so that pilots can be taught to take off and fly and land safely. A 747 new pilot is now given around thirty hours on the simulator and four hours on the aircraft itself, basically only to give him confidence,

197

as against the thirty-odd hours on the simulator and fourteen hours on the aircraft on 707 training.

In 1978 the Federal Aviation Agency (FAA) decreed that 90 per cent of checks could be done in the simulator. This was also approved by the CAA.

Fire, engine failures on take-off, generator failure and explosive decompression were all practised. On average one pilot dies (usually from heart failure) on the flight deck every year. Taking over from a dead or incapacitated pilot was one of the practised drills. Engine failure at altitude presents no problem on the 747. On two engines at normal height and temperatures, 10,000 feet can be maintained.

The savings generated by using mainly simulator time were enormous. One hour on the DC10 simulator costs £300 as against £3,000 an hour aircraft flying time.

The next step came in 1981 when Zero Flight Time pilot conversion was introduced in America. There the pilot is converted to the aircraft without ever having flown it. After 25 hours in the simulator, including a check flight with an inspector, the captain takes over a passenger-carrying service and flies in command, never having felt the controls of a real DC10 or 747.

This is approved by the FAA, but not yet by the Civil Aviation Authority. In Britain, some flying on type must be done and approved before the pilot is considered safe to carry passengers.

This is the sort of course that the candidate will have to run before he reaches the left-hand seat. As a First Officer he will probably have shared the take-offs and landings almost 50/50 with the captain. Every six months all pilots are given a medical, a check in the simulator and a short session in the ground school.

Eventually a First Officer will be considered for a command and given one on a small aircraft, working his way up to becoming a 'wide-bodied captain' – the man in charge of a Jumbo.

198

10
The Taming of the Sky

It was the atmosphere rather than the physical and mechanical problems that proved to be the most daunting in man's climb up into thin air.

An aircraft with a pressurised cabin was flying before the Second World War, eliminating the need to suck oxygen above 10,000 feet. Supercharged engines lifted Flying Fortresses up to 25,000 feet. Heating improved and cabins became bearable.

What still remained were rain, hail, snow, ice, fog, lightning, turbulence and wind.

Wind was the main cause of having to carry so much fuel. It could blow slow aircraft miles off their track and reduce their speed to zero.

Fuel in the tanks is like money in the bank, and the early pioneers stuffed their flimsy machines full of it, depriving themselves of radio, clothes and even sandwiches just for a few more ounces of life-blood.

It was as though they carried their own life-spans in their petrol tanks, and they loaded themselves up so heavily that many of them crashed on take-off. What they feared was becoming lost or losing their speed against heavy headwinds. Or, like Saint-Exupéry, being caught above cloud over mountainous territory, not knowing where they were and doomed to chasing stars or flying in vain from one fog-bound aerodrome to another.

Yet the ironic thing is that ever since the earliest days of the aeroplane, except for one inept performance over the Caribbean, practically no civil aircraft has run out of fuel. The fear was far more dangerous than the actuality.

Nevertheless, fuel was a necessity – and a nuisance. The whole point, commercially speaking, of getting up into the sky is to carry things. The airframe and the engines are heavy enough. If the possible payload had then to be mostly fuel, the future of civil aviation in the early days looked bleak. Few governments would help. 'Civil aviation,' declared Winston Churchill, with the politician's profound ignorance of things aerodynamic, 'must fly by itself. The government cannot possibly support it up in the sky.'

The obvious way round was just to do short trips needing little fuel. London-Paris, Amsterdam-Berlin, such tiny little journeys were the beginnings of civil aviation. Anything longer was out of the question commercially for what was called the 'engineering curse' that limited an aeroplane's range to around six hundred miles. Politically this was acceptable, especially to Britain, who could get round her Empire, except across to Canada, on such a range. Much longer routes than that, and the fuel required would be so weighty that the wings would have to be huge to lift the aircraft off the ground. In any case there were no runways long enough to get it airborne. The beginnings of long-range flights across the nearly two thousand miles of the North Atlantic strong westerlies had thus to be done in flying boats.

Various expedients were tried to conquer this curse. The Germans tried catapulting their seaplanes off ships. The British tried the piggy-back. A small floatplane was attached to a lightly loaded flying boat, and the combined power of their eight engines managed to lift them up into the sky, after which the small plane disengaged and flew the Atlantic. It was in this way that D. C. T. Bennett took the first mail across in 1938.

The British also tried flight-refuelling across the Atlantic both before and just after the Second World War, where a grapnel was wound out of the aircraft's tail, and a tanker aircraft would then fire a cable by rocket to

200

catch the grapnel and haul it in. A hose was then wound in from the tanker to the receiver and connected to fuel pipes in the tail. The tanker would then fly above the receiver while 800 gallons of fuel were transferred in twelve minutes. After transfer, the hose was flushed with anti-ignition chemical, contact was broken and the hose wound back into the tanker.

The French were particularly partial to the idea of seadromes supported in the Atlantic by buoyancy tanks and having a runway, refuelling and repair facilities, wireless stations and even an hotel.

The problem was considerably lessened by the production of bigger and more efficient airframes and more powerful engines, and by streamlining and polishing. But even in the 747/200B at long range, its weight of 778,000 lb will include 341,700 lb of fuel, far heavier than its payload and a dead loss commercially. Perhaps the engineering curse will not be finally removed till aeroplanes are flying for hours on a few ounces of atomic fuel.

Early engines and airframes could behave villainously. 'In those days,' wrote Saint-Exupéry, 'our planes frequently fell apart in mid-air, and because of this, the African divisions were always flown by two ships, one without the mails trailing and convoying the other, prepared to take over the sacks in the event the mail plane broke down.'

Much of the engine trouble ceased with the civil advent of the jet engine on the Comet in 1953 – for then there were no plugs to oil up giving a revolution drop (the most common cause of trouble) and far fewer reciprocating parts than in piston engines. Airframes were made much stronger, and their design is now tested in huge water tanks and by continual hammering for months on end.

The atmospheric problems have taken longer – especially that villainous trinity: fog, ice and turbulence.

The first attempt to beat fog and cloud was through radio in the 1930s, when at last it was becoming standard equipment on aircraft. These were QDMs (courses to steer). The radio operator pressed his key, the ground station took a bearing and the pilot was told to fly the reciprocal.

This did not take account of any mountains that might be in between, and was extended to a procedure called a QGH (descent through cloud), where the aircraft was brought over the station and given courses to steer on a pattern of heights to fly. Alternatively, bearings could be taken off beacons by the radio operator, and a similar sort of let-down carried out. This got a pilot under cloud safely, but was not nearly accurate enough to bring him down on the runway. Towards the beginning of the Second World War, on the same radio principle, the Lorenz company invented the first 'blind landing system'.

A signal in morse As ($\cdot$—) was transmitted to one side of an airfield, Ns (—$\cdot$) to the other. There was a steady signal in the overlap over the runway. Later there was a left-right indicator on the instrument panel. This idea remains the basis of most sophisticated blind landing aids today.

The next development was the radio range, where the transmitter broadcast universally. Now there were four 'legs' where there was a steady signal, separated by morse As and Ns. Like identifying an object blindfolded, the pilot could tell from the As or Ns in his ears that he was in one of two quadrants.

Selecting the most likely one, he took up a course to cut the most likely leg, turning down his volume at the same time. If the sound diminished, he was in a different quadrant from the expected one, so he had to turn right round. Eventually he identified the leg, got on to the steady signal and continued to the centre of the range, the noise building up all the time. If he flew dead over the transmitter, suddenly the noise would die away to nothing. He was over the 'cone of silence'. Now he knew exactly where he was and from his 'plate' (range and aerodrome map), he let down on a laid-down course to the runway. This was the standard training procedure after the Second World War, and the best test of blind flying ability ever invented.

This simple range is at the basis of all the more complicated omni-directional ranges called VORs (where courses to steer and bearings can be found straightaway). Most of the world's airways are formed by the legs of radio ranges which form an intersecting pattern, like a road system, along which aircraft fly, reporting at various intersections along their route. In this, they are helped by Distance Measuring Equipment (DME) which clocks in the mileage flown. There is also the support of the radio compass, where the needle simply points to the station or beacon after it has been tuned in.

The early ranges were subject to heavy static, as was the radio compass where the needle often flickered in a perplexed way round the dial. For really bad visibility, something better was necessary. To get bombers into unexpectedly fogged-in fields after their raids in the Second World War, Fog Investigation and Dispersal Operation (FIDO) was invented. Here pipes were laid on either side of the runway with hundreds of holes in them. These were connected to a fuel tank. When turned on, the fuel was lit and literally burned the fog away.

It was certainly the most impressive blind landing aid ever devised. For miles before you got there you could see a great bronze smudge through the cloud. As you came nearer, this became red-gold, and it was like letting down into hell. Then, suddenly, there was the runway, and you landed between two long lines of fire.

FIDO could only be a wartime expedient, for the expense was phenomenal. There had also been invented two radio radar let-downs – one, called BABS, on the aircraft's own radar was quite effective, provided you had a good operator, and the other was called Ground Controlled Approach, where a radar on the ground picked up your blip on a screen.

This last was developed from the 'Darkee' (the Allies

and the Germans always used the most expressive code names) emergency system to help a lost bomber home. The pilot is given a height to fly and a course to steer to join the circuit by the controller over the radio telephone. He is then lined up with the runway and literally 'talked-down'.

These controllers spoke the same patter in a quiet, authoritative way, every now and then giving a course correction ('steer left, left on to 271°'), or a height correction ('you're a little below the glide path') or an encouraging pat on the back ('half a mile from the runway now. Your rate of descent is good. Your course of 271° is quite OK') till the pilot could see the runway.

GCA used to be universal at most international airports. Now it, too, has virtually disappeared. For what finally destroyed the terrors of fog was the Instrument Landing System, the most universal blind landing aid throughout the world. Instead of As and Ns, now on the dial was blue to the south and yellow to the north.

In the old simple form, there is a round indicator on the instrument panel, one half of the round orange-yellow, the other half blue.

Two needles – one vertical, for the 'localiser' or runway direction, one horizontal for height on descent – give the instructions visually that the GCA controller used to do aurally. What the pilot must do is to steer the aircraft along the localiser and down the glide path so that those two needles make a cross in the centre thus +.

He corrects his direction and height by their indications, which is not so easy as it sounds, particularly on a heavy aircraft in bumpy weather. But this manoeuvre is practised more than any other, regularly and persistently throughout a pilot's flying career. Guided by his 'plate' (his airport let-down map), he comes to the Outer Marker, puts down his wheels and does his before-landing check. Then a 3° glide path brings the aircraft below the

204

cloud and down to the ILS limits (on good airfields 100 feet cloud-base and a quarter of a mile visibility).

The pilot holds the aircraft at that height. If he still cannot see the runway, he opens up the thrust levers and carries out an overshoot procedure.

The 747 ILS let-down is more sophisticated but basically remains the same as it has done for the last thirty years. Now an instrument called the Flight Director, still equipped with two pointers, gives commands to the pilot to turn left, right or go up or down, but is attached to a computer that does much of the pilot's work for him. The aim still remains to keep the vertical and horizontal lines in the centre of the instrument.

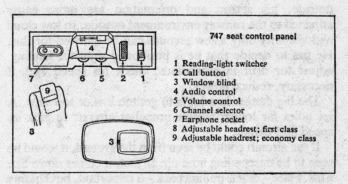

747 seat control panel

1 Reading-light switches
2 Call button
3 Window blind
4 Audio control
5 Volume control
6 Channel selector
7 Earphone socket
8 Adjustable headrest; first class
9 Adjustable headrest; economy class

In British Airways it is usually the First Officer who flies the ILS pattern in bad weather. This technique was pioneered by BEA (now the shorthaul side of BA). It leaves the captain free to check and cross check, particularly speed and altitude. He makes sure that the aircraft does not go below the glide slope, that the aircraft is at the correct height over the Outer Marker (where a flashing green light is seen and an intermittent blipping is heard) and the Middle Marker (a flashing amber light and blip).

While he monitors throughout and does the R/T, the

Captain is really holding himself in reserve for the sudden break out into visual conditions just before landing. He checks the aircraft when it has reached minimum safe height (varying with the airport and the high ground above it). He stares ahead looking for the approach lights, still not letting the aircraft descend.

If he sees nothing, he initiates missed approach procedure. There is a roar that goes through the whole aircraft as the thrust is increased, and then the 747 flies off to the missed approach holding point.

If he sees the approach lights, he takes over. Instead of having the inevitable delay of adjusting his eyes from staring at phosphorescent instruments to the muzzy lights outside, his senses and orientation are more easily adjusted to the runway environment outside. In low cloud and visibility only a few seconds can be allowed for this. He has to decide that he is positioned right for landing, adjust for drift in crosswinds, check his speed and, if necessary, reduce power.

The big danger in a jet is to get too low or too slow. A jet takes far longer than a propeller aircraft to pick up speed and height.

If the aircraft could be seen from the ground, it would be seen to be descending nose up. In fact, it comes down like a lift. Flare – that is pulling back – is important, but holding off not so necessary as with earlier aircraft. The wheels may connect harder with the runway, but if the approach has been carried out at the right angle that should be all.

The ILS together with the automatic pilot forms the automatic landing system by means of which aircraft can take off and land in near zero visibility.

Coming to land on a visual approach, the checks and speeds will be approximately the same as on ILS. The normal circuit is flown at 1,500, descending to around 800 on base leg. If one engine is out, speeds and heights are higher and flap is used later.

The First Officer monitors the rate of descent, altimeter

and airspeed right to the flare, where there should be a 700–800 feet per minute descent. Higher and he warns the Captain. An airspeed decaying below Vref (optimum threshold speed+gust factor) also has to be prevented.

At the flare, the 747's pilot's eye is seventy feet above the ground and as such is conducive to undershooting. The captain aims to touch down 1,000 feet down the runway.

Co-pilots call at a hundred feet, fifty feet and thirty feet levels from the radio altimeter. The gentle pull back initiating the flare should be started just after the fifty feet level.

After the flare, the thrust levers are fully closed and the Jumbo is allowed to sink on to the runway. Auto-brake – automatic braking – is preferred to normal foot braking.

The spoilers come up from the wings and reverse thrust is applied. Nose wheel steering is only used when the aircraft slows below forty knots.

One of the most unexpected villains, and one that pilots refused for many years to recognise, is the fact that without a horizon, man does not know whether he is upside down or sideways. The early RFC pilots in the First World War believed that it was a sign of skill to be able to fly through cloud or in dense darkness. Since it is physically impossible for a man to do so for long without adequate instruments, these pilots spun down to earth with monotonous regularity, thus contributing to the idea that flying was dangerous.

But in Britain so confirmed was this belief that it took a Central Flying School instructor to *demonstrate* on aerodromes throughout the country in 1928 the truth that man couldn't do it, before the belief was abandoned.

Once the pilots had cottoned on to the idea that they couldn't fly without a horizon came the problem of what would be adequate instruments to give them. Spirit-levels were the earliest indications of fore and aft and left and right attitude.

But now the gyroscope came to the rescue in 1928. The property of a gyro, which is essentially a spinning top, is that it takes up and maintains a position relative to space. So if a pilot turns to the left or right and the wings tip, or he puts the nose up or down, the gyro remains unaffected. So the pilot is given an 'artificial horizon'. Even though the 747 has a Flight Director, it is still equipped with artificial horizons, operated by other sources of power.

Added to this is a 'directional gyro' – useful because in a turn the magnetic compass needle, in spite of dampening by alcohol, spins so much that it is not possible to change course accurately and cleanly. The gyro gives a completely steady indication of turn from 0–360°.

The gyro is undoubtedly one of the main heroes of flying. It compensated for man's innate inability to know his own attitude without a horizon. Other contributions made by the gyro such as automatic pilots and inertial navigation systems were to come later.

So now 'blind flying' came into being and was taught on a 'Link Trainer'. The pilot was shut up in a machine on the ground with a black lid over the cockpit that turned right and left and went up and down. Since he could not see out, the pilot was forced to rely only on his instruments in carrying out complicated let-down patterns and blind-landings ordered by the instructor sitting at a desk outside. The pilot's every movement was plotted on a plate of glass in red ink by something that looked like a miniature machine for marking tennis courts.

So a pilot couldn't say he didn't make *that* mistake when he came out. There it all was, staring back at him in the same colour as his face. The little Link was the mother of the huge and complicated simulators of today.

Blind flying was further tested in the air. Green screens were put over the captain's windscreen, and the pilot wore dark goggles. He was unable to see out. An instructor or 'safety pilot' sat beside him.

Night flying was the same as cloud flying. If a pilot couldn't see the horizon, he could soon turn turtle and spin down. But night flying was vital for the future of civil aviation.

'It's a matter of life and death,' said Rivière, the stern Line Manager of Saint-Exupéry's *Night Flight*, 'for the lead we gain by day on ships and railways is lost at night.'

The first thing needed was lights – lights to see and lights to give the pilot orientation, direction and his aeroplane's attitude as he flew forward in the darkness.

During the First World War and afterwards, haystacks were set on fire to take off and land and the route was marked by burning tar barrels. Then in the middle 1920s, the American military pilots flew the air mail across the continent from revolving electric beacon to beacon set up by the Post Office.

At the same time, the Germans had lined up one of the first flarepaths – 400 yards of green lights, white lights and red lights at Tempelhof airport, Berlin, for the night mail to take off on. They flew from lighthouse to lighthouse and the lighthouse keeper, since there was no adequate radio, as soon as the plane passed over him would telephone to the next lighthouse.

It was the Germans who inaugurated the first night passenger route in the world. On 1 May 1926, a three-engined JU24 took off with three crew and nine passengers wrapped in rugs to fly to Königsberg (now Kaliningrad). Chimneys round Tempelhof were lit up with spotlights; churches and masts were marked with red lamps. Every five kilometres, there was a gas light on a rooftop. The aircraft was fitted with the first landing lights and carried electrically triggered magnesium flares on the wings.

Saint-Exupéry gives a vivid description of passengers travelling in this era in South America. 'Nine passengers,
209

huddled in their travelling rugs, had pressed their foreheads on the window, as if it were a shop-front glittering with gems. For now the little towns of Argentina were stringing through the night their golden beads, beneath the paler gold of the star-cities. And at his prow, the pilot held within his hands his freight of lives, eyes wide open, full of moonlight, like a shepherd. Already Buenos Aires was dyeing the horizon with pink fires, soon to flaunt its diadem of jewels, like some fairy hoard.'

In 1930 the first international airline conference on uniform airport and route lighting was held at Berlin. By now the pilots were used to flying on the gyro direction finder and the gyro artificial horizon. Cloud and night flying became normal skills under the name of instrument flying.

Even so, few airlines flew passengers at night. The trips to India and through Africa and to Australia were daytime ones and the crew and passengers kipped down in comfortable hotels for the night along the routes.

When I started night flying in 1940, we learned on a grass strip laid out with paraffin flares. Otherwise there was total and terrifying blackness. Over one-third of all RAF casualties were caused by accidents during the war, most of them at night. There were electric flarepaths on the bigger aerodromes, though for operational reasons these were sometimes not used. In Malta during the siege, JU88 night fighters used to prowl on Luqa aerodrome approaches. As soon as any airport lights were shown, they would know that an aircraft was coming in to land, and would position themselves for the attack. So we landed to the right of two 'glide-path indicators'. These were simply made up of three lights: a red one on the bottom, a green one in the middle and a white one on the top. The green was angled at 3° for the correct glide-path. Red and you were too low, white and you were too high. The object was to stay in the green. These were hooded so they did not shine upwards and therefore were
210

difficult to be seen by the circling night fighters. They were the forerunners of the present Visual Approach Slope Indicators (VASIs).

As identification of aerodromes in wartime England, there was an aerial lighthouse called a 'pundit' which flashed out a morse call sign in red on a bearing of so many miles from the airfield, the position of the pundit regularly changing like the colour of the day cartridges that had to be fired off for identification. A 'Chance light' which produced a high-powered beam down the runway could also be turned on.

By the middle of the Second World War, aerodrome lighting had improved out of all recognition. Now there were lights round the circuit, and a funnel of lead-in lights to position the aircraft directly in line with the runway and at the right height.

Ice was a further villain. The first indication to the pilot that ice is around is a thin white piping on the leading edge, followed by a rapid falling-off of airspeed. Even the smallest amount badly affects the airflow over the wing.

Clear ice – equivalent to what is called 'black ice' on the roads – is even more dangerous. Now and again an 'inversion' takes place, which means that warmer air overlays colder air. Down comes heavy rain on to cold wings and freezes into thick ice very soon, not only spoiling an aircraft's aerodynamic qualities but forcing it down by sheer added weight. Then huge pieces of ice are slung off the propellers to hit against the fuselage like cannon-balls. The stuff forms on the air intakes of the engines, and literally throttles them to death. In addition, ice forms over the pitot-tube and then all airspeed indication is lost.

It took a long time to know how to cope with ice in the sky, for it struck in various forms. In the 1930s, a Kilfrost paste used to be applied to the wings. Then rubber 'boots' were put on the leading edge ('a large rubber tube,'

211

Churchill called it when he first flew the Atlantic in 1942, 'which expanded and contracted at intervals'), which were alternately inflated and deflated to crack the stuff off. Alcohol was sprayed on the propellers, and hot air was diverted into carburettors.

These measures had some effect, but the best thing was to run out of its way. 'Watch your air temperature gauge,' we were told in training for flying the Atlantic after the war. 'Next to your artificial horizon, it's your most valuable instrument.'

The danger areas in temperature were considered to be between $+1°$ and $-10°$ centigrade. You had to avoid that zone like the plague if you were in cloud or if there was bad weather ahead. So you climbed – going down was too risky – trying to get colder than $-10°$, for the colder the air, the less moisture it can carry and therefore the less ice can be formed. Unfortunately, due to super-cooled water-drops, minute amounts of moisture held up by up-currents could be found well outside the 'safe zone'.

Another expedient was hot air from the engines along the leading edge of the wing, which proved far more effective than 'boots'. With the advent of jets, it was hoped that engine ice anyway would disappear. But on turbo-props like the Britannia, there were endless icing troubles and all four engines would now and again fail simultaneously in flame-outs that were very frightening.

But once the pure jets came, aircraft flew so fast through icing conditions that airframe icing ceased to be a problem. Wing leading-edge heat is still provided, together with floodlights for checking, but the leading edge itself becomes so warm through fast air friction that ice rarely forms. Jets fly so high that they are far out of range (at cruising height in temperate zones, the temperature will be around $-25°$ fahrenheit), even of super-cooled water-drops. No propellers, so no need of alcohol. No carburettors, so no fear of engines choking.

212

Ice has tried one last fling. It froze the aircraft's kerosene into wax and stopped the engines. The danger was so great that originally the 707 was going to be powered by petrol. But De Havilland and Shell had had this trouble on the Comet and had devised a new kerosene fuel with a freezing level of −50° C. Even so, there is considerable free water present in aircraft kerosene and that can freeze, causing fuel starvation of the turbine engines. To combat this, hot bleed air from the compressor is directed through ducts around the fuel chambers upstream of the fuel control system. Engine nacelle heating is also used to ensure that the airflow sensor devices, essential for efficient turbine running, do not ice up.

There are still pre-departure anti-icing operations to be carried out (usually with alcohol spray-ons and de-icing compounds) on the airframe. The sheer size of the 747 makes this a considerable task. There are also electric heater elements on waste water drains and water supply lines.

On take-off, the wing tips can be seen to flex sharply upwards about ten feet. In turbulence, they waggle up and down so much that the vivid impression given is almost that of a bird flapping its wings. It is fortunate that they *do* move, because if they were rigid, not only would the ride be uncomfortable, but it would be dangerous in turbulence.

For the sky looks still, but never is. The air moves constantly in currents, up and down and sideways. As regards the horizontal currents or winds, the aircraft simply drifts with them and the streamlining copes, but it resists the up and down currents which, particularly in cloud, are often very close together.

So the effect is of a hammer coming down on the underside of the wing one moment and the topside the next. During the day the ground is heated, and this causes the air to become warm and rise, so causing 'bumpiness' which is not so apparent or intense over the sea. It is also carried by the windflow over mountains.

Bumpiness is more evident therefore over hot or mountainous countries and it usually disappears in clear weather the higher you climb away from the ground. It is sometimes uncomfortable, but its quick irregularity is so unlike a ship in high seas that it is not nearly so sick-making.

Its bigger brother turbulence occurs in clouds, especially the 'cauliflower' or cumulus clouds where up-currents can be more than sixty miles an hour. The aircraft actually reacts by pitching and rolling.

Unpressurised aircraft had sometimes to fly continually for hours in the middle of cloud. The aircraft would toss, heave, soar, dive, waggle its wings and all but stand on its tail.

The warm air lifts in the central cells of storms, finally exploding at the top, spreading, cooling and descending in downdraughts. There are continual violent vertical currents up and down – and it is these that are dangerous. The whole effect is like going over a series of humpback bridges at very high speed. The wings take a fearful pummelling, first upwards then down. Throttled right back, aircraft can still be carried upwards at 7,000 feet a minute.

Such a hammering may be too much for the fuselage. Or the aircraft may achieve a speed above its maximum permitted, as so much lift upwards is being produced. Or it may get into a jet upset, a dive downwards difficult to recover from. A downdraught can tilt one wing at the same time as an updraught hits the other, causing the aircraft to turn turtle or loop-the-loop, as a DC3 did (and survived) in 1941. Gusts can cause the airspeed to fall back as much as 50 knots, bringing the aircraft near the stall.

A DC8 dropped 13,000 feet over Miami. Looking up, the pilot saw his briefcase on the ceiling. In 1963 a 720 jet was literally encircled by a squall in Florida and crashed
214

into the Everglades swamp. In the same year, another 720 in a downdraught went through the sound barrier – but though subjected to stresses well above what they were designed for, the wings held.

However, aircraft are now very strong. A 747 on take-off hit an approach light pier. With three out of four hydraulic systems out, two of the undercarriage trucks and part of the tail plane broken, and with the cabin punctured by steel girders, it still landed safely.

Cloud on aircraft radar

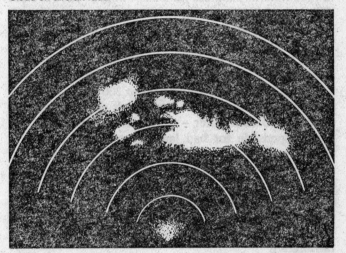

Courtesy of David & Charles Ltd and MEL Equipment Company Ltd

In December 1977, a DC8 over the Bimini islands lost 10,000 feet and twenty-six passengers were injured. The same year, a DC9 entered a severe thunderstorm over Georgia between 14,000 and 17,000 feet. The engines wouldn't rotate due to the ingestion of massive amounts of water and hail which in combination with thrust lever movement induced severe stalling in the compressor. Seventy were killed. Hazardous weather information had not been sent to the crew.

The principal way of dealing with turbulence is to keep out of it. From 35,000 feet storm heads can be seen far away. The radar on the left of the captain shows storms clearly, and their intensity can be gauged if the set is properly tuned. Nevertheless, the best thing is to use the radar to keep at least a dozen miles away.

If the aircraft is caught in heavy turbulence, the captain will slow right down. Then he will ride the up and down currents, never forcing the aircraft to maintain an altitude or speed that it manifestly does not want to do. He rides it like a bucking bronco.

There are other forms of turbulence of which Clear Air Turbulence (CAT) is the most frightening. This is invisible to the eye and does not show up on radar screens. It is caused by a massive wind shear, usually associated with a jet stream wind of anything up to 300 knots at 36,000 feet, though a wind shear – two winds going in opposite directions to each other – can occur anywhere and has been responsible for bad landing accidents, notably at Kennedy.

There is invariably, however, a marked temperature change that gives warning, and CAT is being forecast now with increasing accuracy. The CAT 'river' is in any case very narrow – often only a mile or so – and provided it is cut at right angles has only a momentary effect on the aircraft.

A further form of turbulence is the Mountain Wave, where wind pours over the summits of high mountains, particularly the Alps and Andes, causing fierce downdraughts in the lee. The moral is to fly well above mountains, which in jets is usually easy to do.

Hurricane hunters of the USAAF continually fly in and out of squalls and tornadoes, gauging their power and the best way of negotiating them. It would be wrong to say that turbulence has been conquered, but due to stronger fuselages and wilier ways of coping and avoiding them,
216

accidents due to turbulence are considerably fewer now than they used to be.

The vast majority of snow stays up in high cloud, but the rest does descend, although it has no real effect on an aircraft in flight. Coming in to land, like fog, it obscures visibility and can be a nuisance on runways. Vast snow ploughs and snow-clearing blowers have cured the latter on most big airfields. Hail can still damage aircraft skin or the radome up front. There have been twenty-five accidents due to hailstones since 1946. A DC9 was damaged in this way in 1977, a 747 the year before. Heavy rain can still play a tinny tune on the fuselage roof, but the days when pilots had to put their hats on to avoid condensation drenching over their eyes – as they did in the Stratocruisers – are over.

Even further back are the days of aircrew having to pass written notes to each other so as to be understood. In 1919, the noise of the engines in the open cockpit of the Vimy was so bad that Whitten Brown, the Navigator, had to write notes and pass them over to his pilot on the first North Atlantic crossing, even though Alcock sat close beside him.

Lightning used to be a real hazard to aircraft because of possible sparks. Now copper strips connect all metal parts. Lightning arrestors placed on the electronic systems divert the potentially destructive energy away from delicate components and down to the airframe.

Aircraft are still struck by lightning, but nothing particularly serious results. A DC9 was struck in 1977, causing partial electrical failure. A 727 lost a tail cone through lightning over Seattle. A DC8's radome fell off near Pottstown, Pennsylvania, in 1977. Radomes in the nose appear to be particularly susceptible.

I was once struck by lightning over Greenland. There was an enormous flash, a sound like a land-mine going off, the propeller engines coughed and then it was over

217

and everything was quite normal again. The magnetic compass may be affected but little else will be.

There remains man himself. The vast majority of aircraft accidents have been caused by simple human errors, such as turning left instead of right, selecting the wrong switch or lever, cutting corners to save time or trying to become visual in instrument weather.

Over Toronto in a DC8, a co-pilot called out, 'Three greens' (mainwheels and nosewheel down), 'four pressures, spoilers on flare!' Spoilers are devices on the wing which 'spoil' lift and help stop the aircraft on the ground. On this occasion they were activated at sixty feet, the aircraft hit the ground so hard that number four engine broke loose and burst into flames. Two similar accidents occurred, one in a Japanese and one in an Icelandic DC8 a couple of years later.

Instruments are misread. With the old three-needle altimeter this was easy. The 10,000 feet needle could easily be hidden. At least a dozen accidents, one at Hurn when an experienced training captain thought he was at 10,000 instead of the actual 1,000 feet, have occurred over the years. The new 747 altimeter with one needle and a milometer window is a great improvement.

Altimeters can still indirectly be causes of accidents. Before an aircraft lands, the pilots ask for the QNH or aerodrome pressure. This is usually given in millibars and is set in the window. If correctly set, the altimeter will read the aerodrome height above sea level when it lands. If the QNH is incorrectly set (as happened at Nairobi when the co-pilot set up 938 millibars instead of 839 as he had been told) the altimeter will read wrong, in the case of Nairobi by 3,000 feet low. Being 3,000 lower than they thought they were, the aircraft hit the ground nine miles short of the runway – but fortunately landed with everyone safe.

Also at Nairobi, in 1974 an aircraft was cleared to descend to 7,500, QNH one zero two zero decimal five.

218

The pilot repeated back the QNH right, but descended to 5,000 – again the aircraft, though damaged, got away with it.

Half the accidents occur on the approach and landing, usually being caused by undershooting. An undershoot warning operating off the glide-path of the ILS has been introduced. In addition – also helping on undershoots – is the Ground Proximity Warning System, mandatory in the USA for the last three years. If the aircraft approaches a mountain a voice warns, 'Ground! Ground! Pull up!' If the aircraft starts to sink, it calls 'Sink! Sink!' It works in conjunction with the radio altimeter, and in the US it has been dramatically successful.

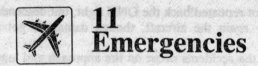

11
Emergencies

The demonstration donning of the life-jacket by the smiling stewardess is the only thing in the emergency drill that most passengers watch and listen to. The instructions are often recorded in English and French and often difficult to hear. Put it on with a double bow at the side, pull red knob sharply down to inflate, top up by mouth tube. Junior life-jackets are available for children.

In fact, the chances of ditching are so near zero that the carriage of life-jackets is sometimes viewed as a throwback to lifeboat drill at sea, as antique to modern flying as carrying a parachute.

Aircraft do go into the water, but usually because the pilot misjudges his height coming into land on a runway that juts out into the sea or overshoots. Once in a notorious case in the Caribbean, a DC9 ran out of fuel through mismanagement. On these occasions, ditching drill as such hardly comes into it. Two DC4s followed each other into the Persian Gulf on successive days at Bahrein. A DC8 was lucky to be cushioned by a mudbank on an approach to San Francisco. Two aircraft simply landed short on the aircraft-carrier-like runway at Kingston, Jamaica.

Sometimes there is mechanical trouble or mismanagement of the controls on take-off, and again, though the aircraft goes into the sea, it can hardly be called a ditching.

In fact, aircraft float quite well. I ditched during the war and the aircraft floated for ten minutes. Several aircraft have floated so long they have had to be sunk by
220

gunfire. Yet in the 1930s there was a demand that aircraft should carry mail only, as it was too dangerous to carry passengers over water.

In 1962, two engines failed on a Constellation in mid-Atlantic. By error, the Engineer failed a third, and the aircraft had to be ditched by a ship, with the loss of twenty-eight lives.

Ten years before, number two and three engines of a Hermes began to behave abnormally and were feathered. Without electrical power and with the batteries depleted by emergency signals, one and four began to follow suit. The aircraft was ditched near Trapani. Four were drowned, two were missing. The enquiry considered that it was the state of mind caused by the knowledge of a power failure accident on the same type of aircraft rather than the engine failures themselves. The emergency drill was not properly followed, especially by the stewardesses.

Neither of these ditchings should have occurred.

Another Constellation came down in the Atlantic from which there were no survivors. There was some evidence of mechanical failure.

The wreckage of a Stratocruiser in the Pacific contained nineteen bodies with carbon monoxide in the tissues. It was thought that a propeller might have come off and a fire started, but there were no distress signals. The aircraft did not go back to Ocean Station November not far away, the flat angle of impact on the sea indicated an aircraft under control and a survivable ditching, the weather was perfect. The captain of a following aircraft said that he had seldom seen such perfect weather conditions. Why then did nobody appear to survive? One theory propounded was that the crew and passengers were deliberately asphyxiated by the CO_2 cabin fire-extinguishing equipment for infamous purposes.

The first ditching of a civil aircraft was a flying boat. The Empire *Cavalier* on her way from New York to

221

Bermuda in January 1939 developed ice on the carburettor air intakes of two of her engines. Little was known about ice in those days, and the power simply faded away. The captain had to land in a heavy swell, and the flying boat was soon sinking. Though all evacuated the aircraft, and in the darkness linked hands in a circle, three died from exhaustion before the survivors were rescued by the *Esso Baytown*.

Half-way between Honolulu and San Francisco, the propeller of number one engine on a Stratocruiser oversped. When this happens, the revolutions go up well above 3,500 with the most terrifying banshee whine. The speed was reduced by flaps and the reduction of power, but the overspeeding continued. Repeated attempts to feather failed. Then number four lost power and was feathered. The speed had fallen right back to 150 knots, not enough fuel remained to go on or go back. On board were seven crew and twenty-four passengers, including three infants.

Though the wind was calm, there was a major swell up to four feet on the sea.

The aircraft went back to the Coastguard Ocean Station *Pontchartrain*. For three hours, the Captain circled while the cabin staff and the passengers took up their emergency positions and prepared for ditching. As dawn broke, a foam path was laid by the cutter on the sea. At 06.15, the Captain circled, descended to just above the waves, slowed the Stratocruiser down with full flap, and ditched alongside the ship. The ditching drill was carried out calmly and efficiently. Everyone had evacuated the aircraft and boarded the inflated rafts at 06.32. The Stratocruiser sank at 06.33.

That was many years ago. Most of the other entries into the water have been caused mainly by simple mistakes on the part of the crew. Since then, actual ditchings at all similar to a ship going down with lifeboat drill can be counted on the fingers of one hand.

The rescue services included an airborne lifeboat. On

222

the difficult 2,000-mile Azores–Bermuda leg, the winds changed on one trip of mine so there was an unforecast headwind on to Bermuda as well as a tail wind stopping me getting back to the Azores. Not believing in waiting till the last minute on that notorious route, I called up the airborne lifeboat which formated with us over the last 300 miles.

Life-jackets have to be carried if an aircraft is over 300 miles from land, life-rafts 900 miles. Radios, water, food, rocket flares, first aid and all sorts of other equipment are carried in the rafts, which are self-inflating. There is some pressure to use cushions of seats instead of life-jackets and have the escape slides doubling up as life-rafts.

The stewardess will also demonstrate the oxygen equipment which automatically drops from the roof in an emergency. In 1973 a DC10 had a pressurisation failure at 39,000 feet over Albuquerque. In spite of some passengers not having oxygen for three minutes and two stewardesses passing out, they got down to the no-oxygen-needed level of 10,000 feet quite safely. The Captain will invariably dive very steeply in these cases.

Far more important to look out for is where the exits are and how they are opened. To open the emergency door on some jets, rotate the handle anti-clockwise and pull the door inwards. The slide comes out automatically. Unfortunately this opening procedure is not universal.

In a planned emergency, brace yourself by leaning forward, wrap your arms round your knees, head down and body tightly compact. In a split-second one, grab your ankles. Rear-facing seats might well help (the RAF and USAAF use them), but the airlines say that passengers wouldn't like them.

The biggest danger is not panic but inertia and tunnel vision. An aircraft turned upside down in a crash in Yugoslavia. Passengers could still have got out but remained hanging by their seat belts. In the Constellation crash at Singapore thirty-four years ago, the passengers

223

crammed round the jammed door, though the aircraft had split open and they had ample time to walk out forward, for the aircraft did not catch fire for many minutes. There were many inadequacies – the fire engine appeared to take the long way round to the crash and many of the firemen had bare feet. On the subsequent findings and recommendations of the very lengthy enquiry was founded the present standards of highly efficient and well-trained procedures.

Aircraft passenger education was called 'the missing link in air safety' by a US Committee of Public Works and Transportation in July 1977. One-third of the people who died in aircraft crashes could have survived. They were alive and usually unhurt after the aircraft had crashed, but did not think and waited to be told what to do. Then the big killers – smoke and fire – moved in leisurely many minutes later.

A comprehensive study of aircraft accidents shows that fire occurred in 20 per cent of accidents. Of the 1,849 people involved, 33.5 per cent were killed and 9.4 per cent suffered serious injuries. Of the 9,473 in the 80 per cent non-fire accidents fatalities were 0.9 per cent and severe injuries 0.8 per cent. Of the 520 US accidents in the ten-year period before 1977, 70 per cent were surviv-able, but nevertheless in those, 505 people – mostly passengers – lost their lives.

Twelve per cent of injuries occur on take-off, 39 per cent in flight, 37 per cent on landing and 12 per cent taxiing (usually getting up too soon to try to get out first).

It is best to travel on an airline where the crew's native language is your own, for people regress to their first language under stress. Language can be an appalling barrier. A DC10 full of Turkish pilgrims crashed at Istanbul. The aisles were filled with Hadji – one who has made a pilgrimage to Mecca – bags, sacks of rocks and five-gallon jugs of holy water. There was no fear what-ever. The Turks stood at the portholes, watching fire get
224

a hold of the wing, while the American stewardesses implored them to evacuate the aircraft.

No sooner had the cabin crew got the passengers out when they tried to get back in again. A flight attendant had to be stationed at the door to throw out passengers who were entering to get their luggage. In so doing, he threw out a fireman. One stewardess tried to get people away from the aircraft by waving her flashlight and running like the Pied Piper of Hamelin with them following off into a field. But when she went back to the aircraft so did they.

When a DC6 crashed at Rikers Island, fire spread slowly. The stewardess tried to get the passengers out, but nobody moved. Twenty out of 102 died needlessly. Twenty-five minutes after an Ilyushin crashed, people were still moving around inside the fuselage, but did not get out. By 1965, British and American authorities demanded the evacuation of all passengers within two minutes. Now it is ninety seconds, and as a result there are far more chutes.

Unfortunately, a chute jammed in the Manchester 737 crash of 1985. Another misfortune is that, now the FAA has authorised the removal of two overwing exits on the 747, British Airways have carried out this modification, against fierce opposition from the pilots.

Even in their own language, again and again, flight attendants in crashes report having to shout and scream at passengers to move. In a crash, they revert almost to babyhood. They will not accept the responsibility for their own survival.

In contrast, generally the cabin crew behave magnificently. The efficiency and courage of stewards and stewardesses before, during and after crashes is legendary. That goes for operational crews too. It is an extraordinary thing, but there is practically no known case of an airline Captain, having made some simple mistake and badly

225

damaging his aircraft, not in the subsequent appalling circumstances carrying out other than a perfect landing.

Of course there should be more emphasis on safety training. Instead of the gourmet-meal-serving and sex-symbol image, instead of beauty care and learning the correct way to direct the titled gentry, safety should be the flight attendants' main expertise. There should be no divisions between flight deck and cabin crew – *all* should be operational. Some airlines allocate certain blocks of passengers to each stewardess who wears a different coloured overall so they can identify her. More often, unfortunately, they still dress her in a highly flammable uniform.

But regular evacuation practices are carried out, including a full cast of pregnant women, babies, the disabled, together with smoke and grinding metallic noises piped in over the PA system. But on average, stewardesses spend only an eighth of their training time on emergency procedures.

It is essential for all passengers to look where the exits are and how they're opened, for unfortunately there is no standardisation. Mentally decide on what to do and think of alternatives. Emergency lights should automatically go on, but it is as well to carry a small pencil-type torch. The CAA has now instructed floor guidance lighting to exits to be installed.

All emergencies have ground plans and a practised drill all ready to go forward with. Air Traffic Control give the alarm from the Tower in the event of an accident and direct the rescue services to the scene.

Fire is the worst and most frightening emergency in the air. On the flight deck, a bell rings. A master fire-warning light and a fire location light both flash on. But it is also one of the rarest emergencies, for, most likely, when the bell rings, it is a false alarm such as a minor electrical fault. If it is 'in anger', the throttle of the engine – it is almost invariably an engine fire – is shut down, the booster pump closed and the fuel shut off. A CO_2 bottle

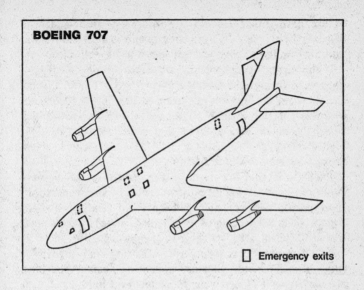

BOEING 707

☐ Emergency exits

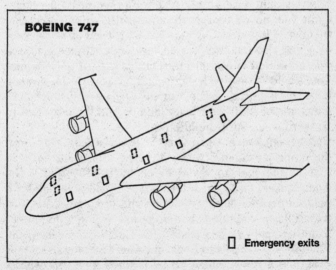

BOEING 747

☐ Emergency exits

Note: Some airlines have removed the overwing exits.

of fire extinguisher inside the aircraft is pulled. If the warning light stays on, another bottle is pulled and the aircraft is made to dive at high speed to blow the fire out.

If the aircraft lands on fire or crashes on take-off, the ground movement controller (if in fog by radar) directs the fire and ambulance services to the exact numbered location on the airfield. The BAA fire service has a complement of 400 officers and men. At Gatwick 74 highly trained men provide a 24-hour service. In 1984 they attended 1,360 emergency calls.

Parked in the fire station are one Meteor vehicle containing over 3,000 litres of water and foam, one Rapid Intervention Vehicle, two Javelin foam tenders – which can provide 45,400 litres of foam a minute – and two Nubian Majors, with two-thirds of that capacity.

The firemen wear protective clothing and proximity suits. These provide thermal insulation against heat and are waterproof. They wear gauntlets and helmets, tough heat-resistant boots and respiratory equipment. Foam from the hoses covers the fire with an air-excluding blanket of bubbles. Carbon dioxide is used as a means of knocking down liquid fires because it penetrates inaccessible areas and is useful in aircraft rescue. If no inflammable liquid is involved, cargo and brakes will be dowsed by water fog. The wheels of the 747 have fusible plugs which melt at 350° fahrenheit and deflate the tyres before dangerous pressures build up.

Rescue teams have to keep at least 25 feet away from operating jet engines to avoid being sucked in, and 150 feet to the rear to avoid being burned by blast. The firemen carry miniaturised radiotelephone units, and use power-operated cutting tools on the fuselage, as well as hydraulically-operated bending and lifting equipment. The principal fire hazards are the fuel in the wings, the oil tanks, batteries and hydraulic fluid reservoirs.

Should a runway have to be foamed for a 747 wheels up landing, a foam path 75 feet wide and 3,000 feet long
228

would be laid, involving 22,500 US gallons of water and 1,250 gallons of foam liquid.

Training is given on a new £100,000 training ground, where Middle East and Far East fire officers are trained as well as British. An old Britannia that was used for training has been replaced by a Trident, bought at a cost of £15,000. Three circular bins simulating aircraft engines into which fuel is injected are used on engine fire exercises. A fire chamber filled with smoke and various obstacles is negotiated by trainees wearing breathing apparatus.

Stansted also has a fire-fighting school, located on what used to be an American Second World War aerodrome. The main lecture room used to be the chapel, and there is still a window in the shape of a glass cross on the eastern wall.

At Heathrow airport, the firemen are called out for almost every emergency. They were once summoned by a work-in-progress gang on one of the taxiways to rescue one of their workers. When they arrived, all they could see of him on the flat surface of newly laid concrete was a round face staring up at them embedded in the concrete. The firemen had to hack him out.

Emergencies on a big airport average one a day, but they are usually small fires in offices. Sometimes an aircraft's wheels begin to smoke through too much brake being applied during long periods of taxiing, and a fire engine goes to stand-by. When an aircraft is returning to the field for any emergency whatever, the fire engines will immediately take up position close to it on the Controller's orders and will follow it down the runway after it lands. There has been no major aircraft fire at Heathrow airport for thirteen years – and aircraft take off and land at an average of one every ninety seconds throughout the year.

All warnings of explosives are treated as genuine. The responsibility of what to do rests primarily with the

Captain of the aircraft – whether to offload the passengers if still on the ground or return to the field if airborne. If the aircraft is to be searched, it is sent to a Remote Search Area. The responsibility of searching the aircraft lies with the airline, but the senior police officer present is designated the Incident Officer. If a device is found, the Incident Officer reports to ATC, who arrange for a Bomb Disposal Squad.

If the air traffic control officer spots a suspected hijack in an alighting aircraft, he calls the fire service, police and the telephone exchange. The Alert Switch alerts operators, airlines, medical centres and the Information Room. The senior police officer will move in with the fire engines. It is his job to decide whether the aircraft should be boarded, bearing in mind the need to follow the wishes of the Captain. Outside police, military and fire services are informed, move in to the Rendezvous Point and take up positions round the aircraft.

It is essential that the wishes of the Captain or those in command, whether lawfully or not, are followed as far as possible so as not to jeopardise lives.

Emergency exercises and practices are regularly carried out, including casualty evacuation, crowd control and preservation of aircraft debris for accident investigation purposes. These exercises are often done at night, with the casualties labelled and provided with simulated injuries.

The Casualties Union, a body of volunteers with branches throughout the UK, provides an agreed number of casualties with realistic make-up and considerable acting ability to add a dramatic touch to incidents. For this, they get their travelling expenses, plus refreshments after the exercise. There are usually three operational exercises a year. The Press are informed and invited, in case they misinterpret the incident as real and report it.

Bird strikes are perhaps the most unexpected emergency. The first bird-aircraft duel was during the First World War where an eagle tangled with an RE8.

Birds, especially plovers, like the grass between the runways because it is never used by humans and contains certain essential foods. Heathrow in the nineteenth century was famous for its plovers' eggs.

Propellers tended to swirl birds away. It was only really when they got sucked into the engines and caused damage that bird strikes began to be news. However, there was a fatal accident in Boston in 1960 when an Electra took off into a flock of starlings. A whistling swan brought down a Viscount flying at 6,000 feet over Maryland in 1962. In the same year, the Captain of an Indian DC3 was killed by a vulture. In 1981 a co-pilot was blinded when a bird came through the windscreen of a Learjet passing through 4,000 feet near Cincinatti. The Captain was injured, the starboard engine failed, the flaps were inoperative, but the aircraft landed safely.

A three-year analysis showed 3,806 reported strikes in Europe, or 3.5 per 10,000 movements. Since the end of the war, there have been 60 major accidents caused by birds.

As was to be expected, the very busy airports had the most strikes. Scandinavia had a better than average bird-strike record because of the bird population going south earlier. Fifty-three per cent of the strikes were caused by gulls, usually the black-headed ones. Lapwings were second, but far below at 11 per cent.

Gatwick has the best bird-strike record in Europe. Because it is in the open country, there are no major sewers or rubbish dumps to attract the birds. The grass between the runways is purposely left long (six inches), which they don't like. At dawn, as the birds arrive to feed, and in the evening before they roost, the professional bird scarers go into action. Exploding cannon-type agricultural bird-scarers were used until it was noticed that crows used to sit on the cannons because they were warm, hopping off when they heard the click that announced the beginning of the activation process to retreat to a safe distance, returning to their warm perch when the explosion was over!

Nearly all accidents have been caused by birds of under four pounds in weight, and the damage is usually restricted to the nose radar cone or the engines. At Kastrup in 1975, twenty-eight blackheaded gulls severely damaged number one engine of a 747. Much the same thing happened in Istanbul in the same year and Tokyo in 1977. In 1978 a Belgian Boeing 737 struck a flock of ring doves just as it was becoming airborne. Unable to remain airborne, the pilot put the aircraft back on the ground where it over-ran the runway, tore away the localiser antennae, and came to rest three hundred yards beyond the end where the undercarriage collapsed and it burst into flames. In 1980 an Airbus 300 hit a blackheaded gull in a heavy rainstorm. Fire broke out in an engine, which was shut down and a landing made at Lyons.

Another bird strike occurred on a DC10 on 24 March 1983 at Kastrup. The aircraft returned and landed overweight because of the fire risk, and the engine damage was safely contained.

Predictably, the bigger the aircraft, the more bird strikes. Worst was the Tristar with 10.1 strikes per 100,000 movements. The 747 had 4.5, the Comet only 0.7. September to October are the worst months because of migration, with twice the average number, while during the winter there are very few. About 75 per cent occur by day; 74 per cent are below 200 feet; 25 per cent occur during the take-off; and 35 per cent during landing, and almost always at speeds between 100 and 150 mph.

They cost the airlines over a million pounds a year. Bird-scarer teams are in action in most busy airports, firing shellcracker (bird-scaring) cartridges, broadcasting from loudspeaker vans tapes of the distress calls of the most common types, or using salvoes of automatic gas cannon. A special bird-strike form (CA1282) has to be filled out after every incident, and the Bird Impact

Research and Development Committee (BIRD) considers all aspects of control.

Apart from bird strikes, what were the causes of civil aircraft accidents?

There is rarely one cause. Sometimes there are more than a dozen. Pilot error used to be bandied about as the single cause as soon as there was a crash; then human factors began to be better understood, but recently the term has again begun to rear its single misleading head. In about 50 per cent of accidents a mistake by the pilot *is* involved, but the question, 'Why did he make the mistake?' is frequently ignored. When it is examined a number of other causes, some of them major, become immediately apparent.

One of the most serious and persistent causes is collision with high ground. Over-running the runway accounts for over 1,500 mostly minor accidents since the war. In the same period there have been nearly 400 in-flight fires , over 200 occasions when all the engines failed, over 60 airframe failures, over 90 mid-air collisions, and nearly 250 major engine disruptions. Instruments have been incorrectly set, misused, failed or malfunctioned over 50 times. Hail damage, ice-accretion, cargo breaking loose, lightning strikes and electrical system malfunction were involved in over 250 accidents.

These figures should be seen in the context of the hours flown and the millions of passengers safely carried. The aircraft accident rate is in fact still minimal. The fatality rate in cars per million passenger miles has remained fairly constant at 0.6. The accident rate on Imperial Airways from its inception in 1924 to its demise in 1938 was one passenger killed per 4,000 journeys (short ones too). The BOAC/BA accident rate from 1946 to 1978 was one passenger killed per 160,000 journeys, and this included one accident that accounted for over half the fatalities during the period.

In 1938, the world scheduled airline safety record was 5.2 passengers killed per 100 million passenger kilometres flown. The non-scheduled figure was 19.7. In 1945, it was 3.3. By 1982 the figure was under 0.1, thirty-three times better in thirty-seven years – and that includes Latin American, African and Asian records, which are worse than the American, European, Australian and South African.

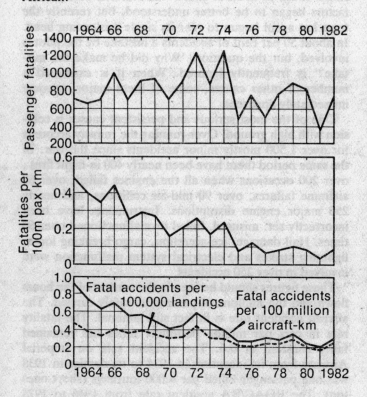

1983 was dominated by the shooting down of the Korean Air Lines 747 over Eastern Russia. A Gulf 737 crashed after two distress calls, and 105 passengers were
234

killed. In addition, there was the bad 747 Madrid under-shooting accident in which 181 were killed, and the collision of an Iberia 727 and an Avianco DC9 on the ground at that same airport, resulting in the deaths of 86 passengers.

Ten bad approach phase accidents killed a total of 446 people. There were four ground collisions and twelve incidents of skidding off the runway or overshooting it.

Two 767s lost both their engines, an Air Canada aircraft because of fuel mismanagement. The refueller had used conversion factors litres/pounds instead of litres/kilos. The same mistake was made on an Air Portugal Tristar, the engines fortunately only failing on the runway after touchdown.

But the fatal accident rate remained nil for the Australian, South African and European airlines (except for the Spanish). The only American fatal accident was when a Convair propeller hit a snowbank and a blade entered the cabin and killed a passenger. The British accident rate continued to remain low, with no fatal accidents.

An Air Canada plane had a fire on board behind the lavatories in which twenty-three passengers lost their lives. There was also a fire on an American Airlines aircraft in the lavatory, fortunately extinguished by a flight attendant. Pan American and Air Canada have now installed smoke detectors in all their aircraft lavatories.

The 1984 air accident rate was the best in civil aviation history with only 451 fatalities – none on European, Australian and North American airlines.

In contrast, 1985 was the worst year in air transport history. 2,129 people were killed in forty fatal accidents. There had been no deaths in western civil airliners in the first six months of 1984. In the same period in 1985, there were 639.

Five facts about some of the accidents were particularly worrying. First, structural failure occurred in such a strong and hitherto reliable aircraft as the 747. Secondly, there

235

were uncontained engine failures in the most widely used civil jet engine in the world, the Pratt and Whitney JT8/D in accidents which killed fifty-five in Manchester on 22 August and thirty-six on 6 September at Milwaukee, and risked lives in a number of other incidents. Thirdly, in the first six months there had been seven accidents in which the pilots had simply flown into high ground, killing 288 in all. Fourthly, one accident in particular illustrated the often repeated truth that passengers can be in danger while they are still on the ground. Fifthly, the sheer size of at least two accidents was a daunting warning that accidents in the future might well take on holocaust proportions.

On 21 January 1985 a Galaxy Airlines Lockheed Electra on charter service stalled immediately after take-off. It is thought that an access hatch on the underside of a wing had not been properly closed.

On the recovered cockpit voice recorder, the Captain could be heard calling, 'We need more power!' thirty seconds before the crash.

In the background the Ground Proximity Warning System could be heard, 'Pull up, pull up!' while the First Officer was calling off airspeed and reporting 100 knots, well below stalling speed. The Flight Engineer could be heard saying, 'God, God!'

On 19 February 1985, an Iberia Boeing 727 was about to land at Bilbao at the end of a flight from Madrid. While the aircraft was in the early stages of a procedural let-down to join Bilbao's Instrument Landing System, it hit a 175-foot television mast on ground 3,333 feet high. The chart being used by the crew did not show the television mast.

The aircraft was in cloud at the time. The weather at Bilbao was 4 kilometres visibility, wind 4 knots. At the point where the aircraft hit the mast, it was laterally one mile clear of the procedural let-down path, 1,000 feet below the height at which it should have been at the nearest point on the let-down procedure and 3,500 feet below the sector safe altitude.

It is not known if there was any systems or airframe failure. There had, however, been a bomb scare on that same aircraft, the same flight number, the previous day. The aircraft had been thoroughly searched, but no bomb found.

Traffic Control had not received any emergency call from the aircraft. The aircraft was not fitted with a ground proximity warning device.

The Spanish authorities only issued a Notam (Notices to airmen) announcing the presence of the television mast four days *after* the crash.

Since 1975 there have been six fatal airline accidents which either happened in Spain or involved a Spanish airline. The world's worst airline accident happened in Tenerife in 1977. These accidents have not necessarily been Spain's fault (three were not) but it should be asked if Spain is adequately equipped with primary and ground radar and if its aircraft have adequate ground warning devices. Airports such as Malaga and Madrid are disliked by pilots.

On 17 April 1985, the crew of an American Airlines Boeing 727 at San Diego discovered an engine was missing.

They believed during the flight that number three engine had seized. They had followed normal shut-down procedure which seemed to have gone correctly.

The engine was subsequently found in a remote area of New Mexico. A Boeing spokesman explained that the bolts securing one and three engines were designed to sheer under stress before any damage could be caused to the fuselage.

A passenger said, 'I thought I had three minutes to live, and I thought what a terrible last meal!'

On 24 July 1985, a Colombia Air Force DC9 was sent to pick up passengers booked on an American civil flight

237

but stranded because of a strike. There were unconfirmed reports that the aircraft took off overloaded and that the crew had disregarded technical problems on the way up. Fire was reported shortly after take-off, and the wreckage was found in the jungle. All thirty-three people on board were dead.

On 2 August, a Delta Tristar crashed in bad weather at Dallas, Fort Worth. 134 were killed.

When on 12 August 1985 another 747, this time belonging to Japan Air Lines, crashed, it was at first thought to be a terrorist attack, since two Japanese groups claimed responsibility.

Flight JL 123 took off from Hareda airport at 18.12 local time. Thirteen minutes after take-off, the Captain reported an emergency, descended to 19,500 feet and requested radar guidance, adding that he had lost control of the aircraft. The uncontrollable aircraft now started flying inland towards the mountains. The ATC told the Captain to land at Yocata base, but there was no reply.

Minutes later, it disappeared off the radar screens. It had crashed into the mountains, seventy miles north of Tokyo. There were four survivors, all sitting in the rear. One of them was a stewardess, who had heard a bang three minutes after take-off. The cabin filled with white smoke (a typical decompression phenomenon) and the oxygen masks dropped automatically. The 747 began pitching, rolling and swaying from side to side. The stewardess saw Mount Fuji go past to port, where it should have gone past to starboard. She helped passengers into life jackets.

Ten minutes later the aircraft went into a steep dive and plunged to the ground. Parts of the vertical stabiliser were recovered ninety-five miles from the scene of the crash.

Investigations showed that the aircraft's tail section had been damaged when it had dragged along the runway at Osaka in 1978. Thirty people had been injured. In 1982, the aircraft had scraped the ground with its number four engine. It had done 25,025 flying hours with 18,830 landings.

The flight recorder and the cockpit voice recorder were recovered. Fin failure appeared to be the probable cause.

As a result of the Air India bomb and JAL accident, all 747s were inspected. Four Pan American and British Airways 747s were found to have cracks in the nose. These were elderly ones with more than 10,000 landings. It was believed that constant nose-gear opening and closing might have contributed to the formation of such cracks.

Jumbos are known for their strength. It is true that after the introduction of a new aircraft into service the first phase is the most accident prone. Mechanical snags appear and pilots are at the most inexperienced level of the learning curve on the new machines.

However, this was not so with the 747. The second phase of fifteen or more years of low accident levels was entered into immediately on its introduction. Straight-away the 747 showed its strength after surviving appalling near-disasters, none more horrendous than the one on 20 February 1985, when a China Airlines 747 bound from Taipei to Los Angeles lost an engine over the Pacific.

It stalled, rolled to a point only twenty degrees short of inverted, and dived 60 degrees nose down from 41,000 feet, to recovery at 9,000 feet, spiralling through a skypath no airliner has survived before.

In cloud for most of its dive, it broke cloud at 11,000 feet and diverted to San Francisco, where it landed safely with a wing bent and considerable damage to the trailing edge of the starboard stabiliser. Only minor injuries were suffered.

The Flight Data Recorder when examined was not reading clearly. It stopped at some points because of G forces. The US National Transport Safety Board says that much has yet to be discovered about the incident.

The crew reported the failure of all four engines. On the failure of number four, the autothrottles and auto-pilot were left in and were 'hunting' – trying to maintain speed and level flight at the aircraft's high altitude. The Captain said he had commanded the auto-pilot to put nose down to maintain speed, but the speed continued to drop.

During the descent, the landing gear had come down under G forces, not by aircrew selection. At 9,000 feet the aircraft was levelled. At that stage, according to the Engineer, they air-started engines one, two and three. Number four had to be ground started.

In fact, Jumbos are so strong that their toughness is taken for granted. The third phase of accident prone-ness is when the aircraft is fifteen or so years old. Cracks appeared in the Super DC8 in the summer of 1978, and this led to the grounding for inspection of all 161 in service. In 1977 a Boeing 707 cargo plane approaching Lusaka dived to the ground after its tail plane fell off. Later inspections revealed more than twenty cracks in other 707s.

Cracks in the rib cage at the front of some other 747s, including those at Japan Air Lines, were discovered. But the Civil Aviation Authority maintain that these were not serious and no dangerous risk was involved.

On 12 August, a British Airtours 737 began to take off from Manchester when suddenly there was a loud bang and black smoke poured from the port engine, which then burst into flames. With great presence of mind, the captain braked hard and swung the aircraft to the right off the runway. Fire engines were at the scene within thirty seconds and covered the burning 737 with foam.

Unfortunately one of the passenger exits jammed. Under great difficulties, the Chief Cabin Services Officer managed to get it open and the chute down. But the cabin had become filled with smoke and flames. There were bangs, probably the oxygen bottles exploding.

The engine was the Pratt and Whitney JT8/D, and the

failure was thought to have been associated with the burned section. Of the 131 people aboard, 79 passengers and 4 crew escaped. Fifty-four died, most of them at the rear of the aircraft. One of the injured died in hospital.

On 12 December 1985, an Arrow DC8/63 crashed one kilometre from the end of the take-off runway at Gander, killing all 256 on board (250 servicemen and a crew of 6). The time was 06.50 Newfoundland Standard Time. Cloud-base was 1,200 feet, visibility 12 miles in 'light snow grains', temperature −4° degrees centigrade, dew point −5° degrees centigrade. Freezing drizzle had been reported about half an hour before take-off. The aircraft take-off weight on the manifest was 15,000 lb less than maximum take-off weight.

The flight had originated in Cairo with a full passenger load of US troops from the United Nations peace-keeping force in Sinai. Its final destination was Fort Campbell, Kentucky, where the troops were to be given a big welcome home for Christmas. It was staged through Cologne and Gander and had thus just completed a transatlantic flight. It had been on the ground for 67 minutes at Gander.

The Flight Data Recorder was recovered. 'One of those primitive four parameter metal tape varieties', according to an Aviation Safety Board spokesman. Badly damaged by fire, it indicated that the aircraft got safely airborne but that airspeed began to decay until the aircraft impacted tail first on downward sloping ground.

On 1 February 1986, an Aer Lingus Short's 360 crashed at East Midlands Airport. The weather was 5,000 metres visibility, wind 20 knots. Cloud base 600 feet. According to the pilot, control was suddenly lost on the aircraft, which landed two miles short of the runway while he was carrying out an ILS approach in darkness. The aircraft hit high tension wires, then trees, and came to rest facing the opposite direction to which it was landing, but there were only minor injuries amongst its crew and thirty-three passengers.

In a recent book called *Safety is no Accident*, Bill Tench, Head of Aircraft Accident Investigation from 1974 to 1981, writes that causes of accidents uncovered by enquiries are not followed up. For instance, he points out that the cargo door which came away causing a Turkish DC10 to crash near Paris in 1971 with the loss of over 200 lives had happened before. And the flap warning system deficiency which caused a Lufthansa Boeing 707 to crash at Nairobi in 1975 had happened before.

He is reported as saying that his investigators recommended research into fire-resistant materials for aircraft seats and furnishings in the early 1970s, but the Civil Aviation Authority did not carry it out. Since then there have been some appalling accidents – the accident to the 737 at Manchester is one – when the smoke and flames from burning furnishings were a major cause of casualties.

The CAA deny this, saying they have insisted that all British civil airliners should be fitted with flame-resistant seats by July 1986.

Other safety measures being introduced are passenger masks (a number of the Manchester crash victims were asphyxiated). There is also a special anti-misting kerosene developed by ICI which allows fuel to burn in an engine but not in a crash. A test in the Californian desert was a flop, but there is considerable expert belief that further tests might well be successful.

Then there is all that inflammable alcohol which is transported all over the world. The writer and broadcaster Anthony Smith has estimated that 3¼ million gallons fly westbound, trundled between aircraft aisles to be sold duty-free.

Why not, he asks, just buy a ticket and pick up your alcohol at your destination? BAA, who rent out the duty-free shops, say they don't disagree. Concorde has had no purchase of duty-free liquor for years because of lack of space and weight. The Air Transport Users Committee say they have been advocating the idea for years. But Customs and Excise object to it 'on principle'. They say goods picked up at the other end wouldn't be an export but an import.

The time has surely come when the air passenger should insist on more of a say in his own safety. In the past, the average passenger has been bedazzled by the mystique of flying and has been content to leave the responsibility for his safety to those who transport him, content to suck his duty-free dummy, happy to have Dad drive the bus and Mum bring him his food and drink.

In the glossy package tour brochures it's usually quite difficult to find who's flying you. Recently I heard a woman in a travel agency say, 'I will not fly on a Spanish airline, even though I am Spanish.'

In the *Flight International* safety record of airlines, the Australian airline Qantas has for many years reigned supreme. A researcher called Gordon Redding has put this down to the PD factor – power distance, the extent to which the boss will allow you to dissent. Australians have the fewest accidents because they have self-discipline and will argue with their superiors at the same time as respecting them. In other words, they have a low PD. It is only public opinion which will change the attitudes of governments and big organisations. Air passengers should not put up with unsafe airports and unsafe aircraft.

Scandinavia, Japan and the USA follow Australia's lead. Britain, France and Germany are not far behind. Bottom are India, Egypt, Turkey and Colombia.

There were other cost-cutting worries. A proposal by US airlines and FAA to fit more aircraft into the air by reducing vertical space between aircraft flying above 29,000 feet from 2,000 to 1,000 has been condemned by the US Airline Pilots Association.

Many major airlines are reducing employee costs to

the bone as a result of deregulation and cut-throat competition.

Captain Steve Last of America's Airline Pilots Association commented, 'The public is not saying to airlines, "We will not fly – it is too dangerous" – it is saying to government, "We will not fly – it is too expensive."'

So governments get out of the whole argument, calling it deregulation. But in doing so, they are getting out of technical regulation too. Deregulation, according to ALPA, allows anyone to start an airline and operate anywhere in the US at whatever fare he likes – often with no notion or experience of how to run an airline. Old margins of safety are narrowing, and new problems are springing up, while pilots are 'airline-hopping' for better pay.

Israeli pilots on international flights have reported that they are exhausted because their existing regulations allow up to 24 hours duty time for augmented crews. Pilots are asked to fly while tired. Existing regulations allow Israeli airlines to employ basic crew up to 16 hours at a stretch and on augmented crew up to 24 hours.

There is now likely to be a shortage of pilots up to 50 years old. Ex-Second World War pilots are retiring and those of the Korean War, previously regarded as too old to be recruited, are now being sought after. Experienced veterans are going just at the time when the world's wide-bodied aircraft fleets are showing their age.

In June 1983, an Air Canada DC9 with 41 passengers and 5 crew aboard was on its way back from Dallas to Toronto when fire broke out in one of the lavatories. The aircraft landed at Cincinatti. When the passengers doors were opened, a flash fire killed 23 passengers and crew. This disaster intensified Air Canada's fire-blocking programme on its fleet, despite the fact that the enquiry found Air Canada's operating procedures to be of the highest order. Six years before, Air Canada had installed fire extinguishers in the lavatory waste bins. So have Pan

244

Am, as they're a likely place for people to toss cigarette ends into. At Orly airport, Paris, 124 people died after someone did just that.

After 1983, Air Canada began replacing all 17,500 seats on their aircraft fleet. A fire-blocking fabric is being used, developed by the Burns Division of Fairchild Industries in North Carolina. It forms a complete skin round the cushion under fire-resistant woollen covers. The cost is about £120–£185 per seat.

Acrylic carpets are being replaced by woollen ones. Smoke detectors, fire extinguishers, protective breathing equipment and smoke goggles are being carried. Toilet motor-pumps are being fitted to minimise fire risk due to the present toilet system.

Such safety measures should be widely publicised by airlines instead of the usual free drinks and stewardess nonsense. Safety standards have been eroded in the name of profit.

The travelling public has the power to stop this. Don't fall only for cheapness and advertising gimmicks. Enquire about the aircraft, the airline and its safety standards, whether non-inflammable seats are fitted and whether the destination airport has good landing aids and adequate runways. Airlines will only react by passengers withholding their custom. After the 1985 Rome and Vienna airport killings, American tourist business to Europe dropped by $100 million. A similar downwards effect occurred after the Air India and JAL 747 crashes, the Manchester British Airtours disaster and the Arrow Gander crash. After the American bombing of Libya and further terrorist reprisals, there were further massive American cancellations of holiday flights to Europe.

The time has come for the air passenger to insist that adequate safety and security measures are taken before and not after crashes. After all, it is your life, your safety, your money. And he who pays the piper must call the tune.

245

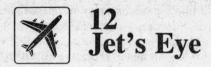

12
Jet's Eye

Up in the sky, the stars shine brighter than they do on the ground. If it is a clear night in the Northern Hemisphere, the Plough is unmistakable on the northern horizon during an Atlantic crossing. Half-way up the sky will be Polaris, the navigator's dim best friend for several thousand years. Polaris gives latitude as well as direction, and the westerly course and approximate 52° North latitude can be visually checked. On the handle of the Plough is the bright star Arcturus.

In the Southern Hemisphere the same easy navigational facilities are provided (though not nearly so clearly) by the Southern Cross. It is often confused with the False Cross beside it.

Shared by both hemispheres is Orion. In the north, it is usually on the southern horizon, looking like a suit of armour with a sword belt in the middle. Top right, Betelgeuse has a reddish glow, while in the opposite corner Rigel is very bright and has a sapphire tinge. Bellatrix and Betelgeuse point to a curve of five stars – the brilliant Sirius looking like a diamond in an heiress's engagement ring at the bottom, Capella yellow as a cairngorm at the top. Further north from Capella is the Lady in the Chair, and the same distance further on will be the Northern Cross and another bright diamond in Vega.

Most star names sound strange. That is because they were named by Arab shepherds. The ones lower down the sky appear to vary rapidly in brightness and colour – that is to say, they twinkle, due to constant changes in the density of the air. In comparison, the planets remain reasonably steady, Jupiter looking like a miniature amber moon and Mars redder than Betelgeuse.

A full moon coming up from the eastern horizon looks bright yellow and enormous. As it climbs higher in the sky, it shrinks and pales, eventually becoming as white as cream cheese. The phenomenon of bigness (the same thing happens with the sun) is due probably to atmospheric density acting like a magnifying lens. The change in colour is certainly caused by the greater profusion of smoke and dirt particles when looked at horizontally.

If the moon is in a different phase from full, it will be waxing (getting bigger) if a semi-circle is visible with the bow on the west. An easier way to tell is by the mnemonic C is D (dying) and D is C (coming). If the moon looks like a C it is waning; if it looks like a D it is waxing. The moon has been blamed for many things from love to lunacy. But the idea that its light (it has none, only the sun's reflection) harms plants is a fallacy associated with those clear winter nights when both the moon and ground-frost turn up.

Rimming the horizon to the north may be the Aurora Borealis (to the south in the Southern Hemisphere). It is quite the most spectacular firework display in the sky, and the further north you go (south in the Southern Hemisphere), the bigger and more frequent the show, which literally changes every second and never repeats itself.

White light shimmers like veils, turns green, sometimes forms a cone of searchlights, can turn both pink and yellow, all taking place between around thirty and six hundred miles up in the sky. Quite why, nobody is sure. Partly it may be due to the reflected glitter of snow, or to sunspots which affect communication, for when the Aurora is bright, the radio is weak. Sunspots are dark spots which irregularly appear on the sun's face and are regarded as disturbances in the sun's atmosphere.

One misses some of the sights by being so high and safe. Very rarely now will St Elmo's fire be seen. In the piston-engined age, the propellers used to be turned into green and white sparklers, fizzing into the night, looking as though the magnesium of the aeroplane was burning. In a storm, bright phosphorescent snakes wriggled over the windscreens, caused by charged water-drops exploding on the windscreen and known as electric rain. Sometimes the propellers would be ringed in blue light and the leading edge would be illuminated. They were all simply fireworks of static electricity, a brush discharge which happens when there is a strong electrical field in the air.

Flying across the Atlantic in the summer, it is never really dark enough for the Aurora Borealis. The orange rind to the north is the sun, just below the horizon in a sort of combined sunset-sunrise.

The sun's light is white – yet on a clear day the sky is blue. This is because as the light waves travel towards us, they meet dust or obstructions of nuclei on water vapour which break them into their constituent colours. The shorter wavelengths are scattered first – so at great heights where there are few obstructions, blue is produced. The closer the earth, the 'dirtier' the atmosphere. So yellow comes up next, then orange, finally the long-wavelength red. That is why the sky is so colourful at sunrise and sunset. We are looking at it through miles of dusty atmosphere.

At sunset the earth's shadow can be seen. In the eastern horizon, clouds that were pink suddenly turn grey, while at higher levels the sky is still blue. This is the earth's shadow greying them out as the sun sinks lower and lower behind the horizon.

Darkness does not fall from the air, as the saying goes. It comes up from the ground. High in the eastern sky as darkness settles on the ground can be seen the twilight arch of the earth's shadow.

248

In the west, above the colours still left on the horizon, can be seen a patch of purple that gets oddly brighter as the other colours fade. This purple light, sometimes called Alpine Glow, can be particularly well observed on snow-covered mountains.

Rainbows occur when the sun shines on water-drops. It is then reflected and emerges in a 42° cone towards the sun. Some of the light does not emerge from the drop till it has been reflected twice, and then the angle will be around 50°, producing a double rainbow. Again, the white light of the sun has been split up, and the bigger the drops, the redder the rainbow. As the drops become smaller, the rainbow colour turns orange, then violet. Finally, in the minute drops of mist, white is the predominant colour, and it is called a 'fogbow'.

Rainbows rarely last more than a few minutes. They can also be observed on a moonlit night, but here, because the human eye has difficulty distinguishing colour in bad light, they appear like fogbows, mainly white.

When the sun is on the other side of the aeroplane to where you are sitting and is casting its shadow on the cloud below, sometimes a rainbow can be seen ringing it. This multi-coloured circle looks so much like the halo painted in old pictures round the heads of saints that it is called 'glory'. The whole phenomenon is called the Brocken Spectre after a castle in the Harz mountains. There a person's shadow thrown on to high misty ground was first observed as gigantic and ghostlike, with the head ringed in rainbow.

Haloes of 22° radius round the sun or the moon are not so spectacular but are much more commonly observed, and are produced by reflection or refraction of their light by the ice crystals in high cirrus cloud.

The weather outside produces most of the sights – the layer cloud below, the cirrus and the towering heads of cumulo-nimbus above. A warm front can clearly be seen approaching as a long grey wall. More spectacular are the jagged battlements of a cold front veined by lightning.

Thunderstorms are quite the most dramatic performances in the sky's repertoire. They occur mostly over land and in warm climates, being practically unknown in high latitudes. An electric field develops in a cloud, and a leader stroke of ionised air makes for the ground like a spark. It is the return stroke back to the cloud which is the one that is usually seen, though perhaps only for a millionth of a second.

Though its speed is far faster, it is also far hotter, reaching temperatures several times the temperature of the sun's surface. This zigzag return stroke is often referred to as 'forked lightning', much more dangerous than the blurred flash type that is called 'sheet'. In fact there is no difference, sheet lightning merely being forked lightning covered in cloud. Sitting safe in their Faraday's cage (as the aircraft is) passengers can now enjoy the sheer beauty of both sorts with equal indifference over their effects.

Waterspouts reaching up a thousand feet from the sea to the cloud-base can very infrequently be seen over tropical oceans. Since aircraft fly well above them, they can do no harm. The same is true for dust-devils – tiny tornadoes above deserts – again not reaching up high. Sandstorms where the air below is turned bright yellow are spectacular sights during the winter in the Middle East.

Above and below, the vapour trails of other aircraft provide interesting designs as they form and decay. These trails consist of fine ice crystals. When kerosene burns, one of the by-products is water, which freezes at a jet's high altitude and makes 'smoke'.

Icebergs can regularly be seen even from high altitude, sparkling white against the grey Atlantic on clear winter days in the Labrador current round Newfoundland. And through the winter, the ice-covered sea joining that province of Canada to Quebec looks like marble. Ice-breakers make black, straight cuts through the wide frozen path of the St Lawrence leading to Montreal.

In the Canadian fall, there is the bright red blaze of the maples in the forests of Quebec and Vermont, and in winter the snow-covered firs on the sides of high mountains.

Man-made things look totally different from the air. Map-reading from the air is not easy. The tendency is to try to make the ground fit the map. If you have ever tried to identify your house in a village or town as you fly over it, even low coming in to land, you will have found it difficult.

The early aviators found it almost impossible. Across the twenty miles of English Channel to Dover, on that first crossing in 1909, Blériot relied on a French destroyer showing him the way with its smoke. When, not unnaturally, he caught the destroyer up and passed it, he did not know where he was when he reached the English coast. Following railway tracks (the stations had their names obligingly painted in big letters on their roofs) was the usual way of navigating. The apocryphal story was that Imperial Airways pilots used to let down for Croydon when from their open cockpits they could smell the gasworks.

Cities certainly have their own particular stamp. The wheel of Paris, the blocks of New York on Long Island, and the snake of the Thames through London are easily recognised. The irregular countryside of England looks quite different from the more symmetrical patchwork quilt of the continent, but finding what is called a 'pinpoint' (your actual position) on either is something else altogether.

A pilot only really learns the art of getting from one place to another in the sky when he can accept with equanimity the fact that he doesn't know exactly where he is for several hours on end. But it doesn't really matter, eventually something recognisable will show up.

Or the sky will give the pilot a good idea where he is. Or the weather will clear. Or radio will help.

Of course these days, everything is quite different. Up front on the flight deck of a jet, what looks like an electronic taximeter is clocking up the actual position all the time. Double-checking the accuracy of that taximeter is another one. And treble-checking those two is another one.

All the Captain has to do is to read off his latitude and longitude in green luminous figures as easily as a taxi driver reads off a fare.

13
Man is Not Lost

The Triangle of Velocities sounds as though it should be marble and stand beside Marble Arch and the Arc de Triomphe. It is in fact the cornerstone of navigation, and its three sides are made up of true course and true airspeed, true track and true ground speed, and wind speed and direction.

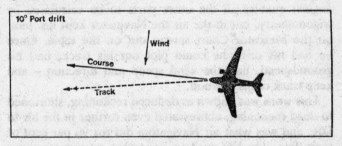

The wind puts its pressure on everything flying free in the sky. An aircraft flying at one hundred knots True Air Speed (because of decreasing air pressure and height, airspeed indicators read low with height and temperature and the indications have to be corrected) into a headwind of one hundred knots will be stationary. If there is a wind of fifty knots on its starboard beam, it will be drifted to port about 40° and will crab along a track above the ground well to the left of its true compass course (magnetic compasses point to magnetic, not true north. The amount of variation between magnetic and true varies over the globe and is plotted on charts. There is a further error in the compass itself called deviation, and this also has to be taken into account before the true course is found).

A pilot knows his true course and true airspeed. What is in doubt is the wind and how much he is being blown off his course and his speed reduced. Therefore he wants to keep track of his drift – if you look out of the window and the wind is at all on the beam, you'll see against the cloud below your Jumbo drifting crabwise. Drift used to be measured during the war by the rear gunner, who threw out aluminium dust (a flare float by night) and kept his guns on its mark in the sea, reading the drift off on the quadrant marked on the turret.

A triangle has three sides and three angles. A knowledge of any *three* of those six parts (except the three angles) enables all the other parts to be calculated by trigonometry, but in the air the Navigator kept his 'plot' on the Mercator Chart spread out on the table. Once he had his drift, he could plot out his track, find his groundspeed, find the wind speed and direction – and keep track of his position.

This work was known as deduced reckoning, shortened to dead reckoning, abbreviated even further in the air to DR, and was what air Navigators did for 90 per cent of their time. The DR position due to the many factors was always suspect – a little or a lot, depending on conditions.

Often the ground could not be seen for hours on end, and drift had to be based on the met wind the forecaster had given you. Particularly in wartime, with so few reporting stations, this was often inaccurate. The effect of a wrong but strong wind on a slow aircraft can make its position hundreds of miles out after a few hours. It is therefore essential to get a 'fix' or position.

Once you got a fix, of course, you could solve your triangle of velocities straight away by joining it up either to your last fix or your DR position. It was obtained, if you were lucky, by recognising the ground below you (called 'a pin-point' because you put your pencil point on the chart and drew a circle round it). A DR position was plotted as a square, an air position as a triangle. Or

254

position could be found by radio. The aircraft carried a loop aerial by means of which bearings of known (from their morse call sign) radio beacons could be obtained. Three accurate bearings should give what was called a 'cocked hat'. The smaller the 'cocked hat', the more accurate the position in the centre.

Or the position could be found by astro-navigation, another of the many things inherited from the seamen by the airmen. Position was found by 'shooting' stars. Three intersecting position lines produced the same sort of cocked hat as three bearings from radio stations. But a steady horizon was necessary for the sea sextant, so in the middle of the 1920s a 'bubble' sextant was introduced on a similar principle to the bubble in the spirit level. As in that instrument the bubble had to be kept central. A perspex dome was built on the flight deck, and from there the air Navigator 'shot' his stars – difficult enough on the often unsteady bomber platform. A little light illuminated the bubble and there in the centre he tried to keep the even smaller light of the star while a clockwork mechanism averaged out readings over two minutes. The reading was then checked out by tables and plotted on the Mercator Chart.

All the time they were airborne, the Navigator kept a meticulous log of courses, airspeeds, wind velocities and positions.

Those bare bones of navigation seem so simple and so very like that used at sea for hundreds of years that at first glance it is difficult to appreciate why air navigation remained much of a mystery for so long. There were, of course, many complications: all the instruments used – airspeed indicator, altimeter and compass had a number of corrections that had to be applied. Until the coming of the gyro compass at the beginning of the war, the needle used to swing very erratically, particularly in turns. The only 100 per cent accurate instrument the navigator had was his watch on GMT. Even so, in the early 1930s there were very few air Navigators, never mind skilled ones. Inaccurate navigation was one of the biggest headaches of air forces during the Second World War. Many wrong targets were bombed or right targets never hit at all.

There were weird ways of navigation. On Amelia Earhart's first trip over, the crew bombarded the *Majestic* with oranges round which were fastened the message *where are we*? Chamberlin and Devine had the bright idea of carrying the *New York Times* giving the shipping list on their day of departure. Spotting the four red and black funnels of the *Mauretania*, they ascertained she was outward bound to New York, calculated her position from the sailing date given and set course along her length eastwards to England.

It was radar and radio that came to the help of the navigator. Radar gave actual 'maps' of the country below. Gee and Loran were used for obtaining fixes – hyperbolic navigation systems based on measuring the time taken from the transmitters to reach the aircraft. Since radio waves travel at 186,000 miles a second, it is possible to obtain a position line from the time interval between the arrival of the two signals. In this way, the Atlantic was first commercially navigated. There were also many more direction-finding beacons on land and on the weather-ships at sea. As a last resort, a QDM (course to steer) could still be obtained from the ground by the radio officer.

The carriage of radio was from compulsory in Europe from 1922. But now from high flying aircraft, the pilots talk to bases right across the Atlantic, and in the early 1950s the Radio Officer was phased out of the crew on most international airlines.

Overland, aircraft now flew radio airlanes along radio range legs, reporting at one station after another as they passed over. As additional aids to safety, further refinements of radio altimeters were developed: terrain warning was given by flashing lights and bells. Phase comparison
256

systems, called Decca and Dectra, were introduced. Then an entirely new idea, Doppler, was introduced which gave the pilot not only his drift but his groundspeed and the distance in nautical miles that he had travelled.

Up front in the 747 on the left of the Captain is now a radar with thirty, one hundred and three hundred mile ranges. The beam can also be directed ahead, left or right. Radar shows storms ahead which can then be circumnavigated. Coastlines, lakes and rivers are clearly indicated up to around one hundred miles ahead. Other aircraft show up fifteen to twenty miles away as little bright pimples. In addition, there is the Distance Measuring Equipment working on VHF Omni-directional Ranges, and this again gives an accurate fix that need not be plotted. There are quite separate ones on the flight deck of a 747, showing the miles from a VOR station.

With the introduction of so many jets on the Atlantic (500 and more a day) travelling so fast, it was essential to ensure that pilots knew where they were all the time with even greater accuracy in order to maintain their allotted airlanes. And so an entirely new system of navigation came to be introduced, first on the 707s and then in a more advanced form on the Jumbo. The Inertial Navigation System has been hailed as the greatest advance in aviation since the artificial horizon.

It is, in fact, on the same system as that invaluable instrument, the gyro. Three gyros maintain a platform fixed in space, but it is balanced to move freely, north or south, east or west. Also fitted are two detectors which monitor every movement and feed them to a computer. Into this computer is fed all relevant navigation information, such as course and airspeed and time. At the start of the flight, the engineer of a 747, by means of push-buttons, sets up the latitude and longitude of his position which registers on an instrument. This setting is checked independently by both other members of the crew, since it is of course absolutely vital that the starting position is registered correctly. As the flight progresses, the INS registers like a taximeter the new latitude and longitude in neon-light type numerals, and the windspeed and direction can be found at any moment by turning the appropriate switch. The automatic pilot is connected to the INS, and the flying of the course and the logging of the trip are both entirely mechanical. And there is not just one of these machines – there are three of them. One steers the aircraft and is on watch. It 'reports' if it becomes unserviceable. The second monitors the first. The third machine is the 'hot spare' – all ready to be brought into use if either of the other sets fails. And now even simpler navigation systems have been introduced like the Collins AINS 70, where all the routes that may be required, amended up to date, are contained in a cassette which is simply slipped into place as though into a tape recorder, and the aircraft flown according to its stored information.

It is this type of navigation system that is in operation on the 'new technology' aircraft, the 757, 767 and the Airbus. The ground speed, wind speed and direction are continuously registered on the screen on the instrument board. The aircraft's track, the radio beacons and turning points – all are shown. Any change of plan, such as diverting to an alternate airport, has simply to be selected – and there on the screen is the course to steer and the distance to go, which the automatic pilot will immediately obey.

Now instead of the painstaking navigation logs, a condensed flight log is kept with much of the information already printed on it. Gone is the Mercator Chart with its arrow-headed position lines and its little cocked hats of fixes. Gone, too, is the astrodome and the bubble-sextant.

Also gone is the quiet Navigator, his work now being shared between the First Officer and a machine. The machine will be much more reliable and accurate than the First Officer.

In the future then, will we be lost without machines? A test was held for people going into a certain profession. They were given a map of the world and told to put a number of places on it. Some put Manchester in Sutherland, Killarney in Greece and the North Sea in the middle of the Pacific.

And the profession for which they were being tested? Travel agents!

14
Bigger, Faster
and Further

Every hour there is a slight change in the engine note. The Flight Engineer is pulling back the thrust levers progressively as the aircraft becomes lighter. 45,000 lb thrust is now total on the four dials, instead of 46,000 lb. The fuel consumption has dropped on each engine by 120 gallons an hour, but the speed is still 480 knots true (Mach .82, 82 per cent of the speed of sound).

For the first ten years of civil aviation in Britain, speeds were generally around 100 mph. Speeds in America were higher, and doubled with the introduction of the Lockheed 14 just before the war. DC7Cs brought the speed higher still up to 300 knots during the piston-engined heyday of the 1950s and early '60s. But the real big step forward was the introduction of the jets.

The idea was an old one. The Greek mathematician, Hero of Alexandria, made a hollow ball mounted on two pipes so that it would spin. Steam was fed in through the pipes and allowed to escape from several jets on the ball. Since every action causes an equal reaction in the opposite direction, round went the ball. Just before the Second World War, engineers in a number of countries were thinking about the possibilities of making jet engines. Whittle invented the jet engine, but the first jet aircraft to fly was German. But it was not until the Korean war that they really proved their worth in combat. In 1952, the British produced the first jet civil aircraft, the Comet, that was to revolutionise air travel, flying almost twice as fast and high as its predecessors.

The principle of the 747 jet engine is extremely simple.

Air sucked in through the front of the engine by the rotating fan is compressed and mixed with fuel in the combustion chamber. The mixture is then set on fire and the expanding gases rush out through the rear of the engine, striking the fan blades on the turbine.

The turbine turns the compressor, which is also in reality a fan with hundreds of blades that draw in the air and compress it. The force of the hot exhaust exerts a thrust power of 43,500 lb propelling the aircraft forward.

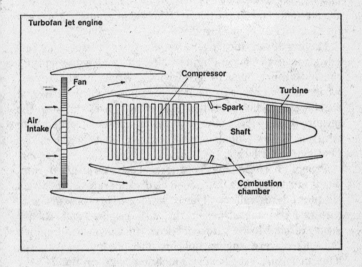

Turbofan jet engine

The 747 engine gets almost double the thrust power than earlier jet engines and 10 hp per 1 lb of weight, compared to the Wright Brothers' first engine of 1 hp per 10 lb of weight.

Because of the by-pass design and the low speed of the fan at the front of the engine, much less noise and smoke is produced and there is 20 per cent less fuel consumption. Sound absorbent lining is also installed in the engine cowling.

When it is taken apart, the engine resembles a never-ending collection of hoops of various sizes – yet it is only 128 inches in length and weighs only 8,470 lb. The problem of very high temperatures inside the engine up to 3,000° centigrade was solved by using titanium and high-alloy nickel steel. Non by-pass jets have that shrill siren sound that sometimes resembles a revolving saw running at speed on insufficient oil. The Jumbo sounds deeper, more rumbly but less grating on the teeth. The engine was tested in the best possible way – in the air. One engine was fitted in a B52 bomber and flown for many hours at high altitudes.

Having fewer moving parts, the jets produce far less vibration than piston-engined aircraft, and being simpler there is much less to go wrong. What Saint-Exupéry wrote fifty years ago is now even more true: 'In the machine of today we forget that motors are whirring: the motor, finally, has come to fulfil its function, which is to whirr as a heart beats – and we give no thought to the beating of our heart.'

Propeller engines' revolutions were only 2,000 rpm. They are 9,000 in a jet and if it disintegrates, pieces get shot out like bullets. There were early problems with turbines disintegrating in the JT9 engine, but British Airways shutdown rates are low. In the piston-engined era, there were engine failures once every 1,500 hours. The jet failure rate is very much less, and on the 747 the engine can be changed in five hours. Fuel consumption is ninety passenger miles to the gallon.

It was not only the engines that pushed up the speed. The streamlining of the airframe did, too. Pound per pound, four and a half times as much thrust was required to pull Alcock and Brown's strutted bi-plane Vimy across the Atlantic than a 747.

The new jet age is a boon to passengers – twice as fast, much more comfortable, high above almost all the weather and comparatively cheap to operate. Tristar is advertised as being 10 per cent cheaper to operate than its brothers, the 747 and DC10.

There was one big problem. Jumbos became status symbols. Some Eastern and African countries ordered more big jets while making few efforts to ensure they had the ground equipment and personnel to operate them. Airports, lighting, radar, landing aids, fire-fighting and ATC took second place to having the aircraft.

Studies are in progress to make the second generation 747s hold 700 by extending the body by fifty feet. The third generation is likely to be a double-decker carrying 1,000 passengers. This would mean a wing area of 7,000 square feet and a wing span increased from 195 feet 8 inches to 258 feet 10 inches.

The seats can be easily dismantled and the whole aircraft, or part of it, can be turned into a cargo carrier, capable of transporting 170,000 lb of freight across the Atlantic in fully automated holds. For the whole essence of survival in the competitiveness in the sky is flexibility – rearrangement of an aircraft interior to carry out any combination of demand for first-class or economy seating, together with every shape and size of freight.

An enormous customer-relations exercise went into the Jumbo. Boeing teams visited airlines all over the world and listened to their requirements before they built anything. And then having decided what the majority of long-range customers wanted, they went to town. An entirely new manufacturing complex was set up, and the total production bill for the 747 – borne by the company, for like most ventures into the sky it is a private enterprise aeroplane – was a billion dollars. In two and a half years, on 30 September 1968, the first Jumbo emerged from the hangar.

Such a revolutionary aircraft required revolutionary maintenance procedures.

The old idea was so many landings for a tyre, so many

263

hours wear in an engine, so many checks to be made ritualistically at such and such a time. Aircraft used to be regularly dismembered every year and after it was found to nobody's surprise that everything was working well, they used to be built up again. A time limit (either flying hours or calendar time) was set for all components and the airframe structure. At these predetermined periods the aircraft and components were overhauled. The overhauls were carried out in predetermined work packages. Such a system is still carried out on 707s and 111s. The checks are done like a car's servicing – one at so many hours flown. On older aircraft, extensive checks are not made, but in a 'progressive maintenance' scheme, parts are overhauled and if necessary replaced when the aircraft comes into the hangar for routine checks.

This system proved adequate at the time, although a school of thought voiced the opinion that aircraft generally proved less reliable following extensive strip down and rebuild until a shake-down period had elapsed.

However, such maintenance proved costly in resources, both human and equipment. Tests also showed that many components removed for inspection/overhaul during these major checks had no defects or any symptoms of incipient failure. They could have safely continued in service.

Economic pressures plus the necessity to improve on aircraft utilisation meant a new approach, one which did not rely entirely on experience and judgment but which used technological techniques such as oil spectrographs and engine borescopes to detect the worsening of components/systems.

This is the basis of a system known as 'condition monitoring' and, in collaboration with a statistical analysis of aircraft defects, can be used gradually to escalate check cycle intervals until the optimum is reached. Certain components are checked at certain times on certain checks and their condition inspected before replacement.

This is the method that has been used to maintain the

747. Some idea of its value can be gauged by the fact that an Intermediate Check occurred at 1,000 flying hours in 1972 – now the same check occurs at 4,000 flying hours.

Use is made of *all* technical information when determining how a system or component is performing. Defects which are noted by the flight crew are monitored and any trends analysed by a group specifically set up for this task. Strip down checks are inspected by the regulatory authorities. All the information is collated, discussed and used as the basis for negotiations between the airlines and the Civil Aviation Authority. Only 10 per cent of components still have a fixed or hard life allocated to them.

As a result, aircraft utilisation hours have increased rapidly – and since it costs over £2,000 an hour to keep a Jumbo on the ground, this is a big economic advantage. Flying boats had a five-hour-a-day utilisation, Stratocruisers and Constellations around seven. Jumbos have a mean of around thirteen and a half hours and peaks of fourteen and three-quarters have been achieved.

Modern techniques are used to discover wear before a part breaks down. All 747s are fitted with Flight Data Recorders and Airborne Integrated Data Systems (AIDS). Blocks of data from each engine operation – take-off, climb, cruise – are reduced to a single 'snapshot' of exhaust-gas temperature and other parameters and converted to standard conditions for comparison with the engine brochure. This is called engine condition monitoring and gives adequate warning for engine changes.

Cracks still appear in wings – they did in the Trident, slight ones in the Concorde and in the middle of 1978 the DC8 was affected, leading to all 161 of these types being grounded for inspection. Now the 747s are being affected.

Yellow fluorescent dye is sealed in the centre of bolts or rivets which seeps out to the surface if the part starts to crack. Dye is also used to penetrate minute cracks and illuminate them.

Ultra-sound is also used, similar in principle to the sonar echo-sounding detection used on ships. A pulse of sound is passed through the object under test. The pulse bounces off the back of the object and its return is received and analysed. Should there be a defect, the pulse will bounce off the defect and not the back of the object. The pulse return time will therefore directly relate to the presence or absence of a defect.

Both X-ray and gamma-ray methods are used, gamma for the more dense type of materials. Film negatives are produced, similar to hospital X-ray plates, which show up any defect.

The eddy current technique is also used whereby minute electrical currents are induced into the object. Any defect will modify the pattern of the induced currents. This modified result is compared with a known defect-free sample. The result of the comparison will determine the size of the defect.

These techniques have been described as extensions of engineers' senses in that they help in the detection of the existence of defects which normally cannot be seen, heard or felt. In addition to this, there are test points built in throughout the 747 where test equipment can be fitted in and spot checks made. An optical borescope is plugged in and spot checks made to inspect wear on engine compressor and turbine blades.

It is a pity that the phrase 'sound barrier' was ever invented. A picture of a wall is produced, a sort of Iron Curtain. Sonic boom reminds you of a bomb going off.

Actually, when an aircraft approaches the speed of sound, or Mach 1, the air in front is compressed and its density changes. Disturbances build up and eventually cause a shock wave. This caused a rapid increase in drag, and difficulties in control, but these are now largely eliminated, and there is no great change in supersonic to subsonic flight.

266

This is just as well, for the next step had to be supersonic. After twenty-five years of difficulties, the Concorde began its passenger service in January 1976. There were further noise and environmental problems but a regular service London – New York started in 1978. Now the time taken to cross the Atlantic was cut to three and a half hours, one hundred passengers flew at a height of 60,000 feet and a speed of 1,150 mph in smoothness and comfort. Built for strength, weighing rather more than half a 747, basically it resembles a dart. This is particularly evident on the flight deck, which is long and thin, and in the passenger cabin with its narrow aisle.

The Concorde's appearance is now well known – the prehistoric-bird-like take-off, with its tiny head and down-pointing beak with outstretched wings, has figured in the news the world over.

The 'beak' is the visor nose lowered to give the pilot better visibility. Flying twice as high and two and a quarter times as fast as a Jumbo, on a clear day it provides for the passenger through inky blue light a perfect picture of the rounded flank of the earth.

The portholes are small and (when flying supersonically) warm to touch. The comfort is the same as that of a first-class Jumbo. It is perhaps a little quieter in the cabin. Navigation aids and blind-landing aids are much the same, and it is operated by the same number of crew – three.

No films are shown on board, though there are five radio channels. The Concorde's appeal at present would appear to be mainly to businessmen whose time is big money.

There have certainly been problems with the Concorde. Its cost is enormous, for again it is a one-off and custom-built with no military ancestors, as with all British civil aircraft. At present only Air France and Britain operate it, and it is cleared to Category III on landing – cloud height on the deck and visibility almost nil. The speed of the aircraft – Mach number – is shown in the cabin.

The sonic boom on Concorde is heard on the ground like distant thunder as it flies over. Because of this, some countries prohibit supersonic flying over their territories.

The environmentalists have also accused Concorde of air-pollution. Coils of black smoke could be seen streaming from the early engines. Even though this pollution was minimal – apart from electric vehicles, aircraft are the cleanest forms of mechanical transport, much more so than the totally accepted motor car – concern was naturally felt by those living round airports. Then concern has been expressed in the theory that oxides of nitrogen emitted into the stratosphere by supersonic exhausts might cause a chain reaction with the ozone, thus depriving the earth of protection against excessive ultra-violet radiation, though a major survey shows no real evidence of this effect.

Some authorities were worried about radiation. We are exposed to some radiation from many sources, such as luminous dials, television and X-rays. In addition, there is cosmic radiation which is composed of stripped atomic nuclei particles that normally do not penetrate the shield of the earth's atmosphere. In the Concorde this is around 0.8 millirems per hour at 60,000 feet against colour TV of 0.6, and living in London 120 annually.

However, about twice a year, often connected with the appearance of sunspots, the sun ejects streams of particles in a solar flare, some of which may have sufficient energy to reach the thin top of the atmosphere through which both subsonic and (higher still and therefore more vulnerable) supersonic aircraft fly.

All jets are, in fact, regularly tested for radiation activity, but in addition on the Concorde, there is a radiation meter which continually measures radiation and gives an early warning system to the crew. If the needle points to rising radiation, all the Captain has to do is to descend under the thickness of the atmosphere shield.

The Concordes survived a long period of being called

expensive white elephants, and are now not only in profit but in high demand on the Atlantic and Australian routes. There are tourist trips to see Halley's comet and a special day trip to the Arctic to see Santa Claus and have a bonfire on the ice at a cost of over £600 a seat.

In 1971 Boeing completed the engineering research into the supersonic 2707, a bigger aircraft than the Concorde designed to cruise at 1,890 mph. Then it was shelved because of the expense. But now there is interest again in supersonic civil aircraft, fuelled by President Reagan's State of the Union speech in 1986, in which he spoke of aircraft being designed to fly from Washington to Tokyo in two hours.

Not to be outdone, the British then produced their Hotol project. Hotol is really an unmanned satellite, but under a £2 million programme, the possibilities of making it into an aircraft are being explored. It uses a runway and accelerates to 290 knots take-off speed, climbs at an angle of 25° and reaches Mach 5 at an altitude of 26 kilometres. It descends unpowered and touches down at 170 knots. If the project succeeds, it is said that Hotol will fly from London to Sydney in an hour. There is no doubt at all that the air passenger of the twenty-first century will be flying regularly at supersonic speeds.

Meanwhile Concorde continues to prosper, but the main airline work is being carried on by the 727s, 737s and 747s, which are still selling in their updated versions.

Coming up fast, of course, are the high technology aircraft – the 757, 767 and the Airbus. The European consortium which involves British Aerospace builds the A300, A310 and A320, and plans to spend £1.85 billion developing a four-engined 260-seater A340, with which it hopes to put out of business the hugely successful 747, of which six hundred are still operating.

The European consortium has sold nearly 500 aircraft, but have had government support running into billions. They have infiltrated the American market and with the twin-engined A320, due to fly in 1988, they have produced what they call a new generation jet.

The engines are completely electronically installed. There are no sticks between the pilots' legs, only a six-inch-high lever to the left for the Captain and one to the right of the co-pilot. The throttles do not move on take-off, indeed they thought of doing without throttles completely.

When the A320 is switched on, computers test the aircraft for defects. It has the latest Airborne Integrated Data System, recording a large set of engine and systems performance parameters from which the maintenance engineers work. It stores defects and has two systems of fault recording – either translated into plain language and printed on hard copy entirely during flight or in code which directs the engineer to the place in the manual that tells him how to correct the fault. All data goes to the airline's main computer to be stored. When any component is changed, the new one is automatically tested and any defective part rejected.

Built In Test Equipment (BITE) monitors instrument and equipment function. And computers will forecast any trouble ahead. The Engineers on new technology aircraft these days say all that's necessary is an index finger that can press the computer buttons.

As a result of the tourist boom, airlines began doing much better. Pan American made $52.4 million profit in 1983. British Airways made a £315 million profit in 1984. 1,373,000 million passenger kilometres were flown in 1984/5 and 892 million new passengers were flown world-wide. Cheap Laker-like no-frills airlines like People Express and Virgin Atlantic appeared to be thriving.

Virgin Atlantic, under Richard Branson, the pop record millionaire businessman, is following in Laker's cheapness footsteps and carried 270,000 passengers in 1984 with 90 per cent loads and are hoping to buy a second 747. The fare from Gatwick to Newark at present is £129 on the day of departure, £159 for a confirmed booked seat. If the passenger can sing or do a comic turn, he or she is allowed fifteen minutes to entertain the passengers. If they succeed, their fare is refunded. Branson says, 'Some were pretty horrendous, but others had old ladies crying in the aisles with laughter.' Businessmen booking first-class fares get an economy return free. They also get a free helicopter ride from Newark to Manhattan.

Such gifts and bonuses are likely to become more frequent since world competition is hotting up again. A crucial passenger capacity agreement between Britain and America expires in July 1986. The increase in terrorism and the uncertainty of the market after the price of oil plummeted has had a dire effect on American passenger traffic to Europe. In June 1986, British Airways gave free seats to 5,700 lottery winners to induce Americans to cross the Atlantic. Virgin Atlantic was selling seats for £56, and People Express for £66.

In addition the airlines are faced with the enormous cost of replacing their ageing fleets. The big Tristars, DC10s and 747s will still be flying, but it will inevitably be the smaller high technology aircraft like the 757, 767 and Airbus 320 which will eventually be taking over. And each one costs more than $30 million.

This necessary buying of new equipment will give a big boost to the aircraft companies. So far 160 757s and 195 767s have been sold. Aerospace have sold 260 A300 Airbuses, 106 A310s and 40 A320s. The big sales fight will take place in the Far East where aviation is expanding even more rapidly. Here Boeing have the advantage in that the 767 (with 27 per cent better fuel economy than the 737) is already in service, while the Airbus 320 is not. Customers will have to wait till 1988 for it. Boeing forecasts jet sales of 287 in 1988 rising to 519 in 1989, and then falling back.

British Aerospace is again in private hands and the

government is planning to sell off to the private sector not only the airports, but also British Airways with its 165 aircraft.

The attempted privatisation of the government airline, first announced in 1979, is a saga all on its own. First there was a massive legal fight alongside a number of other international airlines, after Laker had gone into liquidation, which was only resolved after a settlement worth $64 million had been agreed in July 1985. Then there were other problems. July 1986 was announced as the new date for privatisation, but whether this would take place was open to debate. The new date is early 1987.

Independent airlines are already vying for BA routes. Another struggle between the old Jumbos and new technology aircraft is whether the latter can match the former on the really long-range routes.

In March 1984, El Al pioneered the non-stop Atlantic route in a twin-engined aircraft with a 767 that flew from Montreal to Tel Aviv in eleven hours and eight minutes. Other airlines began to follow suit. International rules laid down that the track should be within sixty minutes of an airport, so they were routed well to the north to keep within that range of the Greenland and Iceland airports. There appeared to be no problems. But Air Canada, which had followed suit with non-stop North Atlantic flights, suspended its North Atlantic winter operations. This was really for commercial reasons and to monitor weather availability of alternate airfields on the route. They had made 200 crossings, having had no diversions, no engine shut-downs and no electrical power emergencies.

It would appear on the face of it that the safe two-engined operation over 2,000 miles of water has been proved, with a clear victory of the 767 over the 747.

Not so. The new 747/400 will operate with only a two-man crew and carry 414 passengers over 7,000 miles at a higher speed than her limited-range sisters.

Then there is considerable feeling against flying across the Atlantic on two engines, which I share. I spent much of the early part of the war out over the Atlantic on an aircraft that would not maintain height on one engine. Most of the pilots who qualified with me on the RAF twin-engined training course and accompanied me to Coastal Command were lost, not through enemy action, but through coming down in the Atlantic after losing an engine. The Constellation aircraft which flew across the Atlantic after the war were continually losing engines.

Engines, of course, are now very much more reliable. But there have been engine failures on the 767. The International Federation of Airline Pilots don't like the idea of twins operating the North Atlantic. When one engine is shut down, there is more pressure on the survivor. There is also the matter of pilot workload, especially in an emergency. Though such aircraft operate well to the north to keep close to Greenland and Iceland, no international standards have been laid down for weather at alternates; a minimum of 800 feet ceiling and two miles visibility is considered necessary by the pilots, a weather state often absent during the Atlantic winter. TWA had four major diversions in its 767 North Atlantic operations.

Against that view, the protagonists point to an in-flight shut-down rate of the JT9/D and the RB211 engines of .03 and .04 per million hours. And Qantas are going to fly from Brisbane to Tokyo (3,870 nautical miles) in the 767, allowing a maximum diversion time to an above limits alternate airfield of 104 minutes.

If one engine *does* go, that will seem like 104 years to the pilot.

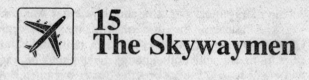

15
The Skywaymen

Enter the hijacker, at first sight, the airborne version of the old highwayman. But close to, a very different breed. Though several hijackings have been for gain and (more difficult to deal with) for political asylum, the hijacker of the 1960s and 1970s was like the old highwayman only in the fact that he was a product of his times, and that he operated on the innocent vulnerable passengers of those times. The ease with which a terrorist or hijacker could take over aircraft was foreseen by some of the airlines several decades ago, but, as with Britain in its first fall of snow, hijacking seemed to catch the world with its pants down.

The first hijacking was in 1930. A PAA aircraft flying over South America was forced to land at Arequipa, Peru. There it was held for several days. The Captain refused to take off, so the hijackers did, raining pamphlets over the town. The Captain was then allowed to proceed without them. Not till 1960, however, did hijacking really begin to take a hold. Nine Cubans took over a national-ised Cubana aircraft and forced it to land in Florida. Four were wounded and a Cuban guard was killed. They were hailed as heroes and granted political asylum.

So frequently were Eastern Airlines planes hijacked and flown to Cuba that special restaurants and gift shops sprang up to cater to the hijacked passengers' needs. Castro began to charge airlines landing fees and charges for passenger buses and accommodation. Back in New York, the long-suffering commuters said of the Long Island railroad, 'At least you never wind up in Havana!'

One of the most embarrassing hijackings was that of Vassilios Tsironis, the opponent of the Papidopolous Greek junta. In the summer of 1969, he took his family on a domestic flight aboard an Olympic Airways jet, and singlehandedly hijacked the plane over the Bay of Corinth, forcing it to fly to Albania. Then he made his way to Sweden, which had taken no uncertain stand against the policies of the Papidopolous junta, and, like the Cubans in the USA, was given a hero's welcome.

But Sweden had also taken no uncertain stand against hijacking, so Nemesis came in the shape of a prominent Swede's love of the law – Jacob Sundberg, who taught law at the University of Stockholm. He wrote to the chief state prosecutor pointing out that Tsironis had violated Sweden's anti-hijacking law. Prosecution of Tsironis followed. Argument raged for years. If a free country grants political asylum to refugees of a repressive régime, can it also prosecute them for crimes committed while they struggled to free themselves?

There were also hijackers who were really robbers. D.B. Cooper hijacked a 727 by showing the stewardess a cylinder connected by wires. He forced the Captain to land and collected $200,000. Then he jumped by parachute into the Cascade mountains. Neither he nor the money has ever been seen since.

Meanwhile hijacking intensified. It was said that a passenger was more likely to be involved in a hijacking than a crash. Airlines racked their brains for devices to combat hijackers. A profile of a 'safe passenger' was built up, like the picture of an average man. And from this cardboard cut out, therefore, a profile of the hijacker, the deviant, was also built up. Gas, poison, sleeping draughts in food, armed guards disguised as passengers, the carrying of guns by aircrew, besides more intricate ones which airlines are unwilling to disclose, have all been in some instances adopted. America, with its early spate of hijackings to Cuba, has spent vast sums on anti-hijacking methods.

275

Specially trained, specially armed men called sky-marshals watch out for that odd man out among the passengers, the possible hijacker. If you get into conversation with a sky-marshal, he will have a cover story. But he won't drink or watch the film. And he won't talk more than necessary unless you happen to be the one he has his eye on. He will be carrying a revolver armed with 'airline special' bullets which minimise damage.

Just after the war, several airliners were hijacked from Czechoslovakia to West Germany. Former Free Czechoslovakian pilots were treated as heroes in the beginning. My wife, an ex-BEA stewardess, knew many of the Czech airliners' crews and the talk was frequently of how to escape.

Then there were the psychotic hijackers like the one on an Eastern Airlines shuttle between Newark and Boston. Once airborne, he appeared on the flight deck brandishing a gun and, clearly bent on suicide, ordered the Captain to alter course and fly out over the Atlantic till his fuel was exhausted. When the Captain protested, he shot him in both arms.

First Officer James Hartley tried a rugby tackle. In the struggle, Hartley was killed and the hijacker injured sufficiently to keep him quiet. The Captain managed to land the aircraft at Boston. Here the hijacker was taken to a mental hospital. He was examined, pronounced sane, but subsequently hanged himself. A post-mortem discovered that he had an old bullet lodged in his brain. Eastern Airlines crews now attend the James Hartley Training Centre in Miami.

There was also another Eastern Airlines incident, aboard a 727 which had just landed at La Guardia. This time the hijacker told the Captain and First Officer that he had explosives strapped to his person, and a vial of acid in his hand.

He ordered them to go to the Bahamas, where he wanted $500,000, a gift from the IRA, waiting for him. His wife,
276

summoned along with swarms of police and FBI and FAA officials, said he was mentally unstable and a heavy drinker.

John O'Neill, the President of Eastern Airlines, took a brave decision. He flew by fast plane ahead to the Bahamas, and tackled the hijacker singlehanded when the 727 landed, overpowering him.

Nowadays many airlines keep the door to the flight deck locked to guard against such sudden apparitions. The stewardess has a key. One stewardess swallowed the key rather than hand it over to a would-be hijacker.

But the best way of all is to stop today's more deadly hijacker boarding the aircraft. Passengers are now used to, and should be glad of, the airport search. There are various metal scanners and beams. Magnetometers isolate solid lumps of metal such as guns and knives.

There is a system where the passenger walks between poles, which trigger off an alarm, or he is briskly run over by the 'electric truncheon'. On many occasions, the alarm simply indicates loose change or keys, but otherwise it will indicate the presence of a gun – unless it is heavily wrapped in lead, when it will be felt by the security guards when they frisk the passengers. At one small Greek airport I was at in the early 1970s, all the women were suddenly led one by one into a booth and frisked. They had had, an official said, a 'tip-off'.

Yet despite the precautions, the hijackers and terrorists got through. For twenty years after the war, hijackings were few. Then suddenly in 1968, there was an epidemic. 1969 was twice as bad, with over eighty.

A tougher breed of the politically motivated hijackers arrived – those with a 'cause'. They wanted the world to sit up and take notice. It did so in September 1970 when four jetliners were hijacked by Arab guerrillas. An El Al 707 with nearly 150 passengers, a TWA 707 with 145, a Pan Am 747 with over 150 and a Swissair DC8 with 143 were almost simultaneously hijacked as they flew in the skies above Europe.

277

With swift presence of mind, the captain of the El Al 707 threw his huge aircraft into a steep dive. In the passenger cabin a terrorist with a gun and a girl holding a hand grenade were thrown off balance. The passengers unstrapped themselves. They and the security guards overpowered the terrorists. The man was shot, the girl tied up with string and a passenger's necktie. The aircraft returned to London, where subsequently the British police found themselves able, under pressure, to release the girl.

The Pan Am plane was forced by its hijackers to fly to Cairo. The passengers and crew were removed, and the plane blown up.

The TWA 707 and the Swissair DC8 were made to fly to a remote airstrip in the Jordanian desert near Amman. There, with great skill, the pilots brought the heavy machines to a safe landing, while between Bombay and London another aircraft was being captured, this time a British VC10 with 117 passengers on board. It, too, was forced to land at the desert strip. It, too, made a perfect landing.

For six days 429 passengers and crew sweated it out in the desert, while international negotiations went on. The heat was unbearable, the sanitary arrangement nauseating and humiliating. There was very little water and practically no food, while over it all was the menace and hysteria of the hijackers, the knowledge that the aircraft were wired up with explosive, and all the frictions and miseries and misunderstandings of an amorphous international multitude poised on what must have seemed like the very brink of hell.

Eventually all the passengers and crew were told to get out. The aircraft were blown up.

Millions and millions of dollars, pounds and Swiss francs went up in smoke – but the hostages survived.

Because the guerrillas are outlaw groups no one could make an insurance claim against them.

Then in 1974 there was the massacre at Lod International airport in Tel Aviv of the passengers from the Air France jet. As the passengers collected their baggage from the conveyor belt, three Japanese passengers working for the Popular Front for the Liberation of Palestine (PFLP) opened fire on them with machine guns and three hand grenades.

Within minutes twenty-four passengers were slaughtered and seventy-six wounded. The following month, a German aircraft was hijacked over Turkey to secure the release of the perpetrators of the 1972 Olympic Games outrage.

One of the most noticeable aspects of hijacking is the extraordinary courage with which both passengers and crew behave in the long-drawn-out agony. Repeatedly it comes out that the hijackers themselves are the most nervous. And thereby, of course, even more dangerous – particularly as the hijacker is almost certainly a social misfit, a failure determined to prove himself.

All airlines have instructions to their crews on how to deal with a hijacking. The USSR, some Soviet bloc countries and some small African states have instructions to resist takeover 'at all costs'. Every airline has its own particular drill. But the passengers are totally unprepared and yet behave well, so long as the hijack is not too extended.

One would also expect there to be crashes resulting from flying mistakes. Surely no pilot could fly properly with a revolver at his head, or pressed into his back, but quite the reverse is true. Bound from Schipol to Tokyo, KLM 861 was hijacked by Palestinians and forced to land at Damascus. The Syrians flatly refused to refuel, so the KLM pilot, Captain Risseeue, had to fly to Cyprus and eventually to Libya.

The hijackers expected an enthusiastic welcome, similar to the one Sweden accorded to Tsironis. But instead, Libya played it according to the law. The hijackers were told to give themselves up. They refused. Instead, Captain Risseeue was ordered to take off at gun point. Two of the hijackers held up hand grenades in the passenger cabin. And as the Libyan army moved up tanks on to the runway, Captain Risseeue took off.

The hijackers seemed unable to decide where to go next. Finally, the captain was told to land in Malta. I've landed at that field many times and it was a feat of tremendous skill to get a Jumbo down on to it. But it would be impossible to take the aircraft off again fully laden, and with commendable calm Captain Risseeue managed to convince the hijackers of that.

The passengers were released. Fuel was taken on. The Jumbo took off at dawn. Then began the long, hot search for a landfall. One by one the Mediterranean and desert airports closed against it.

Dubai reluctantly allowed a brief refuelling stop, and finally the following day allowed them to land again. The Captain had been flying for nearly seventy hours, the tyres were scorched, and it was impossible to take off again. So finally the hijackers were persuaded to give themselves up. All countries had stood together and turned their face against them.

Not so with the Entebbe hijacking episode. In July 1976 the Captain of an Air France jet was forced to alter course and land at Entebbe. There President Amin gave every sign of welcoming the hijackers. Armed Ugandan troops as well as terrorists guarded the hostages in the overcrowded airport lounge.

Like Sweden before, the government of Israel was in a cleft stick. It had protested against the West German government for negotiating with hijackers when they had released some of the Black September group. But relatives of the captives besieged the Defence building in Tel Aviv and demanded that they negotiate.

For days the agonising continued. The Israeli government appeared to bargain. The hijackers' demands
280

escalated. It became clear that a terrible fate would indeed be meted out to the hostages.

Then came the famous Entebbe raid by Israeli commandos. Hijackers and Ugandan soldiers were cut down by machine-gun fire. The hostages were released. Like was met with like. Terrorism with military tactics. There are those who argue that this is the only way – as Yehokel Dror wrote, 'a readiness to accept pain' in the face of terrorism, fanaticism and blackmail.

Fanaticism takes all sorts of forms. There were the five Croatian nationals who hijacked the TWA airliner to Chicago in 1976. They forced the pilot to fly to Charles de Gaulle airport in Paris by way of Montreal, Gander, Newfoundland and Shannon, dropping leaflets along the way explaining their cause. They claimed to represent three million exiles – Croats under-represented in the Yugoslavian government.

They appeared to be armed with bombs and explosive devices strapped to their bodies. At Charles de Gaulle airport the police shot out the plane's tyres. The hijackers were given the ultimatum. Surrender and be sent back to the US or be seized, tried and perhaps executed in France.

The terrorists gave in. The explosive devices turned out to be fakes. The passengers said they had been treated courteously. They applauded as the hijackers left the aircraft.

One hijacker was given the money he demanded, but secreted with it was a small automatic radio transmitter. Its signal was followed by F111 fighters and the man was captured within three hours.

But what does happen up front when a hijacker attempts to take over an aircraft? A pilot is advised first and foremost to try to calm the hijacker and humour him. As soon as possible he presses the emergency hijack transponder. This blips the aircraft's radar image on the air traffic controller's set and sets in motion the wheels of help from the outside world.

281

Then the pilot has to try to acquaint the hijacker with the dangers and needs of the flight, the limitations of the aircraft, the need for fuel. He tries to win the hijacker's confidence, to glean as much information as he can. Are there more hijackers back in the cabin? If not, should the Captain tell the passengers, and if so, how?

The Captain of the aircraft is at the spearhead of the terrorist attack. Much depends on his personality as well as his flying skill. He takes the brunt of the terrorists' hysteria. In the Mogadishu hijacking of the Lufthansa jet in 1977 the Captain was slain and his body thrown out on to the tarmac.

Specially trained German assault troops finally foiled the raid and rescued the hostages. As a result of the failure of the hijack, three of the Baader Meinhof gang committed suicide in gaol. In the Jordanian desert hijacking, because Captains and crew had responsibility, they survived the ordeal better than the passengers who, under such acute stress, tended to disintegrate. There was rivalry for food, and water, and to some extent for approval from the hijackers themselves. Passengers formed groups according to nationality. But though the aircraft were eventually blown up, they all came out alive.

Other skywaymen have operated in different ways. The bomb-on-board made its appearance in 1946 on a British European Viking, but, due to the skill of the Captain and the stewardess, with no loss of life.

Then two ex-convicts put one on a Manila DC3, probably for revenge.

Next came the insurance and 'family' crimes – insuring of wives and relatives and blowing up them as well as the aircraft. In 1949 another DC3 was destroyed for this reason, and all twenty-three on board died.

There were further instances of insurance crimes (basically the plot of the film *Airport*) and in 1963 the International Federation of Air Line Pilots (IFALPA) at their

Conference made a bid to stop the selling of insurance over the counter before take-off.

The criminals were often caught, and on several occasions, though they went off, the home-made bombs did not cause sufficient damage and the aircraft landed safely. Some airlines had armour-plated their cargo holds.

Then came the political bombings – bigger bombs put on board by rival warring factions. A Comet was destroyed over the Mediterranean during the Greece-Cyprus struggle. A TWA 707 was blown up over the Ionian Sea in 1974 with eighty-eight on board. About fifty bombs have exploded in civil airlines since 1946, the majority of them since 1967. In December 1977 a Malaysian Airways crew on approach to Kuala Lumpur radioed that it was overshooting and proceeding to Singapore with a hijacker and bomb on board. When Singapore cleared the aircraft to descend to 7,000 feet, all radar and radio contact was lost. The aircraft had impacted swampy ground at high speed. In 1981, two explosive devices went off on a Tripoli-Malta-Cairo flight, seriously injuring crew and passengers.

The bombs were often of the explode-at-a-certain-altitude type – or that was what the blackmailers said. These would mean that the aircraft could not descend below that altitude to land unless the bomb was found and defused. Ransoms were demanded on such threats.

Some countries are under pressure to reintroduce the death penalty for terrorists in that many hijackings and bomb attacks have been motivated by attempts to release them from jail.

Then there is the other political skywayman, shooting down unarmed civil airliners from the ground or by fighters. The first one was during the Berlin airlift in 1952 when a DC4 strayed over the Soviet zone and was attacked by Russian fighters. The skin was punctured by bullets, two passengers were injured, but the Captain managed to land safely at Tempelhof.

More recently tension in Africa and the Middle East have fuelled these atrocities. At the end of 1977, a DC4 going from Rhodesia to Zaire was shot down and the two crew captured. Nearly a year later, a Rhodesian Viscount was apparently shot down by a SAM missile. Then ten of the survivors were reported massacred by guerillas.

On 20 April 1978, a Boeing 707 of Korean Air Lines on a scheduled flight from Paris to Seoul wandered a thousand miles off course, and began flying over Russian territory. An intercepting Soviet fighter opened fire, puncturing the pressure cabin. The Captain made a rapid descent from 35,000 to 5,000 feet, regained control and made a crash landing on a frozen lake in which two passengers were killed and thirteen injured. It seems possible that the Inertial Navigational System was set up wrongly, or not connected to the auto-pilot, and the track of the aircraft was not monitored by the crew.

On 16 May 1981, an aircraft was shot down by a heat-seeking missile over Angola.

On 1 August 1981, a DC3 near Beira, Mozambique on a magnetometer survey with full permission of the authorities, deviated from its route and was shot down by a fighter. All six crew were killed.

On 3 May 1982, an Algerian-registered Gulfstream left Cyprus for Tehran with the Foreign Minister of Algeria on board. The aircraft reported to Ankara Area Control Centre: 'Passing Van [Turkey] at 13.20 G.M.T., estimating Bonam at 13.28, cruising Flight Level 370 [37,000 feet].'

A few minutes later, the operator of Air Defence Radar called, 'Turn 360 degrees. Two aggressor aircraft have appeared.'

Shortly afterwards, the operator called, 'Turn left to 300 degrees and return to Ankara. The two fighters are about to attack.'

The Captain confirmed that he would go back, but did not turn for three minutes.

284

At 13.31, the aircraft disappeared from the radar. Shot down, it crashed at Givoran, one mile from the Turkish border.

Sixteen months later, on 31 August 1983, passengers and crew boarded a Korean Air Lines Boeing 747 at Kennedy, New York to fly to Seoul, Korea, via Anchorage. Nothing went amiss with the flight as it left Alaska heading west, except that (apparently unknown to the crew) the aircraft was twelve miles north of track.

That in itself would be nothing, except for the fact that there was the highly efficient Inertial Navigational System that by means of inertial forces electronically geared to what looks like a taximeter on the flight deck instrument panel, continually registers the aircraft's latitude and longitude to within a mile or so.

Yet no correction was made. This was even more serious in that Flight 007 was going to have to skirt very accurately round a huge area of Soviet-controlled air space. Worse, it was going to fly over a secret base, Petrapavlovsk, where there was an air base, submarine pens and rocket launching pads, from which, apparently, a new weapon was about to be tested at dawn.

The same incorrect course of 246° magnetic was maintained into Soviet air space, the crew nevertheless reporting being over the right checking-in points. By now an American intelligence 707 had also entered Soviet air space. Close by, Soviet radar watched both.

KAL 007 continued on a course of 246°. Soviet fighters were scrambled. Eventually, when the aircraft was over Sakhalin island where there is a major naval base and a number of military airfields, the 747 was shot down 365 miles off course by two heat-seeking rockets. Two hundred and sixty nine passengers and crew were killed.

The only explanation that appears possible is that the auto-pilot was switched to a heading of 246° (which the aircraft maintained throughout) instead of the next position just below it on the selector, locking it on to the

285

Inertial Navigation System. Why the pilots were not monitoring with their radar remains a mystery. It would appear that the accident of 20 April 1978 of the KAL Boeing 707 had virtually been repeated. One hopeful development to follow these tragedies has been the agreement reached between Japan, US and the Soviet Union to establish an emergency communications line linking Anchorage in Alaska, Tokyo and Khabavovsk in Siberia.

Terror attacks on airports and civil aircraft continued throughout 1984, but it was in 1985 that they reached such monstrous proportions. There were 263 airborne terrorist attacks reported in the period 1970–9. In contrast, by the summer of 1985, 310 acts of terror had occurred, and 341 people had suffered in aviation-related attacks.

There were 46 actual hijacks in 1970 – an all-time high. As a result, passenger and luggage scrutiny was set up at major international airports, and this pushed the annual total back to 28, 40 per cent of which was against the USA.

There were a number of bombs exploded on airports. Three people were killed at Frankfurt. On 1 July 1985, several people were injured when a bomb exploded at Rome's Leonardo da Vinci airport. Three weeks later, there was another terrorist explosion at the Madrid office of British Airways, which killed a woman.

With increasing viciousness came the indiscriminate shooting of Israeli passengers at Rome and Vienna airports by Palestinian terrorists which killed sixteen and injured 120.

So prevalent had these terrorist attacks become by the end of the year that there were tanks patrolling at Heathrow and the police on airport duty carried submachine guns.

There were also bombs left to explode on aircraft. On 23 June 1985, Shannon Air Traffic Control lost the transponder echo from an Air India 747 on a flight from

Montreal to Bombay via London. It suddenly disappeared from the screen at Flight Level 310 (31,000 feet), 150 miles south-west of Ireland.

No distress message was received. Nothing more was heard.

Also on 23 June 1985, forty minutes after a Canadian Pacific 747 carrying 390 passengers had landed from Vancouver at Narita airport, Japan, a bomb had exploded in a container loaded with cases from the plane, killing two baggage handlers.

So the first conjecture about the Air India aircraft coming from Canada was that there had also been a bomb on board. The other possibility was that there had been a sudden disastrous structural failure resulting in an immediate explosive decompression in the pressurised cabin. But the Air India 747 had only done 23,638 hours and 7,522 landings and would not have been considered elderly.

A massive sea search was organised, and the wreck was discovered on the sea bed at a depth of over 6,000 feet by an unmanned television-carrying submersible from the French cable-laying ship *Leon Theverin*. Its beacon was heard, uttering *ping* signals once a second. Bodies were found in the sea, giving no indication of having been affected by a bomb explosion. There had been 371 people on board, none of whom survived. Pieces of the aircraft, including the Flight Recorder, were brought up and taken to Cork for examination. Clearly there had been a sudden catastrophe, probably causing total electrical failure. This could have been caused by a bomb or by structural failure.

Then a report came out that Sikh terrorists had planted both the bombs on the Air Canada and Air India 747s. A passenger calling himself Singh had checked in a suitcase at Vancouver, saying he wanted the bag checked through Montreal, Toronto and Heathrow to Delhi on Air India Flight 182. The check-in assistant told him this could not be done, but when the waiting queue became restless, relented and told Singh to check with Air India at Toronto.

But he never boarded the flight to Toronto. The bag, however, was transferred to the security area at the terminal outside, where the Air India 747 was waiting. Two security officers were checking the bags, but before Singh's bag was examined, the X-ray machine broke down. So the bag was checked with a hand-held explosives sniffer. Apparently a day's training is needed on these machines, which work by detecting fumes from explosive devices. The security officer was apparently given only a demonstration by a senior, who lighted a match under the device which then let out a screaming sound.

When the security officer checked Singh's bag, it only let out a low bleep. So the bag was passed through and stored in the forward cargo compartment of the Air India 747. Apparently the security officer should have pressed the bag to get a sample of air from inside.

After the tragedy, the Canadian government tightened its security on all airports. Both the Indian and Canadian governments examined the wreckage and declared that the aircraft had disintegrated after the bomb had exploded in the nose of the aircraft.

On 14 July 1985, TWA Flight 847 left Athens for Rome. En route, two Lebanese Shia Moslem terrorists hijacked the 737 and forced the pilot to fly to Beirut airport. There passengers and crew were kept in the aircraft under threat of being blown up. One American serviceman was shot dead. There were continual comings and goings between the terrorists and their supporters to decide on further action to free Shi'ites held by the Israelis.

At times hysterical, at times anxious to please and explain their point of view, the terrorists went around with grenades in their hands. They forced Captain John Testrake to fly to Tunisia, then back to Beirut. Tired and
288

under continuing stress, Captain Testrake showed the most commendable courage, diplomacy and resource, as well as a life-saving sense of humour. When asked by Terry Wogan on BBC television what he thought about during those horrifying hours, he said he was lucky, much luckier than the passengers, because at least he had something to do to occupy himself. And when he'd levelled off after taking off yet again under pistol point, he remembered saying to himself, 'Well, you joined TWA because you always did say you wanted to fly.'

Eventually, with Syrian intervention, the thirty-nine passengers and crew on board were released on 30 July. Throughout their ordeal, they had been subjected to worldwide publicity by the media, when under gunpoint they expressed gratitude for their kind treatment by their captors and sympathy for their cause. Considerable anger was aroused that such action by the media was giving free advertisement and actual encouragement to terrorism.

Strong pressure was put internationally on isolating Beirut. The hijackers boarded at Athens airport, which came under considerable criticism for lax security. The boundary fence was incomplete, and other security lapses had been noted. More airport security was introduced worldwide to stop arms being smuggled aboard airliners. Glass fibre covering, it was said, would not hide a weapon from security radar – only heavy lead packing, which would make itself apparent to the body searchers.

Then as a reprisal against the murder of three Israelis on board a yacht in Cyprus, Israeli jets bombed the PLO headquarters in Tunisia. On 6 October 1985, four young students supporting the Palestinian cause hijacked the Italian cruise liner *Achille Lauro*, killing a 69-year-old American passenger. After negotiations, the four were flown out of Cairo on 11 October to go to Tunis. But on the way, the Egyptian 737 was intercepted by US F-14 fighters and forced to land at Sigorella in Sicily, a base shared by the Italians and the Americans.

The Palestinian Liberation Organisation claimed that this was air piracy. Egypt condemned both the ship hijacking and the American interception and Italy declared the hijackers would face an Italian court.

The same 737 was again in the news a month later when it was hijacked by Palestinians and forced to land at Malta. The Maltese government refused to refuel the aircraft, and the hijackers shot seven hostages, threatening to kill all the passengers and blow up the plane unless their demands were met. The US aircraft carrier *Coral Sea* was ordered to have F-18 fighter-bombers in readiness to protect C-130 transport planes carrying Egyptian commandos to Malta to liberate the passengers.

A bloody encounter resulted. Sixty people died, and only one of the hijackers survived. The PLO condemned the incident.

After the Christmas terrorist attacks at Rome and Vienna airports, the last twist in a horrific twelve months was when Israeli fighters forced a Tunisian airliner to land in Israel under the misapprehension that it was carrying known terrorists. In fact only Syrian politicians and diplomats were on board.

This upward trend in terrorism bodes ill for the future. What is additionally worrying is that governments are now committing similar acts to terrorists. Forcing down civil airliners on civil routes, no matter what the provocation, *is* an act of piracy. It was worse still when the French blew up the Greenpeace *Rainbow Warrior* in New Zealand and killed one of the crew.

The sad fact is that terrorism often springs from frustration, despair and injustice. Governments' illegal action may in turn spring from despair as to how to deal with it. But so many of these actions have relatively harmless, seemingly justifiable beginnings, such as the need to escape oppression, or smuggling (how many of us have smuggled in that extra pack of cigarettes, that odd extra bottle of wine, out of a sense that it was all rather harmless?).

Now we have international hijacking, international crime, international drug rings and smuggling – with governments as well as terrorists shooting down and forcing down aircraft. So to governments as to individuals, in the words of St Thomas Aquinas, 'Resist beginnings, all too late the cure.'

Since this was written, the Americans have not 'resisted beginnings'. As a result of a bomb attack on a Berlin disco which killed and injured American servicemen, a bomb outrage aboard a TWA airliner and numerous other terrorist acts, American Army and Navy planes bombed Tripoli and Benghazi in Libya, killing and wounding about a hundred people, including civilians, and using anti-personnel cluster bombs. An unspecified number of those aircraft were F-111s which took off from British airfields, with the Prime Minister's permission. The British public woke on 15 April 1986 to the news that they too were involved in the tightening spiral of terrorism. Yet economic sanctions had not yet been imposed by Britain against Libya. Libyan pilots and engineers are still allowed to train at Heathrow and Gatwick.

Pilots still call for boycotts against countries harbouring terrorists. International agreements against terrorists are not sufficiently pursued. And the core of the problem in the Middle East – the Palestinian question – is not tackled.

Protests and reprisals have followed the American attack. Two British teachers, Mr Leigh Douglas and Mr Philip Padfield, were murdered in Beirut; a pregnant Irish chambermaid was persuaded by her Jordanian boy friend to fly to Tel Aviv, where he would marry her. Due to the meticulous El Al security screening, a plastic bomb was found concealed under the false bottom of her holdall. The Jordanian who had accompanied her to the airport awaits trial in London. A bomb has exploded in

Oxford Street. Letters of protest have poured into Downing Street. There have been demonstrations all over Britain and Europe against the American attack.

And while the Common Market countries seek to take such measures as will placate America and avoid a repetition of their bombing attack, Britain and America are castigated by almost the entire world, and Americans stay away from Europe in their thousands, badly affecting airlines and the tourist trade. Terrorist attacks are also affecting tourists elsewhere. In May 1986, a bomb exploded at Colombo, Sri Lanka, killing several people – the product of another bloody battle, this time between Tamils and Sinhalese.

At the beginning of September 1986, a Pan Am 747 was hijacked and held at Karachi airport. Eventually the passengers were released by Pakistani commandos, but twenty were killed in the fight. Responsibility appeared to point to Colonel Qadhafi of Libya, but it is at present believed to be the work of the Abu Nidal Palestinian group of terrorists.

16
Be Your Own Weather Forecaster

Most passengers know from the television that those lines on the screen join places of equal pressure and are called isobars, that the wind follows the isobars clockwise round a High and anti-clockwise round a Low (opposite in the southern hemisphere), so why don't airlines tell their passengers more about the weather?

On holiday flights a Captain may tell the passengers that it's raining or is sunny at their destination. But why not something about the weather on the route and what to look out for, because the clouds themselves can be spectacular and their portents are easy to understand?

Clouds (see also Chapter 5) come as flat plains (*stratus*) or as cauliflower hills (*cumulus*). Their different heights are indicated by the addition of cirrus (*cirrocumulus, cirrostratus*) for high cloud from 18,000 to 50,000 feet, alto for medium cloud (*altostratus, altocumulus*) between 6,000 and 10,000 and without prefixes for lower cloud, except for rain clouds which are called *nimbostratus* and *cumulonimbus*. Cumulonimbus is the unpleasant bumpy cloud, full of rain, hail, snow and ice and towers up to the troposphere where it is cut off sharp to show its well-known anvil.

The wind blows the clouds around as though they were sailing ships. In altostratus and cirrus can be seen the long lines through which the wind has torn a path and they show wind direction. On the ground, smoke gives the same indication, and over the sea, the number of wave-tops and the way they break (*away* from the wind) arrow the wind direction and indicate its speed. The cause of wind is two-fold: cold air rushes to fill up the space caused by rising hot air, and the rotation of the earth exerts its own pressure on this movement and deflects it to the right in the northern hemisphere and to the left in the southern.

For that reason the greatest wind is the west wind. As Conrad says: 'There are no North and South Winds of any account upon the earth. The North and South Winds are but small princes in the dynasties that make peace and war upon the sea. They never assert themselves upon a vast stage. They depend upon local causes – the configuration of coasts, the shape of straits, the accidents of bold promontories round which they play their little part. In the polity of winds, as among the tribes of the earth, the real struggle lies between East and West.'

As we saw earlier, there are a great many local winds caused by the funnel effect of valleys and by rising dust or by circling and tightening air pressure and by cold and warm air 'warring'. Often from the centre of a pressure system on the telescreen can be seen emerging a line or 'front'. When warmer air is overtaking cold air, it is called a 'warm front', and when colder air is moving in, it is called a 'cold front'. When a cold front overtakes a warm front and embraces it, the resultant mix-up is called an 'occlusion'.

Such fronts have their own characteristics and cloud patterns. A warm front will give low cloud, mist and the 'small rain down may rain' of the poem about my love and the western wind. A cold front will give heavy rain, hail, thunder and lightning, but reasonable visibility underneath. A warm front is damp and sticky to fly through, smooth but foggy.

A vanguard of feathery cirrus at 30,000 feet gives the first indication of a warm front three or four hundred miles away.

The cloud lowers to cirrostratus, altostratus, nimbus – and it starts raining. A two- or three-hundred mile belt of

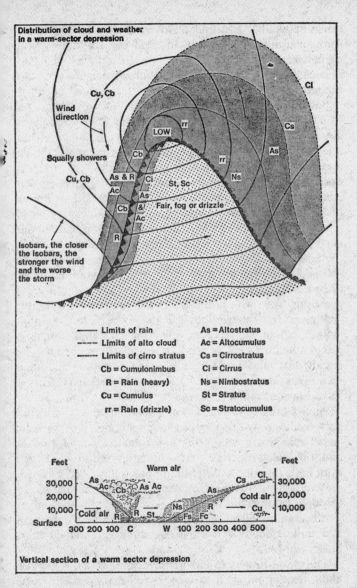

Distribution of cloud and weather in a warm-sector depression

Cu, Cb

Wind direction

Squally showers

Cu, Cb

As & R

Ac

Cb

R

Isobars, the closer the isobars, the stronger the wind and the worse the storm

Cb

Ci

As & Ac

St, Sc

Fair, fog or drizzle

LOW

rr

rr

Ns

As

Cs

Cl

—— Limits of rain

- - - Limits of alto cloud

-·-·- Limits of cirro stratus

Cb = Cumulonimbus

R = Rain (heavy)

Cu = Cumulus

rr = Rain (drizzle)

As = Altostratus

Ac = Altocumulus

Cs = Cirrostratus

Ci = Cirrus

Ns = Nimbostratus

St = Stratus

Sc = Stratocumulus

Feet

30,000

20,000

10,000

Surface

Warm air

As

Ac Cb As Ac

Cold air R R St

300 200 100 C

Ns

Fs Fc

W 100 200 300 400 500

As

Cs Ci

R

Cu

Cold air

Feet

30,000

20,000

10,000

Vertical section of a warm sector depression

295

low stratus and small rain follows. Then the air temperature suddenly rises. Except for mist hugging the ground, the cloud melts away.

But two hundred miles or so ahead may be seen the altocumulus and high cumulonimbus of a cold front. Heavy rain and turbulence occur inside it.

Then the temperature drops sharply. The visibility becomes very good and the cloud begins to dissipate.

Typhoons, hurricanes, dust-devils, depressions, tropical revolving storms, tornadoes and cyclones are basically local variations of such Lows and fronts, the violence of the winds increasing with the high temperature differentials of the air masses involved.

Some indication of where the Lows are can be obtained by Buys Ballot's Law. If your back is to the wind, low pressure will be on your left (right in the southern hemisphere), but the ground deflects the wind about 30° through friction.

Winds rise with altitude. Normally westerly in the northern hemisphere, they can reach speeds of 200 knots and more at the troposphere (around 38,000 feet in temperate zones). The very strong jet-streams are narrow bands of wind only a few miles wide, but their surrounds can cause clear air turbulence, when sudden violent air currents can affect the aircraft. Jet streams are almost invariably found in the cold air behind a cold front. They can easily be avoided by skirting such air masses or not approaching the troposphere height. Some pilots seek them out to get a tail wind, adding enormously to their speed.

Winds will affect your trip. The North Atlantic is dominated by a High over the Azores which moves north in summer, south in winter, and by the resultant westerly winds. The head component (the amount of headwind in knots that decreases the aircraft's groundspeed) of a Jumbo's cruising altitude will average 60 knots, adding an hour to the westerly crossing in the winter and forty

296

minutes in the summer. Eastbound trips will be almost that much faster.

Winds are westerly in the Mediterranean; on the trip to Australia, you can expect a +25 knot component to the Middle East and up to +60 knots from there to Calcutta, till the monsoon arrives in July. From there to Rangoon, the tail wind lessens. For the rest of the route to Darwin, the winds are usually easterlies, though the component is small.

The South Africa route is dominated by the Inter Tropical Front which moves from north of Khartoum in July to south of Salisbury in January. Bad weather can often be seen coming hundreds of miles before it arrives. Haloes round the moon or the sun show that they are covered by the high cirrus of an approaching front.

Thunderstorms will occur over hot land masses, far more rarely over the sea. Local winds can be predicted at certain times: the hot Khamsin over Egypt in spring, the Mistral from the north down the Rhône valley in the winter, the Haboub blowing up the sand in the Sudan five days a month from May to July (see also p. 123).

Sky lore helps. 'Red sky in the morning, shepherds' warning' – a rosy dawn often gets its colour from frontal stratus. Broken cumulus is more likely to give the red colouring to the sun sinking in the west. Hence 'shepherds' delight'.

'Long notice, long past, short notice, soon past' is usually reliable. A sudden quick shower will soon go. If due warning has been given by cloud patterns for hundreds of miles, the bad weather will persist.

'Out of the blue' is a phrase originating in the fact that winter radiation fog forms very fast out of a clear sky. There is also a Japanese saying, 'When the sky is blue, Fuji is angry', referring to the dangerously high winds that tear the cloud on the mountain's slope to pieces.

'Backing is a bad sign' simply refers to the wind changing direction to move anti-clockwise. Under Buys

Ballot's Law, this means that the low pressure area is to the left, and in the northern hemisphere will be approaching from the west.

'Too cold to snow' refers to the fact that really cold air does not contain enough moisture to produce snowflakes.

It is better, of course, to rely on professional forecasting which has made enormous strides in forty years. This is particularly so in relation to upper air winds, which used to be unknown. Once again, it was the needs of war that spurred the development of weather forecasting. Radiosonde balloons were sent up that bleeped information on weather. The latest development is satellite pictures.

Meteorological readings are taken all over the world, small clues that fill in the total face of the weather. The radio telegraph sending this data off immediately was the first necessary stepping-stone in achieving a world weather map. For meteorology, like aviation, must know no boundaries. It must be international.

Nowhere is this better illustrated than by the enemy meteorological flights of the last war. Twice a day, two JU88s full of meteorological equipment and with meteorologists on board would leave occupied Norway and head out west, sending back readings by radio.

The RAF referred to the morning one as 'The Atlantic Mail' and the afternoon one as 'Weather Willie'. Their pilots must have thought they had charmed lives. For in spite of being continually intercepted by Spitfires from the squadrons based on Orkney, they always managed to evade them. The fighter boys eyed them longingly, but let them go.

The reason was simple enough. The German code on their wireless signals had been broken, and the JU88s provided the British with invaluable meteorological information to make up their Atlantic weather charts. The Spitfire pilots were under strict orders *never* to attack.

* * *

Weather has always been among the first suspects when an aircraft crashes. The worst offender used to be fog and low cloud, but neither these days is so dangerous, because of both improved landing and particularly the introduction of automatic landing.

On 10 June 1965 a British Trident landed at Heathrow under full automatic control. The pilots did nothing. This British pioneering was taken up all over the world, so that now most modern airliners and airports are fitted with the necessary equipment.

Aircraft can be landed automatically in nil visibility, but as a safety precaution weather limits are imposed of 50 feet cloudbase and 220 yards visibility (called Category III limits).

Turbulence has always been a potential killer, but for many years this was only associated with storms and big cumulonimbus build-ups. Only in the last twenty years has a phenomenon called Clear Air Turbulence (CAT) really become recognised as we saw in chapter 10.

Formerly pilots could apparently avoid turbulence by seeing the clouds and avoiding them, but then it was discovered that dangerous turbulence could be encountered at high altitudes around 35,000 feet in complete clear air. Two weather systems side by side may produce opposing winds, and there can exist a narrow jet-stream corridor between them in which there are hurricane-speed winds and violent turbulence.

Potential CAT is forecast on weather charts given to pilots, but inevitably on occasion some areas are missed. Some warning is usually given in a sudden onset of turbulence for which there is no other explanation than CAT, and the pilot turns away.

Ice used to be another killer. Aircraft could become encased in ice, spoiling their aerodynamic qualities and forcing them down by sheer weight. It was supposed that ice accumulated only at temperatures around freezing, but after the discovery of super-cooled raindrops, that is unfrozen rain at low temperatures, it was realised that ice could form at hitherto unsuspected temperatures.

The new weather hazards that have reared their ugly heads are wind shear and what are called microbursts. Thunderstorms were always considered dangerous and caused a number of take-off and landing accidents. But now wind shear has caused at least six accidents or serious incidents, including Pan Am Flight 759 which crashed at New Orleans with the loss of 153 lives.

Wind shear causes winds to change direction and speed, turning headwinds into which aircraft are flying into tailwinds, thus suddenly reducing airspeed below stalling; and they are frequently associated with microbursts, or mini-storms. The danger from a microburst is that air moving downwards from cumulonimbus bounces off the ground and radiates in all directions.

On 1 August 1983 Air Force 1, with the US President aboard, landed at Andrews Air Base, Washington. Five minutes later a huge weather build-up appeared on the radar, and microburst winds gusted to 130 knots, with a wind relativity maximum of 50 knots, a lethal wind shear for landing. The disturbance swept over the airfield in three minutes.

On 2 August 1985 a Delta Airways Tristar crashed at Dallas Fort Worth airport, killing 134. The FAA attributed the accident to wind shear, and increased the number of airfield perimeter wind-shear sensors from 5 to 14.

Research has been undertaken and Boeing are presently working on an electronic attitude director indicator, which will present the correct attitudes to survive wind shear, thus enabling pilots to overcome adverse effects of rapid loss of airspeed during take-off and landing.

Pilots are given a microburst on the simulator to show them what they might have to cope with, resulting in not a few 'crashes'. There is also a Wind Shear Warning: an amber light on the panel and a voice calling 'Wind shear!'

It is believed that eventually wind shear and microburst detection will be carried out by Doppler weather radar. Currents moving away from the radar screen appear red or yellow. The danger is a purple patch that indicates wind shear.

17
Controlling the Traffic

A small piece of thin white card, six inches long and one inch wide, is the mainstay of Air Traffic Control. It has always been, ever since Flying Control (as it was called until the end of the Second World War) began in the 1930s. It is called the flight progress strip.

It is produced by the BM 9020D computer half an hour before departure, after the captain files his flight plan and the controller has considered other aircraft movements; it emerges from a metal dispenser like a ticket in numerous airport offices.

On the Outbound strip is estimated time of departure, actual time of departure, requested flight level, type of aircraft, call-sign, time requested clearance, time given clearance, route and destination airport, air traffic control clearance, flight level given and control instructions.

On the Inbound strip is aircraft's estimate for the destination radar beacon, altitude instructions, departure airport, aircraft call-sign, type of aircraft, estimated time of arrival and control Flight Level instructions.

This strip is still the basis of air traffic control today, though in the future with more computers it is possible that electronic data displays may replace the flight progress strip.

The Civil Aviation Authority (CAA) was founded in 1972, and looks after both civil and military aircraft, using hundreds of navigational beacons, radars, landing aids and a wide communication network. The controllers are civil servants and their terms of employment are as such. Over Britain, they control a protected airspace containing airways which are corridors ten miles wide extending from 5,000 to 24,500 feet long.

Everyone flying in that airspace has to be a licensed pilot flying a certified aircraft equipped with specific navigational and communication equipment. In it are also aerodromes and terminal areas containing main airports like Birmingham and London, round which there are control zones. Above 24,500 up to 66,000 feet, civil and military aircraft also have a full air traffic control service. Aircraft are separated from each other on airways vertically by 1,000 feet and horizontally by a minimum of 5 miles when radar is being used.

The wishes of the Captain regarding route and height through this protected sky are passed to the controller for that airspace at the Air Traffic Control Centre (at Heathrow it is at West Drayton). Other requests will have been received from aircraft both coming in to London and going out of it. The outward Captain will certainly want to make use of pressure patterns giving him more favourable winds. But so will all the other aircraft Captains, and since at any one time there can be as many as seventy aircraft over that part of the Atlantic, this outbound Captain may not get his choice. There are six main lanes over the Atlantic and some are longer than others. It may be that a Captain will have to take not only a longer route but also a different height.

An Atlantic flight's progress strip will be dispensed to forty offices, the three most important of which will be the airport Control Tower, Approach Control and the main Operations Room of the Air Traffic Control Centre, from which it will be passed to the sector controlling Green 1, the trans-Atlantic airway.

In Britain, the Tower controllers usually work three shifts: 07.30–14.00, 14.00–22.00, 22.00 to 07.30, each with an hour's break for a meal or a rest. In particularly busy control rooms, the period before a rest is shorter, for it is an extremely busy and taxing job. In bad weather,

303

total concentration and alertness are needed, together with flexibility and quickness; at the same time the controller must maintain an unruffled calm and always speak in a reassuring voice.

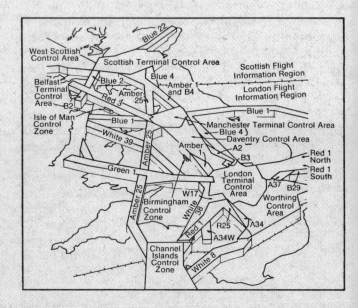

All the controllers can take over any of the positions. The most difficult is probably the number one radar director's, the most high-loaded the ground movement controller's.

Since jets use a great deal of fuel even taxiing, the ground movement controller will not give clearance to start up if there is any likelihood of too great a queue waiting to take off, or too much traffic *en route* that other controllers wish to filter down. Many passengers, kept waiting in the cabin after scheduled departure time, blame the airline for inefficiency. The delay is often due simply to the over-concentration of traffic. If the aircraft did not

304

wait on the departure airport, it would have to wait elsewhere *en route* – and the thinning down is simply a safety precaution. It is difficult to understand why the Captain does not explain it on his public address system, which he rarely seems to do.

The ground movement controller gives clearance to start engines, but since the pilots cannot see behind them, he has also, where necessary, to give clearance for 'pushback' to aircraft nosed into parking stalls. He then gives clearance along the taxiway, at the same time clearing aircraft which have landed to their piers and stalls. He may have as many as two dozen aircraft which he is looking after at one time, inbound and outbound, and the whole thing becomes a fearsome game of chess, playing both black and white at the same time.

Though queues form to take off, the aircraft will not necessarily leave in strict rotation or first-come-first-served order. The controllers have to cope with different aircraft with different speeds from 150 to 450 knots. To get a proper separation balance, the controller may give clearance to faster or slower aircraft to take off before previous aircraft – an apparent injustice which is rarely explained by the Captain to the passengers.

In the Tower, in the darkened Approach Control and in the Air Traffic Control Centre, the flight progress strip is given a plastic holder with a yellow band for eastbound and blue band for westbound. It now resembles a relay runner's baton to be passed on down the line. In a sense, that is what it is, though now it has been slotted in with others underneath the radar sets the whole lot resemble a string of sausages.

The Tower then gives the aircraft's airways clearance to guide it up through incoming traffic on the VHF. In the old days, this was a fearsome business because it was hard for pilots to understand some voices (particularly American) issuing long and complicated briefings, and almost impossible to repeat the clearance back, word for word, as they had to do.

Now the pilots get a Standard Instrument Departure; these charts are published in the *Air Pilot*. Instead of the tongue-twister 'Straight ahead until 1-GG DME 4, then turn left to intercept DET VOR R265. Follow DET VOR RO 73. At SAM DME 20, turn right to intercept GWC VOR R 337 to Kenet. Squawk Ident 6261', the pilot is given 'Kenet One Papa. Squawk Ident 6261.'

The squawk ident is a form of secondary surveillance radar. During the Second World War, because it was necessary to differentiate between friend and foe, a device was invented called Identification of Friendly Forces (IFF). This was a radio device in the aircraft that responded (it was called a transponder) to radar signals it received, enlarging the blip on the radar screen and giving it a sort of halo. So a friend was identified.

It was also used as a distress device. I was once doing trials at 300 feet over the Irish Sea in a heavily aerialled Whitley. The only other crew was a scientist (called a boffin by the RAF). The starboard engine failed, and we gradually lost height till we ditched. The total emergency procedure we did was to put the IFF to the 'distress' position. Even though we were low down, this registered on the Navy's radar screen at Milford Haven, and within a very short time a trawler came to pick us up.

The squawk ident grew out of the IFF. The squawk ident number is selected in the aircraft. A line called a scan goes round the radar screen like a quick hand of a clock, normally burnishing up the aircraft blips with a little orange fizz.

But for identification, the controller can switch on the identification switch on the radar. Immediately beside each blip appears the call sign of each aircraft from its individual flight progress strip. Also registered is the height. For the aircraft's height is transmitted again by
306

secondary surveillance radar from the reading on the altimeter in the aircraft.

The radars have rings round them for distance, and can be adjusted to 10-mile, 50-mile or 100-mile scans. Beside the controllers, if there is a military flight crossing airways, there will be an RAF controller sitting at the London Control Centre who literally nursemaids his 'baby' (which might be a Phantom fighter), talking him safely through each airway and height in consultation with the civil controller.

Approach Control is in charge of an aircraft as it climbs up, separated from incoming and other outgoing aircraft till it is well away from London, when it is told to contact the Air Traffic Control Centre at West Drayton. The pilots call up and report. The flight progress strips of the tower and Approach Control, having reached the bottom of their respective sausage machines, are thrown away.

The baton is now being held by the Air Traffic Control Centre (located in Britain at West Drayton). Over four hundred experienced controllers work here, being fed radar information from six civil stations as well as military ones. As cadets, these men have to take their private pilot's licence, and keep it up at CAA expense, since it is essential that they should know what it 'feels like' to be in charge of an aircraft. They also have to know the operating techniques of many different aircraft.

The flight progress strip remains on the ATCC sausage machines while the pilots report over successive radio beacons, gradually working its way down the desk as other aircraft follow it. Meanwhile into the airspace it has vacated, incoming aircraft are cleared to descend.

At Shannon, the baton is taken over by Shanwick Control located at Prestwick, where the flight progress strip again works its way down the sausage machine as the aircraft flies west across the Atlantic.

All the time, its progress is being monitored. Every hour the aircraft reports its height and position on VHF. Every half-hour, a weather report is sent to it. Notams (notices to airmen) which are regularly issued will have been read by the pilots before take-off, but any new ones will be transmitted in flight.

A 24-hour radar and radio emergency watch is maintained at the Air Traffic Control Centre, ready to alert all the emergency services on the world distress frequency at the first sign of any trouble anywhere.

In the old days, because there were so many intertwined flight paths of aircraft (there are now 120,000 big jet crossings a year as well as a large number of propeller aircraft trips), the Atlantic was referred to in Air Traffic Control circles as 'a bucket of worms'. Then there was no obligation to stay on the planned route and ATC's job became increasingly difficult as one or more aircraft 'followed its nose'.

Now with the daily track structure, aircraft fly virtually along tramlines and are not allowed to deviate without permission. Though there may be as many as fifty big jets over the Atlantic at one time, it is unlikely that – as often happens in ships – passengers in one will ever catch sight of another one. A huge buffer of airspace is wrapped round each aircraft. The nearest aircraft at the same height will be 60 miles away on the International Navigation System.

At longitude 30° West, the baton changes hands again. This time the flight progress strip is taken over and looked after by Gander Oceanic Control, till it nears the New York Flight Information region where the American Air Traffic Control takes over the baton and the outbound process will be repeated but in reverse.

Radars will have located the aircraft 200 miles away from the coast. (In line with the fail-safe policy of almost everything in civil aviation, the aerials are duplicated in case one set fails.) At every sweep of the aerials, the aircraft's position, height and identifying number are transmitted over Post Office lines back to the ATCC in a single digital message. There are limitations – low flying and high-speed climbs will not be picked up by radar.
308

This information is computer processed. It is then stored and gradually fed on to the video maps (rather like television screens) in front of the controllers. The pilot is requested to 'Squawk ident', and he switches on his secondary surveillance radar identification. So there is available to the controller on the screen at the Centre the aircraft's identity and its height.

As the aircraft gradually gets closer to its destination, it is in communication by VHF with the controller, who clears it to descend, all the time watching out for the other blips on his screen till he passes the baton on to Approach Control.

Approach Control sees that the outgoing aircraft have a traffic-free path away and brings the incoming aircraft down, positioning each of them, safely separated, for a landing.

In a fog this may well mean going to one of the 'holding points' or 'stacks'. Bohemia is the main New York stack. In the London Flight Information Region, FIR, there are four, serving each 90° quadrant of the compass – Ockham, Bovingdon, Lambourne and Biggin. Incoming Atlantic traffic go to Ockham, usually to the top of the stack at 13,000 feet. There the aircraft fly a clockwise race-track pattern (the passengers will simply be aware of the aircraft going round and round), being cleared at three-minute intervals to descend to the next 1,000-foot level.

In London Approach, there are four radar screens. Normally only two stacks are used at one time and the extreme left and right screens are manned by controllers watching one of these. One of the middle screens is reserve, one is manned by the controller with the most difficult operation.

His job is to coordinate the two stacks, taking aircraft off each and putting them into a single stream to position them to make an approach to the runway. The flight progress strip is still in front of him, working its way down with the others, till the aircraft is cleared from the bottom of the stack and positioned by radar to make an ILS approach.

In the course of the Atlantic crossing, the flight progress strip will have been handed on like a baton to be guarded by eight controllers. The pilots will be continually talking to the ground right the way across. Ten radar stations will have picked up the aircraft and for most of the 3,500-mile crossing, its blip containing identity position and height will be on the ATC radar system.

No other form of transport is looked after so well and so continuously. *Viatores coeli tutare* is the London motto – looking after the travellers in the sky. In spite of the enormous amount of traffic, there have never been any collisions in the London area or over the Atlantic. The collision risk nevertheless is the big Air Traffic Control fear. Airliner collisions average around four a year, mainly in the USA where nearly a quarter of a million light aircraft invade the airspace.

The American ATC has a computerised 'conflict alert' system which spots two aircraft on collision courses. A buzzer sounds and CA (Conflict Alert) and identification of the two aircraft flash on the radar screens when they are within 400 feet vertically and 1.2 nautical miles horizontally from each other. The trouble is that in very busy centres, like West Drayton, several hundred aircraft may be operating and the buzzer may be sounding all the time. American controllers (like aircraft Captains with their warnings) have been known to shut it off.

Air misses continue to be worrying. The FAA ordered an investigation after a dramatic rise in near-collisions in 1984. The final total in the USA was 592.

The FAA found that 'air miss' was not adequately defined, and suggested that the definition should be when two aircraft pass within 500 feet of each other or when the proximity of another plane makes the pilot feel in danger.

In Britain, a Joint Air Miss Committee examines each
310

case. There was an incident when an RAF Puma helicopter was taking the Prime Minister Margaret Thatcher to Heathrow from Odiham to board a VC 10 for the USA. As it approached the take-off runway a British Airways 757 was cleared to take off. The civil pilot quickly aborted. The RAF said that there was no problem and no risk.

Reported air misses are categorised C (no risk), B (possible risk) and A (definite risk). But incidents are difficult to assess because judgement of distance is so individual.

If a controller is involved, the first investigation is done by his unit, who may suspend him or her (there have been female controllers for twenty years). Then an outside unit looks at the incident and makes a recommendation to the CAA.

The universal language of the air is English. There has been no serious opposition to it, though sometimes French pilots have a Speak-French-Only-on-the-RT day in protest. But they give due warning and they are dealt with by a French-speaking controller.

The phonetic alphabet has changed since the Second World War. Now it is:

	Morse	
A	·—	Alfa
B	—···	Bravo
C	—·—·	Charlie
D	—··	Delta
E	·	Echo
F	··—·	Foxtrot
G	——·	Golf
H	····	Hotel
I	··	India
J	·———	Juliett

K	—·—	Kilo
L	·—··	Lima
M	——	Mike
N	—·	November
O	———	Oscar
P	·——·	Papa
Q	——·—	Quebec
R	·—·	Romeo
S	···	Sierra
T	—	Tango
U	··—	Uniform
V	···—	Victor
W	·——	Whiskey
X	—··—	X-ray
Y	—·——	Yankee
Z	——··	Zulu

The reason for the change was given as being that pilots with English as a foreign language could say the words more easily and clearly. English boy's names took a battering. Gone are Edward, Freddie, Harry, Johnny, Peter, Tommy and William. Roger (still retained on its own as meaning 'received') has given way to Romeo. One misses his sidekick, poor Queenie, the only girl's name in the old phonetic alphabet. Her place as sole female representative has been taken by Juliett (with two ts) and at a decent distance from Romeo. Yankee and Zulu I can never have quite the same feeling for as Yorker and Zebra.

There is a particular airlines vocabulary that adds to the mystique of flying. Most people know that George is the automatic pilot. But many people get hold of part of a word like Mach and reckon they understand it. Mach 1 is the speed of sound, named after Dr Mach, who related the angle of a bullet's shock wave to the velocity of sound, and is around 760 mph at sea level. But it varies with altitude, losing 100 mph up to 35,000 feet, after which it remains constant. The Mach number is the true airspeed of the aircraft (indicated airspeed on the ASI also drops off with height) divided by the speed of sound at its altitude. A Jumbo will cruise at approximately 35,000 feet at a cruising speed of 580 mph, which is around Mach 0.88, and this is what will show on the ASI and what the pilot will fly on close to the sound barrier.

But the 'sound barrier' is not the 'barrier' of popular folklore – as we have seen earlier on p. 266. A fast aircraft catches up with its own sound waves and flies into a build-up of sound and pressure waves which produces shock waves. This compressed air subjects the aircraft to pressure changes that cause turbulence, drag and change of trim. So the pilot has a warning – a horn blast – when his aircraft is approaching this area. Concorde has a specially designed wing and the only way the pilot can tell he has gone through the 'sound barrier' is by his machmeter.

ETA is estimated time of arrival, ATA the actual time. A is changed to D for departure. Pilots talk in initials; IAS is Indicated Air Speed; ASI is Air Speed Indicator; QFE is pressure at sea level; QNH is pressure at aerodrome level (both the latter are set on the altimeter after the figures in millibars have been passed from the ground). ILS is Instrument Landing System; VFR is Visual Flight Rules (five miles visibility, 1,000 feet vertically from cloud and one mile horizontally). Below those weather conditions is IFR – Instrument Flight Rules. A major cause of aircraft accidents is the continuing of a supposedly VFR flight into IFR conditions.

CAVU is Ceiling and Visibility Unlimited; TOC is Top of the Climb; 500 on top is 500 feet above the cloud tops. Charlie Bravo is cumulonimbus cloud; slant visibility is what the pilot can see on the glide-path to the runway – it can be totally different from vertical visibility. From straight overhead a whole aerodrome can frequently be seen in the winter which becomes totally invisible on the

313

approach. RVR is Runway Visual Range which is passed to the pilot by the Tower before landing. It has to give a visibility above 'Company limits', which are minimum weather conditions for each runway. Below them, the Captain has to divert to his 'alternate' – the reserve airport, for which he carries sufficient fuel. Hurn, Manchester and Prestwick are the London airports' alternates. There is reportedly no known case of a civil airliner running out of fuel before it could reach its alternate, and the chances of the alternate's weather also being too bad to land are around a million to one against.

Before a Captain departs, he collects TAFs (Terminal Area Forecasts), METARS (Meteorological Aerodrome Reports) for terminal and alternates, a significant weather chart together with forecast winds and temperatures at various levels up to FL (Flight Level in hundreds of feet) 400 (40,000 feet), and SIGMETS (Significant Meteorological Conditions). The altimeter setting of his destination has to be put on the millibar scale of his altimeter.

Parts of his weather chart will be marked CAT (Clear Air Turbulence), which can be very turbulent and cause damage to aircraft – and does not show up on the aircraft's weather radar. During the flight VOLMETS (actual weather conditions at airports) are passed to the aircraft over the R/T (radio-telephone). Notams are kept up to date – danger areas, new developments, techniques and instructions.

No-shows are pax (passenger) who do not appear before take-off. A slip is where the incoming crew get off to rest and a new crew takes over.

Angle of attack is the angle the wing makes to the horizontal. Too small and there may be insufficient for lift-off. Too big and drag will stop airspeed building up or produce eddies that reduce lift and stall the wing. G stands for gravity – what you feel in the small of your back as the aircraft accelerates down the runway, only a little more than the 1G that holds your body to the earth
314

in an upright position. Acceleration to 2G and for a short time you have to cope with twice your weight. This might just possibly happen in very severe turbulence. Prone, you can stand very high G, but sitting, the blood will either be drawn down from your brain and cause a blackout or, if the pressure is in the opposite direction, a redout. 5G is a pressure that applies only to fighter pilots and even so they can withstand it for only around thirty seconds.

'Gear (undercarriage) up' is indicated by three red lights and a short time later the captain is flying a 'clean aeroplane' (flaps and undercarriage up). Yaw is moving port (left) or starboard (right). Roll is when the aircraft tips port or starboard. Pitch is attitude up or down.

Coming down, the aircraft is cleared from the Holding Pattern to the circuit of the airport. If the weather is good, it may be cleared Straight In (no circuit). On the circuit it is first Downwind (180° to the runway in use). There the crew do their Field Approach Check.

Base Leg is when the captain turns 90° to line up for an approach and intercepts the ILS (Instrument Landing System) beacon. VASI is the visual approach slope indicator that gives him a visual indication that he is 'in the slot' (on the glide-path). 'On finals' is in line with the runway, and the aircraft is cleared 'Number One' (next to land). As it approaches the green threshold lights, the captain initiates the 'flare' – pulling back on the stick to arrest the descent. As the wheels touch, up from the top of the wings come the 'spoilers', spoiling the lift and slowing the aircraft. These have been activated in the air, precipitating accidents. In some jets they can be used in the air to slow the aircraft or for a very steep emergency descent. In a 747 they are auto-activated and the Flight Engineer monitors that they are working. He also monitors the auto-brake system which brakes the 747 automatically. A warning light comes on if the system is disarmed and normal human foot pressure has to be used.

REIL are the red runway end identification lights. Missed Approach is when the engines are opened up and the aircraft goes round again – a rare but rather frightening experience for the passengers, especially if it is initiated low down. 'Touch and Go' is a quick pilot training technique – it means touching down and then immediately opening up and taking-off again, 'cleaning up' the aeroplane at the same time.

Landing has always been something special for a pilot. A good landing leaves him happy, a bad landing worries him. When aircraft had tail wheels at the beginning of the war, they could bounce 'as high as a house' – very frightening, especially as the speed was shed at the same time. But then real 'daisy-cutters' could be brought off – landings so smooth that you didn't know you were down. 'Like a cat pissing on glass' was another description of a propeller-driven aircraft hanging on its props so as to kiss the runway quite imperceptibly.

A 747 comes down on the approach with its nose held high. A bad landing is one in which it hits the runway hard – but it stays there. Almost all landings now are pretty good but a bit rumbly. The expression 'greasing them on', still remains (it means a landing you can't feel), but British Airways specifically forbid Captains to allow the 747 to float and to strive for 'greased' landings, since the landing run might be dangerously increased.

Everybody knows they're down. Daisy-cutters, like the grass aerodromes that grew them, have gone into history.

There is in addition a 'speechless' code mainly used by military pilots in case of bad speech distortion or unserviceable equipment. This presupposes that the pilot can hear the ground. He presses his transmit button one short for Yes, two short for No, three short for Say Again, four short for Request Homing.

The standard of two-way communication between aircraft and ground is exceptionally high. All sorts of different nationalities speaking many different native

316

languages fly the world's air routes and all must speak English. In some South American countries, there are sometimes problems away from the main cities, but on the trunk routes of the world, the only big communication difficulty was when the Russian Aeroflot used to carry interpreters. There was then a delay while the instructions were interpreted to the pilots – but the Aeroflot pilots' English is now improved and interpreters are no longer carried.

Clearly the controllers carry a great deal of responsibility for the safety of the aircraft. As flying becomes more computerised and automatic and radar separation and landing devices more sophisticated, inevitably the question will be posed . . . whose is the ultimate responsibility?

As with pilots, the errors made in ATC are mainly human ones. An analysis of American ATC systems errors put 55 per cent down to judgment, 22 per cent to communications, 19 per cent to attention, 0.6 per cent each to procedures and operations management. This made a total of 97.2 per cent human against 2.8 per cent machine.

British and American airliners have mandatory cockpit voice recorders (CVRs) registering everything spoken on the flight deck. There is talk of a television scan and a video-tape recording of everything the crew do during a trip, but so far this has not been introduced.

There are already the Flight Data Recorders. These are the little black boxes (actually red) in which all speeds and movements and manoeuvres are registered on wire tape. Bad landings, procedure irregularities, poor flying techniques are all therefore preserved.

It has been agreed with the pilots' association that these should be anonymous. Even so, such measures have not unnaturally been resisted by some pilots as being too reminiscent of Big Brother. Captains are required to fill in mandatory occurrence reports (MORs) of anything

317

untoward happening on the flight, including any mistakes that might be made on the flight deck and any too close encounters with other aircraft.

The Captain signs for everything: at present it is all his responsibility. But with the increase of automation he is becoming more a systems manager. It is the men on the ground who have the full picture of all the latest weather and aircraft information and who in effect direct the flight.

After a Pan American 707 crashed twenty-odd years ago near Elkton, USA, in very bad weather, there was a move to give traffic controllers power to bar flights if weather conditions looked unfavourable along the route. Questions were asked about why the plane had not waited in Baltimore where the flight originated.

The airlines strongly resisted the proposal. The Chief Pilot said, 'Aircraft can be flown through heavy rain or snow, frontal conditions or turbulence, with equivalent safety to other conditions of operation, although normal operating procedures call for the avoidance of such conditions to the extent practical. Flight is not less safe in bad weather. Just different procedures and techniques are used.'

But just as the 'Captain Almighty' concept has given way to that of a crew combined operation, so now it is realised that the whole flight is a combined operation in which men on the ground and the men in the air share the combined responsibility and the combined kudos for the safe operation of the world's airlines.

18
The Happy Landing

On descent to his destination, the pilot is passed down the Control line in reverse order to when he took off.

The Air Traffic Control Centre pick him up and give him clearance to descend. He is then cleared to a place in the holding stack. His estimated time of arrival (ETA) and his dock number will also be watched by Tele-move, which monitors all inbound frequencies. At Heathrow, this is located in the Tower. Strips are produced giving details of the aircraft and flight number, expected approach to land clearance, whether there is a VIP on board, and gate number. This information ticker tapes out to the airline and all services required to meet it and turn the aircraft round. Gatwick movements are more modern and radar equipped.

As he reaches the bottom of the holding stack, the Captain transfers to Approach Control to be given his landing weather, Runway Visual Range (RVR), and to be led in to land.

The Runway Visual Range (RVR) is the pilot's visibility when he pulls back the aircraft to become level with the runway. RVR used to be done simply by an observer. Now it is done by instruments. At three positions – touchdown, mid-point and stop, boxes like Daleks' heads project a beam to a reflector twenty metres away. This beam is bounced back, and the Dalek will measure the attenuation suffered in those forty yards by means of a built-in computer. A reading in 50-metre calibrations is then transmitted electronically to an automatic read-out in the Tower.

The machine is sometimes too sensitive. The black smoke from a jet taking off could easily be seen to be nothing by an observer. But the instrument faithfully reports almost impenetrable fog – and no aircraft can land until the smoke has dispersed and an RVR above limits can be obtained.

For aircraft have weather limits for landing. Category II is what most pilots operate to on good airports with ILS. That is 100 feet cloud base, 440 yards visibility. Category III is less than half that and is only used for automatic landings. These in effect make flying impervious to the weather. Aircraft can be landed in totally blind conditions.

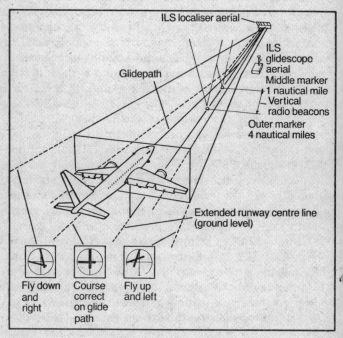

Three auto-pilots connected to the ILS carry out the auto-land. If he is landing in bad night weather on runway Zero Four (043 is the magnetic heading of the runway) at Kennedy, the Captain will be brought down to the bottom of the Bohemia stack by Approach Control, given Number One to land and brought by radar towards the ILS.

The First Officer sets the course selector of the auto-land to 043 and tunes the Automatic Direction Finder to the Outer Marker Beacon. The Flight Engineer officer calls out the Approach Check. The undercarriage is lowered. Instead of three red lights, three green lights appear on the console between the pilots – all wheels down and locked. Speed is reduced to 220 knots with 5° flap.

Gradually, the aircraft is brought lower and placed on the extended centreline of the runway. The Captain moves the auto-pilot mode selector from Heading to Land. B and C auto-pilots are engaged, so now *three* auto-pilots are monitoring each other. The chances of a mistake being made are millions to one against.

The aircraft begins turning to starboard to catch the ILS beam. Now the indicator shows the localiser beam central, and the auto-land 'captures' it on 043.

The First Officer calls, 'Nav green!'

Slowly, the glide slope descends on the indicator and is captured in the centre. The auto-pilots and the auto-throttles are now locked on the descent. The Captain's left hand is poised over the auto-pilot/auto-throttle disconnect button on the left-hand spectacle of the control column. His right hand rests lightly on the four throttles.

The First Officer calls, '1,000 feet! No Flags! Landing Flap set!' The needle on the ADF turns right round. 'Over the Outer Marker!'

Controlled by the auto-land, steadily the 747 descends at 600 feet a minute. Nothing can be seen outside, except black rain streaming down the windscreen. The throttles make tiny movements backwards and forwards, keeping

321

the speed at 140 knots. The aileron control moves to starboard as it picks up the port wing caught in a gust.

The altimeter reading is 600 feet. There is still no sign of the ground outside. An amber light flashing on the instrument panel indicates the Middle Marker.

300 . . . 250 . . . the altimeter needle is still unwinding. At 200 feet there is a faint glimmer of a lead-in light.

'100 decision!' calls the First Officer.

Now wisps of dark mist stream over the wing as though the leading edge is cutting the cloud to ribbons. A line of muzzy green lights marks the runway threshold.

'Decision height, sir!'

'Continuing.'

The degree of braking required has been selected on the automatic speed brakes. At fifty feet a green light glows on the auto-land.

'Flare green!'

The nose is lifting for the flare-out. Like great yellow blobs of wet flak, the runway lights can now be seen coming up on either side. Up and up comes the Jumbo to a 4° angle of attack to achieve maximum drag.

The throttles close with a decisive click. The sixteen main wheels touch. The two nose wheels connect. The aircraft is down.

The Captain presses the button and disengages the auto-land. He puts reverse thrust on the engines. Rapidly, the Jumbo decelerates to a jog-trot, and angles off the runway on to the taxi-track.

Flarepath was the name given to the lighted runway for returning night bombers. Since that time lighting has been further refined so that not only is the pilot led to the runway, but all sorts of other information necessary for landing safely is fed to him.

An Englishman called Calvert developed aerodrome lighting into a science. He studied how a pilot uses visual signals on the ground to help him land and produced the 'parafoveal streamer theory'.

If a person is in motion in a straight line to a point X in a pattern of visual signals, all other points in the vicinity appear to stream radially away from the point X. Once in the signal pattern it is as though he is sucked towards X.

In the Calvert system, point X is the aircraft touchdown point. The pilot adjusts his approach so that the lights appear to stream past steadily and symmetrically, If he drifts to the left or the right, the light pattern becomes immediately displaced. As the pilot in the centre of the pattern concentrates on X, he will be getting lower, and the lights will start streaming past him faster, telling him his rate of descent. The eye, being highly sensitive to the motion of objects in the periphery of the visual field, quickly detects small departures from symmetry.

Visual Approach
Slope Indicator

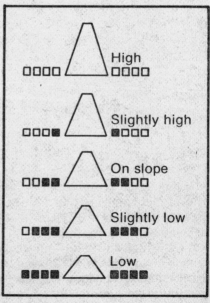

The lighter crossbars, being horizontal to the runway, provide an artificial horizon, tilting left or right as the pilot banks his aircraft. The whole pattern appears like a picture etched in lights (there are as many as 1,200 of them at a big airport like Heathrow) on the black rectangle of his windscreen. Too steep a descent and the crossbars move up to the top and disappear. Too flat and the lights merge together into one blur.

As an additional aid, there used to be two visual approach slope indicators (VASIs) on either side of the runway, basically like the glide path indicators of Malta. Now this is more modern equipment – Precision Approach Path Indicator.

So these days a pilot is led on to the runway. Since he may well have been flying in thick fog down the Instrument Landing System, suddenly emerging very low out of the bottom of it and being expected to reorientate himself visually, such a lighted pattern feeding in immediate information to him is an immense help. It is now used extensively at most big European airports and in Moscow. The Americans at Kennedy use a somewhat different pattern: rows of five lights forming a lane with two cross bars called Alpha.

After all the lights on the approach, the pilot is confronted suddenly with what was known as 'the black hole' – the runway – into which he seemed to be falling. In order to eliminate this, for 300 metres there is a 'mat' of red and white lights called 'barettes'.

It looks like an illuminated halma board and gives textures and light to the ground. The pilot must not land on these lights, but beyond the green threshold lights there are further white lights on which he can safely touch down. It is here that a pilot, particularly on a fully automatic approach where the automatic pilots are flying the aircraft, has to decide whether to overshoot – that is, open up his engines and do 'a missed approach' – on

Zero Four at Kennedy climbing to 500 feet, then right turn to 3,000 feet on 078 to Deer Park VOR and hold.

The lights tell him his exact position over the runway and provide both illumination and a horizon. The use of the displaced threshold is compulsory in the UK at visibility limits below 440 metres.

These lights themselves, like all runway lights now, are embedded in the surface and built to withstand loads of eight hundred tons (twice the weight of any known aircraft) suddenly descending on them at over 150 mph. Built on the same principle as cat's eyes on roads, but looking like small round blockhouses, they are checked every day and serviced once a week.

The intensity of the lights is set by the air traffic controller in the Tower. Recommended intensities for different visibility and weather conditions are provided by the CAA from 100 per cent full bright down to 0.3 per cent. Pilots sometimes complain about the intensities. Almost invariably the British complain that they are too bright and the Americans complain that they are too dim. Intensities are varied on request to the pilots' requirements.

There now remains the taxiway lights to lead the pilot to the apron or dock. On some lighting systems these are blue on the inside edge of the taxiway, yellow on the outside. Modern systems such as those at Heathrow and Glasgow concentrate on a green light centre line, and if necessary white lights or blue lights to mark the edges.

All the time the aircraft is moving towards the ramp, it is being watched by the Ground Movements Controller in the Tower and in bad weather also by the Tower radar (ASMI). Each piece of concrete it moves over has a number, so that all the time its exact position on the airfield is known and can be transmitted to others in case of any emergency. Should the aircraft take a wrong turning in poor visibility or become too close to another taxiing aircraft or work in progress, a line of red lights

325

can be switched on by the controller in front of the pilot to bring him to a stop.

There now remains only the docking problem. Instead of the usual stopping on the ramp followed by disembarkation of passengers and into buses, on modern airports these days there are piers. From these piers, movable corrugated corridors like elephant trunks are extended and manoeuvred like gangplanks to fit into the aircraft's entrances.

It then becomes, of course, absolutely essential to bring the big aircraft to a stop at the stand in an exact position so that the elephant trunk can make the proper connection with the door. This is achieved by what is called the Azimuth Guidance for Nose-in Stands (AGNIS).

The pilot puts his nosewheel as near as he can to a white centre line. But since in a 747 his eye level is twenty-nine feet up and he has a huge nose in front of him, he cannot achieve this manoeuvre to the exactness required. Therefore at eye level in front of him are lights and he positions himself according to their reading.

To tell the pilot when to stop, there are boards on either side called 'sidemarker boards', 3.8 metres long and 1.8 metres high. The pilot keeps going all the time he sees green on the board. As the aircraft approaches the place to stop, the green will appear to narrow and, exactly on the the stopping position, only black will be visible. If the board turns red, the pilot has gone too far. Since every aircraft type has a different height and length, these sidemarker boards are adjusted to give the right reading for each model. The system has been in operation at Heathrow for seven years and has achieved a stopping accuracy of ± 30 centimetres.

Now the engines are stopped. The passengers disembark into the long elephant's trunk and go down a red-carpeted corridor to Immigration. Once through that, they go to find their baggage. At Gatwick, there is a relatively new operation for finding your baggage after
326

your flight. You stay in the waiting room downstairs till your flight number appears on the board with the carousel number beside it. You then go up to that particular merry-go-round and collect your bags.

The hall where carousels are located are being modernised. One of the changes is the shifting of a small raised room in the centre where sits the man on watch. Irate passengers who couldn't find their baggage would sometimes attack this man with sticks and umbrellas, thinking that he was the controller of baggage unloading. In fact he is the engineer supervising the working of the carousels, and he is to be removed from the centre of the stage to a safer area protected by a no-go area.

With the 747, a small army, warned by Telemove-tape officers, descends on it in the shape of six trucks, three fuel tankers and four catering hoists.

Customs men check bars and cargo.

All the undone washing up (in the old days the cabin crew had to do it before the aircraft landed) is off-loaded. So is all unused food, the day-old newspapers, the toilet requisites.

The cleaners vacuum the cabins, including the ashtrays. The tanks are topped up with 47,000 gallons of kerosene. The oil tanks are filled. The maintenance men look at the snag sheet, on which the Engineer has written any mechanical deficiencies encountered on the flight, and carry out their repairs and checks. Three hundred gallons of fresh water are loaded. Food for a further 450 people comes on board.

In two hours, the whole aircraft is turned round. And already the new Engineer is walking down to the ramp to dip the tanks and do his checks for the short trip home.

19
Passport to
Anywhere

Where? That's the problem!

As the tourist industry continues to expand, more and more colourful alternatives are offered to the holiday-maker abroad.

To help him choose, the travel agents' walls are stocked with brochures that blur *en masse* into a cross between tropical fruits and women's magazines, many of them as difficult to read as a railway timetable.

Too often the effect is to stun rather than to assist. The covers are almost identical: obligatory girl in the bathing suit, bronzed couple with kids, snapshots of the beach, fishing boats, swimming pools and hotels. Rarely do you see any sign of the fairy godmother's coach that has made all this possible: the aeroplane.

Tour operators even apologise for the bore of flying in their brochures. Yet the flight – for so many of the customers their very first – could be shown as one of the pleasures of their holiday.

It should certainly be a priority in choosing a holiday. What's the airline, what's the aircraft, what's the foreign airport we're going to land at, what high ground is around it, what are the runway lengths and the landing facilities? You won't get that information in the brochures. Yet airlines, aircraft and especially aerodromes should be starred like hotels. Only thus – Spain and Italy are reported to be particularly bad – will foreign governments spend money on adequate flying facilities. 'Fly the airline that speaks your own language' is a tip not always possible to take, but be thankful that at least British airports are amongst the finest in the world.

328

In most brochures there will be information on whether visas are required. For most popular holidays, a year's passport is all that is necessary, bought at most Post Offices on receipt of the fee, a photograph and birth certificate. In the long run, it's best to have your full passport, which takes longer to get than you might think, so allow plenty of time, especially in the summer. Passport photographs are usually depressingly bad. To quote Sir Vivian Fuchs, 'If you look like your passport photograph, then you're not well enough to travel.' If a visa is required, allow plenty of time for that too (especially American ones, for which a photograph is necessary). Sometimes a visa queue stretches from the American Embassy way down Grosvenor Square.

In many brochures, there is also advice on inoculations and vaccinations. But check with your doctor; or ring Cook's Travel Agency in Grosvenor Square and ask for its medical section; or ring British Airways Travel and Immunisation Centre at 75 Regent Street – it's open Monday to Friday, 08.30 to 16.30, telephone: (01) 439 9584/5. If you should become ill after your return from holiday, always tell your doctor you have been abroad.

Briefly, inoculation against typhoid is generally advisable, unless your travel is confined to N. America, N. Europe, Australia and New Zealand. Everyone should be protected against tetanus, whether they are travelling or not, and it's usually a wise precaution to have protection against polio. For parts of Africa and South America you'll need yellow fever jabs and cholera for much of Africa, India, Asia and the Middle East. But check before you go. And for all countries where standards of hygiene may be low, get protection against infectious hepatitis. You must take with you anti-malarial tablets if you're going to India or Sri Lanka or any area where malaria is rife. Sleep under your mosquito nets in these places. It isn't worth taking chances.

Take with you insect repellent and anti-sunburn lotion.

329

Sun is, of course, what most North Europeans go for. They lap it up and expose their skins to it too rapidly, and are bitterly disappointed if they take their holiday too early and don't get it.

So where is the sun to be found? At least many brochures now quote temperatures, hours of sunshine, humidity and rain. Study that carefully.

The Mediterranean can't really be relied on till May. There are often perpetual winds round islands like Rhodes; and count the windmills in Majorca.

In the brochures, the hotels, like the bathing belles, look almost identical. Look for position. Is it actually on the beach? Will you get a sea-view from your balcony? Are there gardens? Is that a main road between the hotel and the beach? Is the hotel going to be noisy from traffic or discos? Is there a lift? A heated swimming pool in the winter? What children's facilities are there? How far from the nearest town?

There are so many variables that recommendation is the best safeguard, if you can find someone who has been there. Often the choice is so difficult that holidaymakers, having been satisfied once, go to the same hotel every year.

Price is often paramount. It is the philosophy of tour operators to provide the general public with a pre-organised holiday and the economy of the lowest possible air-seat fare. They all work on an 80–90 per cent sale of seats on the aircraft. Many of them are attached to or owned by big companies with airlines – Thomson with Britannia, British Enterprise with British Airways, Intasun with Air Europe.

Likewise some of the big companies own hotels. Beware of swish hotels in isolated places offering very low rates for bed and breakfast in the winter. You'll pay a lot for the meals and drinks you'll have to have there because it's too far and too cold to go out to eat anywhere else.

To try to fill the hotels in winter, additional special rates are offered for children, and two weeks for the price of one, three weeks for the price of two, are also on offer. There will be a reason if the price drops in the brochure, so look for it. Down goes the price of Mombasa in March/April/May – the rainy season. April is cheaper in Delhi – the temperature rises to over 100° fahrenheit. November to February are the usual cheap times, except of course at Christmas, when prices soar. Nile cruises go sharply downwards in our summer in line with the high rise in temperature in Egypt. January and February are usually the cheapest of all, and can be quite nice in the Algarve. Prices always go up at school holiday times.

Not only do the tour operators sell package holidays; they also sell cheap seats on aircraft – an offshoot from the bucket shops that have sprung up. Even if they don't, they have so many hotel nights to bargain with that they can beat the hotel proprietors down by big block buyings, getting a price that couldn't be approached by people on their own. Everything is organised for the client at the highest service level and the lowest contractual price. In addition, of course, the client has the services of the resort representative who should provide maps, information on excursions and the facilities to take up complaints which, being on the spot, he may be able to put right.

The big league of tour operators is headed by Thomson and Intasun. Then come Ingham, Sovereign and Enterprise and Rank Travel. Thomas Cook have their own retail travel shops.

Of the winter travellers, the young half go on a winter sports programme (an area which is fast growing) and the older half usually have a rest at uncrowded resorts (some tour operators offer three-month holidays at phenomenally low rates in order to fill the hotels).

Agents also arrange cheap seats for a new market that has a certain social significance. A segment of the public, having saved enough for a second home, buy a villa abroad rather than the traditional English country cottage. A group of people then organise themselves into a club which lets out the villa when the owner doesn't want it, and obtain cheap aircraft seats for their temporary tenants.

Apartment hotels have also been developing fast – the letting of apartments only with no meals in an hotel-like complex.

Time-sharing is another recent arrival on the scene. A villa is owned by a number of people who have the right of occupancy at certain times of the year. There again is a market for cheap aircraft seats.

These changes are evidence of a richer and more leisured society. The average holiday in the UK today is three weeks plus bank holidays. Personal discretionary income has grown. The Oxford Economic forecasting in 1982 showed an expected increase in Personal Disposable Income from 8.7 per cent in 1981 to 11.6 per cent in 1986. And with increased income and increased leisure come longer holidays abroad.

The number of four-night-plus holidays taken abroad by the British rose from 8 million in 1972 to 14.25 million in 1982. Thirty-three per cent of these holidays started in July and August but the proportion has fallen since the early 1970s, so that now May, June and September are not far behind.

Who carries the holidaymakers?

Thomson Holidays remained on top of the tour companies in 1982 with 13 per cent of the market, but that percentage had fallen from 24 per cent in 1974, largely because of increased competition. Then in 1986, a tremendous advertising push started, led by Thomson and other big tour companies. Holidays were offered at ridiculous prices – some as low as £25, with everyone undercutting each other.

Nobody could make money on such offers which were well below cost. But the free advertising they produced was worth millions. There was a scramble for bookings. As a result, in mid-February 1986, four times as many holidays abroad had been booked in comparison with the same time in 1985.

Where do the holidaymakers go? And what guides them there?

The answer to the first question is 85 per cent to Europe – trips to America and Canada fluctuate erratically in relation to the dollar, and at $1.48 to the pound at present, it's expensive, but better than it was. VFRs (not what the pilot would understand as Visual Flight Rules but Visiting Friends and Relations) keep the trans-Atlantic traffic moving.

In 1984, the fortieth anniversary of D-day, there was a great influx of American and Commonwealth servicemen to Britain and France, and many parties of Britons travelled to the countryside surrounding Arromanches. In 1985, it was the fortieth anniversary of VE and VJ day, and though the British government chose to play down those anniversaries, the ex-servicemen and women and their relatives did not.

But apart from such special occasions and anniversaries, the popularity stakes in choice of holidays abroad is indicated by the passenger numbers leaving the main tourist airport, Gatwick, for the resorts in 1984–5.

Spain was again top of the pops: 793,000 went to Palma (up 3.4 per cent on the previous year); 673,000 went to Malaga (up 19.8 per cent).

From Glasgow, the same pattern emerges, with Palma up 12.8 per cent, Malaga up 43.2 per cent and Alicante up 27.1 per cent.

This provides and illustrates the answer to the second question, what guides them there? *Money* guides them there.

Spain again provides value for the average Briton's money. In 1983–4, however, Spain did increase its charges by 17 per cent. By this, they lost their position at the

333

head of the popularity table to their rival, Greece. The increase pulled their bookings down by 20 per cent. But now they have adjusted their charges again and are back to first place. Certainly no other country has adapted its hotels and amenities so well to the tastes of the tourist.

They build hotels at an economic price, provide cheap menus aimed at the home food of the tourist (for instance, 'English breakfasts' instead of croissants and coffee), swimming pools, barbecues, cabins, and entertainment. And you do get the sun and the beaches are lovely. In spite of gibes of being the Blackpool of the Mediterranean, the Costa del Sol is where everyone can be a millionaire for a week, and no longer is Majorca the retreat of the rich. In addition, the Spanish are good with children and don't resent the serving man's role.

Greece, the next contender (486,000 passengers on scheduled flights in 1985 – up 29.3 per cent) used to be for the more discerning. It has more ancient sites, higher grade hotels in attractive settings, more alternatives in the taverna and the little villas; but it is rather more expensive, and increasingly much more crowded with many more concrete hotels going up.

Italy has a long history of British visitors, and since 1950, its package popularity has been boosted by imaginative lakes-and-mountains holidays. The hotels tend to be smaller and family run, with good food and service. Its art and history and scenery are rivalled in the Mediterranean only by Greece.

Yugoslavia is developing fast – rivalling Spain in value for money, but not yet providing so many of the extras. The scenery is beautiful and holidays on some of the Yugoslav islands are very good.

From behind the Iron Curtain, Rumania is trying to attract tourists with some of the cheapest package holidays. These are excellent value. But one or two words of warning. The Rumanian aircraft tend to be of mature age. On one holiday I sampled, the aircraft was an
334

old Aeroflot Tupolev, very dirty and dingy. The drinks trolley, a simple and primitive one, held little in the way of refreshment except small bottles of whisky. Duty-free perfume was Christian Dior look-alike made in Lublijana. The meal was slightly down on British package standards, but not much. The aircraft departed on time, and the pilot made an excellent landing.

The hotel was comfortable and clean, the food terrible: no salads, no fruit, very hard dry bread. Indeed although this is a fertile fruit-growing, food-producing country and the once renowned bread basket of Europe, people were queueing at fruit kiosks for sour grapes.

The Bucharest hotels we visited were more cosmopolitan, the food much better. Lifts, however, tended to stick. Toilets, except in Bucharest, were grim. I have never before seen a toilet roll secured to the wall with the sort of padlock a bank would have found reassuring. But the scenery is splendid, the people were charming, helpful and very pro-British.

The British have always been strong on the Algarve, which has a climate as pleasant as its inhabitants. From Gatwick, 430,000 holidaymakers travelled to Faro in 1985: an increase of 27.9 per cent. It has not yet reached Blackpool proportions. But in a few years time that may well not be true.

Across the Mediterranean in Tunisia, the tourist industry is expanding, as it is in Morocco, and the Gambia, first opened up by British Caledonian with ex-Laker DC10s, is proving popular. Cyprus is another rapid developer having 15,000 hotel beds, double the number since the Greek/Turkish troubles.

Malta is a favourite resort of the British – good hotels, archaeological sites, a distinct flavour of Britain's colonial past and just a three-hour flight away.

Long-distance runs to India, Thailand, Sri Lanka, Kenya, South America and China are served by a number of tour operators – Kuoni, Thomas Cook, Wings Sovereign etc, operating with 747s. The only Far East airport in the popularity table was Hong Kong – 370,000 passengers (up 9.5 per cent).

Sri Lanka in this market is particularly cheap, with unspoilt beaches, glorious scenery and splendid sights – the ruins of Polonnaruna, Sigiri, the Temple of the Tooth at Kandy. But the present unrest, the fighting between the Sinhalese and the Tamils, is bound to deter tourists. Before that, Sri Lanka was an ideal place for a stopover between Britain and Australia, one of the most popular long-distance destinations. There are cheap tickets to Australia for visiting families and friends, a choice of packages, some with the advantage of a stopover at Bangkok, Singapore, Sri Lanka etc; or the P & O, cruise one way, fly the other.

The value of the Far East long-distance packages lies in their total difference from the European scene. The drawbacks are expense, £1,000–£1,500 for a fortnight's holiday, and length of flight.

Length of flight *is* something prospective passengers take note of. Approximate flying times are: around 2 hours to the Costa Brava; 2 hours 20 minutes to Faro in the Algarve; 2½ hours to Lisbon, Naples and Dubrovnik; 3 hours 15 minutes to Athens, 3½ hours to Crete and 4 hours to the Canaries. Further afield, it will be 5 hours to Agadir, 9 to Barbados, 7 to Nairobi, 9 to Delhi, 15 to Hong Kong and 23 to Sydney.

In addition to checking the length of the flight, check how long it will take you to get to your holiday hotel after you've landed. Some airports are miles from the resorts. It is a 75-mile trip, albeit a beautiful one, after landing at Porec to the Yugoslav resort of Portoroz. Dubrovnik is 15 miles away from its airport. It will take over 90 minutes to reach Hammamet hotels from Monastir airport, Tunis.

All in all, it is likely that air tourists will spend far longer getting to the departure airports from home, and from arrival airports to their hotels, than they will in the air.

Even so, that does not deter people: 21,621,985 passengers went through Heathrow in 1975; in 1985, there were 29,866,164. In 1975, 5,342,560 passengers went through Gatwick. In 1984–5, there were 14,227,954. In the last ten years, Stansted passenger traffic has increased by 50 per cent. East Midlands Airport has grown from 9,500 passengers in 1961 to 1,802,100 in 1982 and is still expanding.

With some improvement in the pound/dollar exchange from the almost par level of December 1984, more passengers went to America: 543,000 to Los Angeles (up 41.1 per cent), 430,000 to New York (up 172.6 per cent).

But the traffic of American passengers coming to Britain and beyond went down sharply in the first few months of 1986. This was due partly to the oil crisis with the oil price falling and less business travel to the Middle East; and partly to American fears of hijacking and the bomb attacks on airports.

But still the boom continues, and operators try to fill the airports and the airliners. With the oil price down to less than half of what it was in 1985, air travel should be much cheaper. British Caledonian have planned a new long-range 747 service to fly non-stop from Gatwick to Japan over Russia. If permission could be obtained from the Russians, this would be a great tourist draw.

Certainly the operators want to know what will draw the customer. Kuoni are refreshingly frank in their brochures, having a Pro and Con list for the countries they serve. This at least prepares people for what they should expect and tends to cut down on complaints afterwards.

Tour operators learn, or should learn, from the complaints they get and from their questionnaires. They report that about one third of the questionnaires they hand out to their clients are returned.

The most common complaints are about food – too

337

Greek or too Spanish, or too anglicised – and slow service. Quality of the hotels is often praised – though there are frequent criticisms too, usually of the plumbing. On a tour of Transylvania, a bus-load of Britons begged the guide to stop the coach in a wood, rather than be subjected again to a stopover at a so-called first-class hotel with its horrific toilets. The guides are criticised occasionally and praised occasionally. But of the flight there is never a mention.

They take the excellence of the aircraft and its crew for granted.

So where will people choose? The main draws are likely to remain sun, short flights and cheapness. On all of these Spain scores. The complaints about its airports are strongly denied by the Spanish government. But now there is another hazard: bombs in tourist hotels placed by the Basque separatist group ETA. So far, bombs have not deterred British tourists, unlike their American counterparts.

**20
Check List for
Passengers**

1: Book early. Tickets for Christmas, Easter and summer resorts and for November–December to Australia go quickly.

2. Memorise your flight number. That is more important than the name of the airline or the aircraft or your destination. That's the number that appears illuminated on the arrival and departure board and on radar screens along the route. Without it, information desks are stuck.

3. Before you leave home, give to people meeting you on your return a note of your return flight number, your airline, the date and place of your return and your arrival time, together with the name of the tour company (if any), the foreign airport and your address abroad.

4. If you are going on a package holiday, the best bargains are out of season. This is usually when there are no school holidays. High season varies with the resort and the temperature. Apart from winter sports, costs usually vary with the temperature – the warmer the costlier – as it is the sun that most holidaymakers are seeking. Look at the temperature, sunshine and rainfall for the period of your holiday at your resort. If the price drops sharply, there'll be a reason, usually because it's very hot (India in April) or very wet (Kenya in April). Some places (the Algarve) can be surprisingly warm in January/February. October is chancy, particularly in the Adriatic.

339

5. Dates are important. Midweek travel is less crowded and is often cheaper. Airport taxes sometimes give a surprise jump at the weekend. On the North Atlantic there are 'shoulder periods' (halfway between low and peak): April, May, September or October eastwards; April, May, June, October westbound. Peak is July–August–September. Not only will it be more expensive, it may be difficult to get a seat.

6. Check that your flight is expected to be on time before leaving home. The worst delays are 'creepers' – an announced delay of an hour becoming two, three, four and then a night-stop. This precipitates total distrust of everything the airline says or does. Free drinks, meals and accommodation do not quite eradicate this feeling.

7. There are so many different fares these days – Excursion, APEX (Advanced Purchase Excursion), IPEX (Instant Purchase Excursion), student fares, wives' fares, children's fares, group fares, shuttle fares, three weeks for the price of two – that the only thing to do to ensure that you get the best deal is to consult your travel agent. In any case, air fares are extraordinarily low in comparison to everything else, particularly on Virgin Atlantic and People Express. Forty-eight years ago the Atlantic fare was over three times the cost in dollars, disregarding the huge effect of inflation.

8. If you book on an inclusive package holiday tour, check that the organiser holds an Air Travel Organiser's Licence from the Civil Aviation Authority – its number will be on their brochures.

An ATOL holder is under bond, so that in the event of financial failure, the traveller will be repatriated and as far as possible refunded for holiday time missed.

9. Obtain your passport as soon as possible.

10. Take all old labels off your luggage and put on only those applicable to your trip, otherwise your luggage may go to an old destination. *Lock your bags*.

Do not pack valuables, cash, passports, cheque books, travellers' cheques or credit cards in suitcases. Above all, do not pack dangerous goods – camping gas cylinders, matches, large aerosols, or other flammable materials. Fires have been started because of passengers' thoughtlessness. Make a list of everything you pack. It will be needed if the luggage is lost and you make an insurance claim. Two checked bags may be taken across the Atlantic on Economy Class, provided that the total dimensions of the two do not exceed 106 inches, and carry-on bags are allowed of combined total dimension of 45 inches. European travel baggage allowance is based on weight (economy 20 kilos, first class 30 kilos), except to France where one checked bag is allowed not exceeding 67 inches and one carry-on bag. Holiday baggage allowance is generally two pieces of luggage with a weight limit of 20 kilos per person.

11. Insure your baggage and your holiday if you are on a package tour and take out cover for possible medical expenses. Now that Britain has joined the EEC, free medical treatment is generally available. If you are self-employed, this will depend on having a form E111 in advance from the Department of Health and Social Security and/or your passport, depending on the country you are going to, and on what they offer their own nationals. In France, for example, you have to pay first and then get the money refunded, whereas Sweden gives you free hospital treatment and you may get travelling expenses to the hospital partially refunded. If in doubt, check with the DHSS. Outside the EEC, medical insurance is vital, particularly in the USA as medical costs there are enormous. Note that for winter sports, cover cost is quadrupled.

341

12. Be careful about your health before, during and after your holiday abroad. Don't work right up to the last moment. If possible, allow yourself time to begin to unwind. Four hundred million people travel the international routes regularly, importing tropical diseases into Europe and America. British Airways publishes a leaflet intended as a general guide to doctors entitled, *Your Patient and Air Travel*. The British Medical Association publishes a booklet, *Health on Holiday*. The Air Transport Users Committee publishes one called, *Care in the Air for Handicapped Travellers*. The DHSS has a pamphlet SA35, *Protect your Health Abroad*. You should be able to get a copy from your travel agent or from the local DHSS office. All these are very useful and helpful.

You will have found out about vaccinations and inoculations from your doctor or from Thomas Cook or from the British Airways centre, but if by any chance you arrive at the airport without the necessary inoculations being done, go to the medical centre there. Although many of the injections take time to work, it is better to have them then than not at all.

If you are taking pills, remember not to pack them in your luggage where you can't get at them. But remember to have them readily available. It is a good idea to take with you soluble aspirin, and anti-diarrhoea mixture, a laxative, insect repellent and antiseptic cream, water sterilising tablets, sunburn lotion and calomine.

If you're travelling with a very young family, remember that babies pick up gastro-intestinal infections much more easily than adults. If your baby is about to be weaned, it might be best to delay this until after you return. If a baby under a year old gets an attack you should immediately summon a doctor.

13. It is sensible to arrive early at the check-in, even well before time, especially if you are travelling Jumbo. Otherwise in spite of probably five counters trying to cope, you will wait in queues, shifting your baggage forward periodically, for quite a time. Being early should eliminate the chance of being 'bumped' (see below) and gets you a better choice of seat.

14. Airline flights may be overbooked, and there is a chance that a seat will not be available on a flight for which a person has a confirmed reservation. A person denied boarding on a flight may be entitled to a compensatory payment. The rules for denied boarding compensation are available at airport ticket counters.

Some airlines deliberately overbook – that is, sell more seats than they have available on an aircraft and 'bump' some passengers. This is their answer to 'no-shows' – when the passenger books but does not turn up.

Overbooking used to be much worse than it is today. British Airways, along with most British airlines, is particularly concerned about overbooking and tried to organise an airline agreement to do away with it – but without success. In the USA alone, 100,000 passengers used to be bumped annually. Some airlines, notably Eastern, upgraded bumped passengers to first class, or sent them on the next flight free. Most others worked on a last-come-last-served basis. Some airlines asked employees to look out for the least inconvenienced. Others called for volunteers.

Then in 1974, an American airline reportedly bumped Ralph Nader from a flight from Washington to Kent How, Connecticut, where he was to make a fund-raising speech for the Connecticut Citizens Action Group. The airline offered Nader $32 in DBC (denied boarding compensation), which he refused. The case went to court and the judge awarded Nader and the CCAG $25,000 each.

This ruling was reversed on appeal, when the big guns of the Air Transport Association and the Civil Aeronautics Board moved in. But at the Supreme Court, the judgment was reversed again to the original ruling.

In 1976, lawyers from nineteen airlines went to ATA's HQ to see what could be done about it. They feared that people might hang around airports, practically begging to be bumped so that they could get hefty damages. They decided that airlines could best be protected by tariffs – notices such as are inside airline tickets or on counters.

This does indeed protect the airline by law. But if a passenger these days is bumped, then provided his ticket is exactly in order and he has checked in at the right time, he should raise hell with the airline until he is offered another flight, either on that airline or another one that is acceptable to him. The Air Transport Users Committee have tried to bring sense into overbooking. This could be eliminated if 'no-show' passengers had their tickets forfeited. But the British airlines say that they don't want to do this, as passengers will then book with another airline. British Airways have, however, agreed to introduce a system of volunteers to stand down in exchange for a later flight plus cash plus appropriate free meals and accomodation. The maximum compensation on European lines has been raised from £100 to £150.

15. A little more concern is now being directed towards the full fare-paying business passenger, mainstay of the airlines before the tourists arrived. His or her status, as apart from discount economy passengers, used to be safeguarded by seating forward in the executive suite of the Jumbo, where the seats are more armchair-like.

But the overspill of cheap fares soon invaded the executive suite, especially in the holiday season. Some airlines have announced seat-selection for full economy fares, priority in-flight meals and service and separate check-in counters.

16. Take good care to be prepared for delays if a known strike is on, and during the winter. There is now a scheme whereby some tour operators will refund days of holiday lost through strikes. In essence, it is the same sort of insurance that operated after a number of tour operators went bankrupt and holidaymakers lost their entire holiday.

17. Seats vary. Some are much better bargains than others, particularly if you are tall and need leg room. Some tour operators pack their passengers in like sardines. The leg-room problem first made its appearance when Juan Trippe of Pan American in 1951 forced through the idea (against the British, who had no adequate aircraft) of cheap Atlantic tourist travel, which later extended to economy: 34 inches economy against 41 inches first class was and is the usual practice. But on some holiday charters it seems more crowded than that.

On some seats, the film screen can't be seen. The ones right at the back of the compartments against the bulkheads don't recline properly.

Avoid being near the toilets. There are never enough of them on any aircraft and in the hot busy season hurried clearing of them during quick turn-rounds can leave an unpleasant smell. Then there are always queues.

Too close to the galleys will mean more to-ing and fro-ing of the cabin staff near you. The best seats for the view outside are the first-class ones right in the nose. The view downwards in the seats around the middle of the aircraft is obscured by the wing.

Airlines say that seats can be reserved ahead and that requests go on to the computer. First-class passengers can usually choose their seats. On some airlines, so can the full-fare-paying economy – but first come, first served. If you are in a party and don't want to be split up, it is essential to arrive early.

18. The luggage racks used to be exactly like the ones above your head in a train. Now they're usually boxed-in containers. Even so, don't put heavy, loose baggage in them. This rule causes annoyance, but it is a very sensible safety precaution against heavy objects falling off and

345

injuring people, especially in turbulence. One piece of hand baggage is allowed per person in economy, two in first class.

19. The passenger seats are direct descendants of the Imperial Airways adjustable chair of the 1930s. The straps are there because Curtiss, the first American aircraft designer, invented them after Commander Towers had fallen 1,500 feet from one of his aircraft in 1919. The commander had miraculously survived by being caught in a tree. Straps have been compulsory equipment in aeroplanes ever since, years before they were first used in cars.

20. The 'fasten-your-seat-belt' sign goes off – but unless you need to go to the toilet, *don't unfasten your seat belt.* Some airlines suggest you keep your seat belt loosely fastened. Don't let the belt be uncomfortable, but at the same time realise that it's there for your protection, so keep it reasonably tight. In turbulent weather, the seat-belt sign will be on anyway.

Just as in a car, it isn't likely that you'll need the belt but you wear it all the same. On an aircraft the same applies. Outside the window, the sky may be blue. Not a tremor in the fuselage. But suddenly, Clear Air Turbulence might turn up out of nowhere, especially around 36,000 feet. This phenomenon is basically a mix-up of jet-stream winds of up to 150 miles an hour in opposition to each other, associated with sharp changes of temperature. Apart from CAT, there can be other sudden upsets. A DC8 over the Atlantic went into a steep climb. The artificial horizon had tumbled. The pilot disconnected the auto-pilot, throttled back and resumed level flight. But as a result of this sudden rotation, passengers at the aft end had been thrown against the ceiling. Four passengers and a stewardess were injured. The Captain had disconnected the auto-pilot without first putting the controls into neutral.

The pilots of two 707s suddenly saw each other on a collision course, while in the passenger cabin lunch was being served. The Captain of one 707 went into a steep diving turn. Food trolleys, bottles, stewards, stewardesses and passengers were flung upwards and stuck to the ceiling in the negative G, descending into the floor again in a crash of broken glass and injured limbs.

Unexpected in-flight turbulence is one of the most common cause of aircraft accidents. Rarely fatal, nevertheless these accidents cause serious injuries. Again and again, the same sort of causes turn up: 'an evasive manoeuvre to avoid an apparent collision potential', 'failure of the passenger to comply with the fasten-seat-belt instructions', 'release of passengers' seat belts in turbulence for an undetermined reason', 'failure of the Captain to use earlier turbulence precautions for cabin occupants over an area of forecast turbulence'.

21. On no account clutter the aisles with baggage or duty-free carriers. In the event of an emergency, it is dangerous, and in any case impedes the cabin staff and their trolleys. Regulations have been tightened since the Manchester disaster. Only items that can be stowed and secured in the approved storage compartments may be brought into the cabin.

22. Don't stand in the aisles chatting. This again is dangerous to you if sudden unforeseen turbulence turns up, and again gets in the way of the cabin staff. Because of the continual use of the aisles by members of a famous orchestra on their way to Los Angeles, the same Captain who had taken them over kept them strapped in with the seat-belt sign on all the way home.

23. Wear loose-fitting clothes in the air. Anything tight can produce discomfort. Take a pair of slippers to slip on. A warm coat can be useful. Have plenty of soft drinks. It's best not to be tempted by alcohol. It's also

347

best to eat sparingly. With the average food that is served that shouldn't be difficult.

24. When the aircraft lands, don't get up to be at the front of the queue to get out. The aircraft may swerve and throw you off balance. Stay put till the engines are off.

25. At most customs, if you have only the allowed amount of goods, you simply go through the green door. Use the red door if you have anything to declare.

26. Absinthe, liquor-filled sweets, firearms and ammunition, drugs, narcotics, lottery tickets, goods from North Korea, Vietnam, Cuba, Cambodia and Zimbabwe, fireworks and dangerous toys need a licence or may be prohibited entry into the USA.

27. Make a list of everything you have in excess of your allowance and pack the goods concerned on the top of one suitcase for easy access.

The following goods can be brought into Great Britain duty free:

Goods obtained duty- and tax-free in the EEC or duty and tax free on a ship or aircraft, or goods obtained outside the EEC:

Alcoholic drinks
1 litre of alcoholic drinks over 22 per cent vol. or 2 litres of alcoholic drinks not over 22 per cent vol. or fortified or sparkling wine plus 2 litres of still table wine.

Tobacco
200 cigarettes or 50 cigars or 100 cigarillos or 250 grammes of tobacco (double for residents of countries outside Europe). Persons under 17 are not entitled to the drinks and tobacco allowance.

Perfumery and gifts
250cc (9fl oz) of toilet water and 50 grammes (60cc or 2fl oz) of perfume and £28 worth of other goods but no more than 50 litres of beer or 25 mechanical lighters.

Goods obtained duty- and tax-paid within the EEC:

Alcoholic drinks
5 litres of still table wine plus 1½ litres of alcoholic drinks over 22 per cent vol. or 3 litres of alcoholic drinks not over 22 per cent vol. or fortified or sparkling wine or a further 3 litres of still table wine.

Tobacco
300 cigarettes or 75 cigars or 150 cigarillos or 400 grammes of tobacco.
Persons under 17 are not entitled to drinks and tobacco allowance.

Perfumery and gifts
375cc (13fl oz) of toilet water and 75 grammes (90cc or 3fl oz) of perfume and £207 worth of other goods, but no more than 50 litres of beer or 25 mechanical lighters.

It must be pointed out that these are individual allowances; and that they apply only to goods carried and cleared by you at the time of your arrival.

The allowance does not apply to goods brought in for sale or other commercial purposes.

You may not mix goods obtained duty- and tax-free or outside the EEC with goods of the same category obtained duty- and tax-paid in the EEC in order to obtain the higher allowance. You can, however, mix duty-free spirits and liqueurs with duty-paid still table wine, as these are in separate categories under the alcoholic drinks allowances.

One litre is approximately 1¾ pints or 35 fl oz.

Into the USA can be brought one US quart of spirits,

300 cigarettes and up to $100 of gifts including some alcohol and cigars.

28. Check that your return flight is booked when you land – that you get OK along with F (First Class) or Y (Economy) on your ticket.

Index

357

358

362

363